« « « « «

I KNOW A GOOD PLACE

» » » » »

I
Know
a
Good
Place

Clive Gammon

DAVID R. GODINE, PUBLISHER

Boston

First published in 1989 by
DAVID R. GODINE, *Publisher, Inc.*
Horticultural Hall
300 Massachusetts Avenue
Boston, Massachusetts 02115

All of the essays in this volume originally appeared in *Sports Illustrated*. "The Shade of a Grayling" was published as "Pursuit of a Grayling Shade"; "Red Star Salmon" as "Czeching on the Huchen"; "Trout and Truffles on the Tarn" as "Truffles and Flourishes on the Tarn"; "Pushed to the Icy Brink" as "Pushed to the Arctic and Beyond"; "Royal Red Setter" as "Bonnie Prince of the Flies"; "The Once and Future Island" as "First Person"; "Invasion of the Red Horde" as "A Fish Story That Was All Too True"; "Deep in the Green" as "Please Don't Fall in the Water"; "The Maharaja Fish" as "In Quest of the Maseer."

«   «   «   «   «   «   «   «   «

Library of Congress Cataloging-in-Publication Data

Gammon, Clive.
  I know a good place.

  I. Fishing. I. Title.
SH441.G36   1989   799.1   88-45290
ISBN-0-87923-764-3

»   »   »   »   »   »   »   »   »

First Edition
Printed in the United States of America

Contents

Acknowledgments

"I know a good place," said Mr. Jeremy Fisher, the engaging and urbane frog created by Beatrix Potter. "For minnows," he added. "Fat minnows." And although Jeremy's fishing trips were restricted to a pond in England's Lake District and this book takes in somewhat more territory, his passion for the sport, which his low-key, throwaway sentence barely begins to disguise, is exactly the same sort as mine. So this book is meant for all passionate, Jeremy-style fishers, beginning with my very small daughter, Lottie, who can hook eight-inch bass in Maryland farm ponds, and my more svelte but somewhat older daughter, Bridie Kate, who came very close to catching a world record rainbow runner in Bermuda once. And it is also for my wife Juliette, who is known to have been momentarily attached to a Costa Rican tarpon and is believed to have captured the smallest barracuda in the history of the Yucatan.

And for all my good fishing friends, too, in so many good fishing places—in school days, Doug Kelly and Billy Nathan, and long after that, but also in Wales, John Barrett and Long Pete Grundel on the high cliffs of Pembrokeshire. Then more high cliffs, the Irish ones, and the shore too, with Des Brennan and Kevin Linnane on the storm beaches of Ireland, and the run of the wild fish in Cork and Kerry. God be with the days, Des would say, and he'd be right. Never mind, though. There'd be more days in Wales with Peter Williams and Michael Begg and Gareth Edwards in magical places like Merlin's green Vale of Towy.

And God knows where after that. Art Brawley and Roy Terrell in the U.S., and a whole company of guides and ghillies from the Florida Keys to the Falklands, from the Northern Territory of Australia to the Northwest Territories of Canada, to the U.S.S.R. and back again. Stick them all on the list. And, sadly, let's add the ones who don't cast around much anymore: Bob Ottum, Les Moncrieff and Ian Gillespie.

Most latterly, though, let's make a place for my son Nick Gammon, whose work illuminates these pages. And who could, if he tries hard, be up there with Mr. Jeremy Fisher one of these days.

All the same, because we have been (literally of course) in so much cold water together over the years, this book I dedicate, with much affection, to my old friend Desmond Brennan.

Foreword

It may seem strange to start off a fishing book with some words about a TV show, but there is a point I want to make and this seemed a good way to make it . . . .

A little more than ten years ago I managed to embroil myself in a television extravaganza called "The Fishing Race." It took place in England and the format was simple: three pairs of anglers (and I was one of those anglers) were given unlimited logistical support, then told to take off and catch as many different species of fish as they could in seventy-two hours of virtually continuous fishing anywhere they fancied in the country. To simplify the rules somewhat, the pair that logged the greatest number of species won a trophy, known as the Golden Maggot, which the BBC rightfully claimed to be the smallest in world sport. In the meantime—and herein lay the originality of the concept—for all of those seventy-two hours the competitors would be under the unremitting scrutiny of the cameras.

The finished product ran over six weeks and was a considerable success. It was repeated over and again. The following year the Golden Maggot was contested in Sweden. But certain viewers were unamused to the point of outrage. They were, of course, members of the Angling Establishment. As they saw it, "The Fishing Race" brought the sport into disrepute. Far from the anglers in the series being imbued with the peaceful, pastoral spirit of Izaak Walton, they revealed themselves as being actually human. They were competitive, sometimes sneakily competitive. They boasted. Sometimes they used profanities that had to be bleeped out. They quarreled and argued and when they snatched brief periods of sleep, they snored loudly.

What the Establishment of the sport failed to realize, though, was that it was by way of their very foibles that these anglers conveyed the strange and powerful passion that fishing induces in its devotees, or, more properly, addicts.

In the meantime, and for very much the same reasons, it seems to me that the inner, conservative core of angling's Establishment may cast a cool sort of eye on the stories which follow. There is no angling purism in them but a catholicity of ways to catch fish. There is as much about people and places as there is about catching fish. And I am afraid that there is not much peaceful, Waltonian philosophy. But I hope there is some passion.

If there is, much credit should go to the editors at Time, Inc., who helped so much to make these stories see the light of day in *Sports Illustrated*, notably Art Brawley, until lately the outdoors editor of the magazine; Pat Ryan, now managing editor of *Life*; and *S.I.*'s present incumbent outdoors man, Bob Brown.

« « « « «

I KNOW A GOOD PLACE

» » » » »

STICKS POOL, RIVER TOWY, WALES

CHAPTER ONE

Home River

Wales has to come first: it is where I was raised and learned to fish. And specifically, I mean its delectable south-western corner, all surf beaches, salmon rivers and toy green hills. It was a fine place to learn because it had the sea and the river both, and it nurtured a fine catholicity of fishing tastes, which I hope will be reflected in this book.

WALES

THE THREE of them were already settled in the drawing room when Peter Williams and I arrived, sitting deep in the chintz-covered chairs, whiskey glasses in hand: Bertram Couch, Howard Gabe, John Mercer. The room had a faint, acrid, medicinal smell. None of the furniture could have been bought after 1930.

Mercer, the lawyer, I knew well. I'd met him on the river bank a dozen times, and now he began to make the introductions. Momentarily, I held cold, brown-mottled hands, the veins standing high. "Give Mr. Gammon a drink," said Bertram Couch from the chair out of which he rarely rose. Mercer poured whiskey from a Waterford decanter. I took the glass and stood there, as nervous as a girl at her first dance.

Howard Gabe indicated a seat. He was very tall and bent, a surgeon retired these twenty years. "I hope you won't be bored with our little meeting," he said. "Just details to be settled before the season starts. You know the river, of course."

I was far from bored, even though Mercer was now standing and reading out the tax assessment of the fishery, 1969–1970, in a dry, courtroom voice. The river meant a great deal to me.

The river Towy, as a geography textbook might say, rises high in the mountains of mid-Wales, by Carreg-y-ast, and flows sixty miles through Cardiganshire and Carmarthenshire to the sea at Llanstephan. It is not a big river. At the widest part it is possible, if you are a strong caster, to lose an expensive salmon lure by dropping it into the trees that overhang the far bank. Neither are its salmon as big or as plentiful as those of its neighbor the Wye, though a very big fish was once caught in the Towy, the biggest fish ever to come from a river in Britain.

A man was trying for salmon at Felinfach when he came upon it stranded on a gravel bank. He threw down his rod and ran to the Greyhound Inn where they laughed at him over their pints until his babblings finally convinced them and they went out to look. What they saw made them go back for a big farm horse, rope and tackle, with which they hauled the thing out in the end. It was a sturgeon and it weighed 365 pounds. Being a royal fish it was sent up to London, to King George V. If he acknowledged it, his message is not recorded locally.

Other strange things have happened in the Vale of Towy. Up river from where the sturgeon was caught, under the shadow of Baner Sir Gaer, the cliff has been cut and riven by storms into screes and deep gullies; and in a hollow of the mountainside there is a black, glacial lake called Llyn y Fan Fach. A man named Rhiwallon, from Blaensawdde in the parish of Llandeusant, was herding cattle on the shore one evening when a fairy woman came out of the water.

As a man he was entranced by her beauty, and as a Welshman by the black fairy cattle that followed her. He offered her some of his hard-baked oaten bread, which she refused, but he courted her the next evening with a soft white loaf that melted her heart, so she married him. She warned him, though, that if he struck her three times without cause she would return to the lake forever. They settled down in Esgair Laethdy farm and she bore him seven sons, but inevitably the three undeserved blows were struck and she disappeared again into the lake, taking her fairy cattle with her. She relented to some extent, however. When her sons were grown, she returned and instructed them in the art of medicine before vanishing again.

So, they became the Seven Physicians of Myddfai, the most skilled in all Wales at that time, which was the twelfth century. It was as recently as 1880, though, that the last Towy Valley doctor claiming direct descent from them died, and only in the last twenty years has the custom of climbing up to the Llyn on the first Sunday in August to see if the fairy would reappear died out.

The fairy woman of Llyn y Fan Fach might be a myth, but Twm Sion Catti was real enough and he lived in a cave high up in the steep valley above Randirmwym, where the Towy, which is here no more than a mountain torrent, cascades through ferns and red-berried mountain ash from one white-capped, swirling, bathroom-sized pool to the next. Twm, though he never gained the same sort of international fame as Robin Hood, was in the same line of work, only he operated single-handed. He robbed the rich sheep farmers to feed the poor, made a hobby of escaping from jails and making fools of sheriffs, and his career was happily crowned when he carried off the heiress of Ystradffin (Ystrad is still there, the walls are five feet thick and you could hold a dance in the kitchen). He ended as a model of respectability, now Thomas Jones, Esq., justice of the peace, of Fountain Gate, Breconshire. That was in the 1600s. The cave where he hid out is still there, though it is hard to find in summer when the oak trees among the white outcrops of limestone are in full leaf.

It is here, far up the river, that the salmon spawn in midwinter, the fish that have been running in from the sea since mid-May. They average perhaps ten or eleven pounds. The native brown trout are not much to boast of either. It's true you can catch dozens in a day but a ten-incher is a good fish. It isn't hard to find the reason. The Towy runs out of high moorland, impoverished, thin in nourishment. Very little weed grows in it. Turn one of its polished stones and there is nothing like the rich, crawling life you'll find under stones in more fertile rivers. There is little fly life either, just odd, sparse hatches of olive flies that seem to surprise the trout so much that they rise to them only spasmodically. Hardly anyone bothers to fish for trout on the Towy unless he wants a few for the breakfast pan.

Fortunately, these are not the only trout that the Towy offers. Somewhere at the misty beginnings of the river, when the glaciers retreated north, some of the little brown trout rejected the bare-bones existence that the river offered and migrated downstream to the sea. They fed richly on sand eel, young herrings and sprat and when they ran back up the river in the summer floods to spawn, they were so utterly changed that until well into this century they were regarded as a distinct species.

In the Towy and other Welsh rivers, anglers called them (and still do) sewin. They go by the name of white trout in Ireland, peal in Devon and Cornwall, finnock and herling in Scotland, and morts in the North of England. When they ran back from the sea they were brilliant silver and pink-flashed, wild to hit any lure which swung in front of their noses—for the first twenty-four hours or so, until the color of the flood which had brought them upstream faded from the water, whereupon they became the shyest fish imaginable, moving only at night.

They are sea-run brown trout that range from first-year babies that dropped down to the sea in May and returned in September as bright little pounders to great, heavy-shouldered fish that have spawned eight or nine times and grown to twenty pounds and more. And according to some, because of its long, winding estuary, and according to others on account of its utter barrenness, the Towy and its tributary Cothi have arguably the finest run of sea trout in Britain.

In the smoky, old man's room in which I now sat, I thought of the first time that I'd seen the Towy. It was after a long, wartime journey in an old double-decker bus, that had wheezed its way up from the city, through small black coal-mining towns and villages named after their chapels. At last the countryside turned green, the hills got higher and the river appeared. I was with another desperate twelve-year-old, Randall Rees Evans. We had a big can of worms and we reckoned we were in for the fishing of our lives.

As anglers, Evans and I had come a long way together. We'd caught mullet from the docks in the seaport city in which we lived, perch and eels from a filled-in quarry. They locked the park gates at dark, so we climbed the railings in the wartime blackout and hammered hell out of the carp in the ornamental lake. Lately, though, we'd begun to encounter difficulties. That spring, in the course of flattening the city, the Luftwaffe had dropped a stick of bombs into the park lake. One of them failed to explode—and so the lake had to be drained, which was the end of the carp. Then one day we went down to the docks and instead of the policeman who knew us, there was a soldier with an automatic pistol, who wasn't letting anybody through.

There was one advantage to the war, though. It cleared away a lot of the competition, so that when our close-range fishing became impossible and we explored farther afield on our bikes, we found that the little trout brooks a few miles past the outer suburbs had been lying fallow for a couple of years. The young men were all away and the older ones couldn't get gas for their cars. The brooks were overgrown with nettles and brambles but we squirmed through;

our worm technique became deadly and we always rode home with hanks of little golden-bellied trout tied to the handlebars. Naturally, in the end, that wasn't enough for us. The trout were small, greedy and easy. We started to look around for something a little better.

Evans found it one afternoon when poor old Soapy Davis was trying to tell us about Ohm's Law or some such in physics. They'd brought him back from happy retirement to teach us because of the manpower shortage, and he couldn't break the habit of spending lunchtime in a pub called The Mountain Dew. Soapy didn't mind what happened in the afternoons, so long as they passed quickly, so that Evans could peacefully read what he chose to. Now he gave me a shove. "Listen to this," he said.

He'd got hold of an old copy of "Where to Fish," a guide published by *The Field* magazine from which he now read to me in a harsh whisper. " 'The Towy: salmon, trout, sewin. Mostly preserved.' " He gave me another hard shove. "Only *mostly*," he said. "We can get a bus to Llandeilo. My auntie goes up there to get black market butter." Evans was short, dark and intense, and his glasses were mended with adhesive plaster.

I said, "I haven't got any money."

"I've got birthday money," Evans said. "You can pay me back."

"What's a sewin?"

"A young salmon," Evans said, inventing wildly. So for the first time in our lives we saw a real river, the legendary Towy, crashing white past the old gray buttresses of Llandeilo Bridge into a deep rocky pool, then broadening into a shining glide shadowed green with oaks.

"Is it all right to fish here?" I asked Evans. There was a little pink-washed farmhouse almost under the bridge.

"We'll ask," Evans said. We knocked on the front door for a while but nobody answered, so we went through the yard to the back. The kitchen door was open and a goose walked out. I hammered on the window. There was a shriek, footsteps and a young woman emerged. She had a pan of boiled-over milk in one hand and a baby in her other arm was hanging onto her hair. It had jam all over its face.

"Can we fish here, please?" I asked politely.

"You can do what the hell you like!" she screeched, slamming the door.

"There you are," Evans said, "Permission sometimes available from farmers, just like it says in the book."

On our bank, pastureland ran down to the river and black and white Holstein-Friesians were grazing. The river was bigger and more baffling than anything we had ever seen before, but we put our rods together, tied on hooks and impaled our usual worms for bait. They plopped into the pool a few yards out and we sat on the grass to await the miracle. Nothing happened for a while. We unwrapped our sandwiches and chewed silently.

"We'll have one in a minute," Evans said with confidence.

"Oh, will you!" roared a terrible voice behind us.

I choked uncontrollably on my cheese. I could only turn around very slowly. Evans, white, put his hands up protectively to his glasses. A huge, ugly man with a red face and a stick in his hand towered over us.

"And who are you?" this ogre roared again.

"Randall Rees Evans," my friend whispered. I still couldn't speak.

"Get out of it! Get out of it before I change my mind!"

Scrabbling desperately for our bits and pieces, we ran like hell across two hundred yards of meadow, over the gate and onto the main road. A small wiry man was leaning on the parapet of the bridge.

"Friends of the Earl of Cawdor, are you?" he asked us pleasantly. We told him we were not.

"I thought I'd ask," he said, "because you've just been fishing his water. I suppose you've got licenses to fish, have you?"

"No," said Evans jauntily, recovering a little now, "but we're not fishing his water now, are we?"

"Ah," said the wiry little man, still pleasant, "I see you're a bit confused. The gentleman you met just now is the keeper. He looks after permission to fish on the Earl's stretch. And I," he said, his voice rising to a sharp bark, "am the River Board Bailiff. I look after licenses, and that is a different matter altogether. Come along with me."

We followed him. Where to? The police station? Jail? Thank God, no. He was turning into a fishing tackle shop.

"These young gentlemen," he told the man behind the counter, "require fishing licenses." He stood behind us while Evans got the rest of his birthday money out.

"That's better," he said. "Even the Earl of Cawdor has to have one of these. Now listen to me. It's a bit early in the year for sewin. Come up again in June, but leave the Earl's water alone. Get a day ticket from the Llandeilo Angling Club."

We didn't go back to the Towy together again, though. Evans seemed to lose his enthusiasm for fishing and eventually ended up as an industrial chemist with an oil company. I lost touch with the river also—college, the Air Force, a job in the North of England . . . it was not until the mid-sixties that I returned to the city, teaching in the Faculty of Education there, and began to think once more of the Towy. Then followed a strange period in my fishing life. From writing odd pieces for outdoor magazines, I found myself running the fishing column in the London Daily Express, which brought with it the chance of occasional, spectacular trips to rivers I'd never hoped to reach, like the Scottish Dee, the Irish Blackwater, the Norwegian Driva. Absurdly, though, there was the Towy running through green Carmarthenshire, only thirty miles from my home, and I couldn't lay my hands on it.

Until, that is, I met Peter Williams, not on a particularly joyful occasion. I got to him because I'd heard he was a good lawyer. I'd been involved in selling and buying a house, and it seemed to me that the legal fees had been somewhat exaggerated. Williams looked at them and snorted like a small warhorse. In the end he saved me $500 and put in his bill for about $20, a man I instantly warmed to, though I would never have suspected him of being a fisherman. I learned that a few months later when we met at a somewhat dull party. I was just back from the Dee or somewhere, and I must have mentioned it because he said, "If you ever fancy a day's fishing on the Towy, please give me a call."

And that was how I saw the Dolgarreg Fishery on the Towy for the first time—as a guest of Peter Williams. After that, our routine was always the same. We'd fix a day and Williams would say he couldn't conceivably leave the office before five thirty. At lunchtime, though, he'd call and announce he'd canceled appointments from four thirty on. I'd get to his office then to find him dancing about like a gnome, half-changed in pinstriped pants and a hoary old tweed coat with flies in the lapel, while his ancient and motherly secretary clucked distractedly. The home-going traffic would thick by the time we got out, and I often feared that Williams would finally blow himself to pieces as he kept up a steady stream of choking, hissing vitipuration at the drivers of all the cars that had placed themselves between himself and Dolgarreg. By the time we got there he would need all the gentle therapy that Dolgarreg could bring.

Dolgarreg would heal the soul of anybody. At the top of the

fishing, the Towy comes scattered in a million points of light over a broad ford, then cuts into the hillside under a stand of dark green pines, running very deep on the far side. This is uninventively called the Top Pool, holding water for salmon and big sewin. The last red kites in Britain, big, fork-tailed birds of prey, soar over the Top Pool sometimes. There are fewer than a dozen pairs left, and they breed higher up the valley, above Randirmwyn. Then the river flows broad and shallow again to the next pool, which is Island Cottage, a great, scoured-out frothing pot that slowly disciplines itself into a fast run. Island Cottage nearly always holds salmon, but they are close to impossible to approach with fly or spinner because the currents are so contrary, making any lure move unnaturally.

But after Island Cottage comes the Flat, a quarter mile of smooth water, consistently four or five feet deep, with a clear white pebble beach on one side and tall overshadowing oaks on the other. When the river runs low in summer, this is where the sewin lie, huge shoals of them that turn your heart over when you climb a tree and look down through sunglasses. The Flat is for night fishing, when the sewin come out of the shadows. It is never touched in daylight.

The Groynes come next, where the River Board has put in a series of stone piers to stop the Towy cutting into the pastures to the north. They have formed a deep, bare-banked, sulky pool which holds fish that very seldom take. It is a dark, mysterious, unresponsive place. But in the next pool, the Sticks, the river comes to life again. Once the Towy undercut a small wood here, and the stumps and boughs still jut out of the water, creating swirls, eddies and deep places. The timber could be hauled out easily enough, but there is no reason to do this. Sewin love the shelter, and they stay in the sticks as long as they can. The pool is nearly always well stocked.

Below the Sticks is Dolgarreg's finest salmon pool, Glantowy. Then comes the Run and, invention flagging again, the Bottom Pool and the Bottom Sticks, until the Dulais brook flows in and that is the end of the fishery, two miles of it altogether, the fishing right that Peter Williams in partnership with Gabe, Mercer and Couch had bought piece by piece from the valley farmers soon after World War II, before fishing values went mad. It had cost them the equivalent of $15,000 then. Twenty years later the value would be more than $100,000, today perhaps five times that.

It may be arguable whether any four men should have the sole right to fish that run up from the sea into a stretch of water, arguable indeed whether any fishing is worth this much. I have no answer to this, only that in the case of Dolgarreg there is no grudging of fishing permission to good and responsible local anglers. As to the value, I think of the first evening I fished it alone.

It was early in May, and three days before, a gale of wind had come roaring in from the southwest and with it big bruised clouds that lashed rain on the mountains for forty-eight hours. The Towy spilled over its banks in a brown flood, carrying boughs and drowned sheep to the sea, and even when I got there, a full day after the rain had stopped, it was still too early to think of fish. I stowed my tackle under a bush, walked upstream to see if the storm had done any damage to the banks, and met Derek Jones, who works at the little railroad halt a half mile from the river — one of those locals who had permission to fish. He said, "Don't go home. The river is beginning to clear up at Llandovery." That was five miles upstream. The clearance would reach Dolgarreg in less than a half hour. This was going to be spin-fishing water, of course. The river would still be too heavy and colored for fly.

I walked back to the Glantowy pool and tied on a No. 5 Mepps spoon, the biggest they make, the kind of lure that would send every sewin in the river scuttling for shelter in normal conditions. I stuck a twig in the bank at water level and watched the river retreat from it by millimeters. I tried an experimental cast. It was possible to see the flash of it a foot or so under the water. It was worth making a start. The fishing cliche on these occasions is that fish could be lying anywhere. Not so. They would not be hanging around in the fast water or in the slacks. They would be pushing upstream, but from time to time they would have to rest for a short while, holding position in smooth water just below the pools. It isn't often in fishing that a theory is dramatically proved correct within seconds, as this one was. I flicked the spoon to the edge of the heavy water, letting it be carried around into the glide. There was no need to wind. It throbbed for a second or two. Then the rod was wrenched down violently.

People make a lot of fuss about telling the difference between a salmon and a big sea trout. They go on about scale counts and imaginary lines drawn from the eye to the jaw, but in fact you know what you have got hold of the minute you hit the fish. A salmon is very slow to be frightened. Sometimes it will keep you waiting a full half minute before it decides to move at all and in the early stages of a fight it may simply proceed, slowly and majestically, in the direction it fancies, leading you like a pet poodle. Later it will go mad, but rarely at the beginning. A sewin, though, knows what the trouble is immediately, and takes to the air.

As this one did now in a series of wild, hysterical leaps that took it across and downstream until it was fifty yards from me and still jumping. Nobody can ever claim to be in control of a sea trout, not even a two-pounder, in the first stage of a fight. I started to run downstream to shorten the line, but the fish changed its mind and ran toward me. I was trembling. This was a huge sea trout, more than twenty pounds. It came straight at me as I wildly reeled to keep in touch. It saw me, leapt high and made off downstream again.

And then the drag of my lovely expensive Italian reel jammed solid. Absurdly, it didn't occur to me to knock off the anti-reverse control and play the fish on the reel handle. All I could think of doing was to follow the fish and I was waist high in the water and almost swept away before the line snapped. As it did, the sewin jumped once more, just to imprint its size on my mind.

I sat down trembling on the bank and looked at the reel. The trouble was in the spool. There was another in my bag, but it was loaded with four pounds test line only, which was going to leave me heavily outgunned with the river coming down big and this class of sewin about. But there was nothing else to do, with maybe an hour of daylight left.

I rigged my gear and cast again in the same place. Immediately came another textbook sewin take, the fish high in the air, cartwheeling away. It was nothing like as big, though — seven or eight pounds maybe — and in ten minutes perhaps I had it damped down and just taking off line in angry buzzes each time I brought it within net range. Then I had it lolling on its side, looking a dull amber under the water, though it would be ingot-bright silver when I got it out.

I didn't get it out. The Mepps spoons I'd brought were a new type made with, so the makers said, instantly detachable hooks for swift replacement. This one detached, right enough, staying in the fish while the spoon blade flipped back to me. The spring clip arrangement had been activated by the incessant leaping of the fish which I now watched sinking, exhausted, into the depths of the Glantowy Pool.

I felt sick. I didn't want to fish any more and I started to walk back to where I'd left my car. But almost at once I saw Derek Jones a couple of fields off, making his way upriver. The Territorial Imperative is what zoologists call what I felt then. I went back to what I reckoned was my patch, put on an old-fashioned undetachable hooked Mepps and went to work again. And again I was in.

Heaven knows how I landed that fish. I did everything wrong, let him have too much slack, tried to bully him into the net. But I couldn't lose this one, which was just as well because I would have slid right into a coma had I done so. Derek came up and we weighed him. Twelve pounds ten ounces, and fresh from the sea.

I rarely fished the Towy alone, though. The syndicate rule was that guests had to be accompanied by a member, except in the case of an emergency. Peter fixed as many emergencies as he could but there was a limit, and there were days of superb conditions when he was marooned in the courtroom without a chance of escape.

This meant that mostly we practiced the other kind of Towy seatrout fishing — the night fishing in summer when the river was dead low and the shoals of sewin cowered in shelter through the day, not moving until darkness fell. We had a rule for those nights. At dusk the big sewin would start to be restless; then, sitting silently in the cover of the trees, you would hear a reverberating crash, as if a boy had tossed a brick into the water. It was essential to do nothing at this stage. Not until the third fish had moved was it permissible to wade slowly and silently into the water, false-cast to get line out and then work down toward the fish as the thick, warm, midsummer night closed in.

On one memorable night in mid-September, 1969, I was wading the Flat below Island Cottage. The sewin were moody and there was the beginning of autumn chill in the air, but a five-pounder had sucked in my Dai Ben, the small, black-hackled, gray-wool-bodied fly that is the most deadly sewin fly used on the Towy, and it now gave a pleasant weight to the bag that hung over my shoulder. I didn't think I would get another to go with him, though. The chill had set up the beginning of a white mist on the river. Once that spread over the water, it would be pointless to fish on. I kept casting fruitlessly until I saw a pinpoint of light wavering down from the Top Pool. Peter was on his way back, and I waded out to meet him, my nailed boots scrunching on the pebbles. He'd had one take and missed it. Not worth fishing on, he said. We took the rod down in the torchlight. I poured coffee and stiffed it up, as was our custom, with whiskey from a little saddle flask.

"I was talking to old Bert Couch today," Peter said. "He's not well. He'll never come up the river again." Not once had I seen him there myself, I told Peter, not in five years.

"He wouldn't admit it until now. Did I ever tell you he took seventeen sewin in one day from this water? In 1950, that was. Not one under six pounds."

We sat silently for a while as the moon started to slide out over the oaks.

"I was thinking," Peter said, "that you might like to take his place."

"I couldn't begin to afford it," I said.

"Ah, well there's ways and means," he said vaguely. We talked of other things on the way home. The subject was not raised again until the next spring. Then he called me. Perhaps I'd be interested in coming to a little meeting of the syndicate, just the pre-season meeting? It was possible that we might be able to come to a more permanent arrangement for my fishing than I'd enjoyed in the past. He was being unaccustomedly formal and lawyerlike. I could tell he had the same scheme in mind as he had that autumn night on the river, but I still couldn't afford it. The Dolgarreg fishing must now be worth close to $25,000 a share. And not long since, I had decided to resign my lectureship to write full-time. But it was a terrifying temptation to borrow it, raise it somehow, get a mortgage. And if they offered it to me and I refused, how could I go on being a guest?

So there I was, in the old man's house, the whiskey glass still half full in my hand, wondering what was coming next.

Mercer had finished with the tax bit; he was going on about the days for giving the locals fishing permits. Then, extraordinarily, he was saying, "And which day of the week are you least likely to come up, Clive?"

I could only look at him.

"If you're coming in next season, we'd like to know that — you don't want to come up and find all the local boys on the river."

Mercifully, Peter intervened. "Bert can't go on fishing," he said, "but he doesn't want it to go to a stranger, somebody none of us know."

"I don't know that I can . . . ," I started to say.

"He wants you to come in at the price he paid in 1948. Let's say $3,500."

The old man was sitting there, smiling and nodding. I still couldn't afford it.

"Yes," I said. "Yes, that's marvelous." My mind was working on two levels. Exultation on one, rapid calculation on the other. There was about that much to come if I drew out what I'd paid into the pension fund when I was a teacher . . . . "That's marvelous," I said again. And to hell with the Earl of Cawdor, I thought.

LOCH KILDONAN, SOUTH UIST, SCOTLAND

CHAPTER TWO

MacDonald's Lament

What follows is only incidentally about salmon fishing in Scotland or even fishing itself. It is mainly about the Nature of the Ghillie (spelled without the 'h' in Ireland and known in North America as a guide). To call a man a ghillie is not demeaning — it is, in any case, almost impossible to make a ghillie feel demeaned. Rather the reverse is the case. It is the provider of his daily fee, tips and whiskey, who is often reduced to currying favor from his ghillie, whose attitude can range from open arrogance to what the Service used to call dumb insolence. Donal MacDonald, the ghillie assigned to Peter Williams and me, was by no means as bad as some, and he actually ended up on our side. But he gives a notion of the profession.

SCOTLAND

Donal MacDonald, resting on his oars, asked passionately, "Have you got a Goat's Toe at all?" His ill-assembled features were screwed up tight and his eyes glittered. He was into his manic phase again.

"No, not even at all," I told him. We were sick of the question, Williams and I. He knew we didn't have a Goat's Toe, indeed that there wasn't a single one left on the island. He was trying to bring us down again, shifting the burden of guilt. He knew as well as we did that Loch Roag, at drought level and now brassily reflecting the September sun, was about as likely to yield up a yellowfin tuna as a salmon. A couple of hours before, a big, weary sea trout had heaved itself through the surface film and collapsed back onto it, but that had been the only vital sign. Until this point also, MacDonald had been fairly silent, as he weathered the early, depressed stage of his normal, monumental hangover; although now and then he would express surprise at his ailment as if it were some act of God or mysterious viral infection over which he had no control. A stranger, overhearing our grunted exchanges, might well have concluded that relations had deteriorated between ourselves and the ghillie. He would have been entirely correct. It is part of the mythology of sport that the ghillie, the guide, the boat skipper, is always a well-seasoned character, full of resource, humor and wisdom, though sometimes he has to speak bluntly to the idiot who has hired him purely for the idiot's own good. Naturally he is infinitely skilled in the ways of fish and game. I have rarely met one like that. I go along with Negley Farson.

Farson was one of those swashbuckling American foreign correspondents who flourished between the World Wars. He took his rod with him when he covered the rise of Hitler, and between despatches wrote the best fishing book that I have ever read, *Going Fishing*, unhappily out of print these many years. He had a lot of trouble with guides and ghillies, especially in Scotland, and in an uncharacteristically ill-humored outburst he wrote, after one of them had broken the tip of his Hardy rod, "Ghillies . . . need firm handling. The local man always knows more than you do. Also, though he may be clever enough to conceal it, he resents your presence: this 'foreigner' he is taking round. I do not succumb to the philosophy of the local man."

Maybe that is not universally true, not even of Scottish ghillies, but after four bad days in the boat with Donal I was beginning to think that Farson could have gone a lot farther. This matter of the Goat's Toe, for instance. Everywhere you go for Atlantic salmon there is a favored fly or lure, and sometimes it has been favored for a half century without any guide or ghillie seriously questioning its supremacy. On the island of South Uist, off the west coast of Scotland, where we were now the prisoner-clients of MacDonald, it was the Goat's Toe that was the only pattern to use.

Oddly enough, I'd come to South Uist as a result of reading Negley Farson, and then only because he'd sneered at it. He'd seen the veranda of the Lochboisdale Hotel paved, he said, with sea trout, but discovered that the fishing was booked up for that and for the following season. "It is a place I have no wish to go back to," he wrote loftily. "The fishing seemed almost a business there. It was too well organized. Still, if you want to be sure of catching masses of fine sea trout, that's the place."

What I should have taken into consideration was that Farson's book came out more than three decades ago. Certainly, as he promised, it had been difficult to book a week's fishing, but the big sea trout were there no longer, or very few of them. Nobody had fouled the water or netted the fish. They had been driven out—by salmon.

Not literally. Big sea-run brown trout are the more pugnacious species, and the South Uist salmon run small, averaging seven or eight pounds. The latter, traditionally, had been outnumbered by sea trout in the lochs by about five to one. In recent years, though, the pattern had changed and the ratio reversed. What happened was that the salmon started to run later in the season than the sea trout. As they moved up into the same hill streams to spawn, they ploughed their way through the redds the sea trout had made, sluicing their fertilized ova downstream. So now, instead of having the finest sea-run browns in Scotland, South Uist has a run of modest-sized salmon. When it has a run at all.

Williams and I, the doctor, the navy commander, the two cattle dealers and the Church of Scotland minister, who formed a fishing party at the Lochboisdale Hotel, reckoned any run would be worth waiting for. The fish, we'd been told, moved from the Atlantic into a handful of small, shallow lochs, and there they rested until the fall. All those weeks they watched artfully tied flies, a thousand Goat's Toes, swim past their noses until they became the most sophisticated fish in Scotland. You couldn't approach them on salmon tackle. You needed a No. 6 line, size 10 or even 12 flies, and a 3x leader. They were well-rested fish, too, not like spring salmon that had fought their way up fifty miles of river, and on what was virtually trout tackle they were a formidable angling challenge. Which was why, through the best part of a bad week, we had put up with the rigors of both the Clan MacDonald and the island of South Uist.

South Uist dangles, like some kind of green afterthought, almost at the end of the island chain of the Outer Hebrides. Northwards, islands like Lewis and Harris have all the trappings of the romantic Highlands: mountains, eagles, stags, heather. South Uist has bog-land, one significant hill, some wet, defeated-looking sheep and the MacDonalds. And the worst of *those* was Donal MacD., and his obsession with the Goat's Toe. For four successive days, Williams and I had flogged the entirely unresponsive waters of Lochs Roag and Fada, the Schoolhouse Loch and the Mill Loch.

And we had caught nothing, which, according to Donal, was on account of us not having Goat's Toes. None of the guests at the Lochboisdale had actually seen such a fly. The last had been cracked off or snagged underneath a stone weeks before we had arrived, and we couldn't even tie one because Donal was vague about the dressing. ("A bit of red wool. A bit of peacock in it somewhere.") The game book on the marble slab in the hotel lobby indeed recorded that until the last one was lost around mid-August, almost every fish that season had fallen to the mysterious killer. Since then, catches had dwindled. In other parts of the world, barroom chat revolves around money or sex. At Lochboisdale, we talked about the Goat's Toe. That was while we were still talking. It didn't take us long to discover that the Goat's Toe was, in fact, a crude alibi. The truth was that four of the lochs — Roag, Fada, Schoolhouse and Mill — had hardly produced a fish all season. Nearly all the salmon had come from Lochs Kildonan and Bharp. Theoretically, this meant that during a week's fishing (six days, since it is illegal, because of some Sabbatarian hangover, to catch a Scottish salmon on a Sunday) you could expect four bad — no, hopeless — days and two good ones.

Possibly. There were plenty of fish holed up in Kildonen, but you needed precisely the correct weather — a moderate blow from the south or the southwest. Anything less and the fish wouldn't move. Anything more, and the sand from the bottom would be stirred up, making it too cloudy to fish. On the other hand, for rocky Loch Bharp you needed a flailing westerly gale.

The guests fished the lochs in rotation and in pairs, Williams and I sharing a boat. And the weather, for those who had risen to the top of the roster and fished the two hot lochs, had been hopeless. Outside the hotel on a long pole was a weather vane, appropriately a wrought iron sea trout, and all week it had stayed still or creaked uncertainly to light airs from the north as the sun blazed down. Nightly, the guests gathered in front of the television for the weather forecast, and nightly it promised more of the same. Surface politeness was maintained, but the early camaraderie soon eroded. Williams and I, with our days on the two favored lochs coming at the end of the week, began to find ourselves alone after dinner except when one of the others was foolish enough to proposition us about changing our schedule. The navy commander, for instance, must have considered us very naive. "Might take a tramp over the moors to-morrow," he said to us, smiling toothily and falsely. "Carry a trout rod with me. Leaves Kildonan free, of course. If you fellows would like to fish it . . ." His smile faded in the face of Williams's steady glower.

Social life, no matter what the state of the fishing, would have been severely curtailed anyway by Miss Morag, an enemy of drink, who presided over the residents' cocktail bar except during her unex-plained, twenty-minute absences which were superbly timed to co-incide with the moment when you were gathering your thoughts to order a fresh drink. When you did get one, it was accompanied by a look of such outraged distaste from Miss Morag that after a couple of attempts, most of us frequented the seedy public bar at the back of the hotel, where it was possible to watch Donal laying the foun-dations of next day's appalling hangover.

You could also watch the early TV weather forecast there, and this was where the evening of Day Four found Williams and me waiting to hear our fate, for the following morning we were to fish Kildonan. There was not likely to be any change, the man said. A light northerly airstream would continue to cover Scotland. The temperature would be above average. The sighs of relief from the two cattle dealers, whose chance was yet to come, were all too audible. We left without offering them a drink.

I didn't bother going into breakfast until nine the next morning. Williams was spooning moodily at his porridge. "Another beautiful day," said the tiny waitress brightly. Williams snarled something inaudible at her. From the dining-room windows of the Lochboisdale Hotel it's not possible to see the iron sea trout, but all of the little rock-girt harbor is in view. Gray Atlantic seals bobbed in and out of the water and a couple of lobster boats rubbed themselves against the wooden pier, a pleasing sight to anyone less jaded than Williams and I. We scarcely noticed it any longer. On this particular morning I must have been staring at it, on and off, for ten minutes before I was aware of a difference on the face of the water.

All week it had been oily, with no more of a ripple than could be raised by a seal's cough. Now it had changed. The surface blurred over. Small wavelets began to slap white at the bottom of the rocks and the sunlight faded as if somebody had turned down a rheostat. And the wavelets were running from the southwest. I stood up and grasped Williams by the arm. "Look at it," I said. We both stared like children watching the first snow of the winter and praying that it wouldn't stop. Then we went outside.

The iron trout had moved. It indicated southwest. Bundles of gray cumulus clouds were building up over the Atlantic. The commander, the doctor, the cattle dealers and the minister followed us out, watched silently for a moment and went in again. Except the minister. He said, feelingly, "Aren't you the lucky ones?" And then, doubtlessly recalling the Tenth Commandment, the one about covetousness, gave us a bless-you-my-children smile and a backslap. We stacked our tackle into the car, afraid to make each other any promises, and drove up the road to meet Donal.

He was waiting on the corner and he looked awful, his face more fragmented than ever, his eyes like coals of fire. He got into the car, moaning softly, and my heart sank. We had this miraculous, God-given day, but we were in the hands of Donal. We drove to Kildonan in near silence. To ask Donal what he thought of our chances might prove too much for him, I feared, but when we'd arrived and were setting up the fly-rods he said, "It is a verra great shame that you have no Goat's Toes. You might have caught a fish today." He lowered his eyelids in response to some secret, inner pain and shuffled off to the boat. I tied on a Connemara Black, size 10, a dark fly for a dark day. There was ninety percent cloud cover now, and the wave on Kildonan was exactly as we had been told it should be, lively, but not big enough to stir up the bottom sand. Donal brought the boat around. "I'll take you to the House of Commons first," he said.

We knew enough about Kildonan to know what that meant. The loch was small and there were two prime fishing areas in it, both on the eastern side, both shallow, stony bays with clumps of reeds stretching out from the shore. The House of Commons was the first, so named in the great old sea trout days because it held just normal-sized fish. But the House of Lords, ah, yes, the House of Lords! That was where the giant sea trout lived, and where there was still just the outside chance of meeting one. Donal's plan, as he unfolded it to us now, was to fish the House of Commons first, reserving the House of Lords until after lunch.

So we sneaked up on the House of Commons, Donal keeping the boat beam-on to the wind and holding her so that we could fish out the casts slowly. On the second drift, about the fourth cast, the light southwesterly wind theory was vindicated. The Connemara Black dropped into a swirl of whiskey-colored water behind a boulder no more than six feet from the shore and was comprehensively engulfed. There was the moment of brick-wall resistance you always get when you hook a salmon, and then a bright eight-pounder was pitching itself out of the yellow foam and Donal, his eyes popping, was hauling on the oars to give me water room away from shore in which to play the fish.

This was a wild one, bright and fresh-run into the loch. The old rule says it should take about a minute to the pound to land a salmon, but this one took three times as long. By then we were almost out in the middle of the loch and the fish had nearly killed itself before Donal put the landing net under it. The same was true of Donal himself. There is an honorable tradition in Scotland, though, that the whiskey is passed around whenever a salmon is killed. We toasted this one in turn and Williams and I looked away politely as Donal uptilted the flask, not wanting to appear curious about the length of his swallow. The reward was just enough. "Verra weel!" Donal shouted. "We'll go back for another. Have you any Connemara Blacks at all?" he demanded of Williams, who was already tying one on. And in minutes Williams was already into a salmon of his own, a twin of mine.

It jumped a couple of times, though, and threw the hook — we'd been forewarned that because of the smallness of the flies, the percentage of South Uist fish that came unstuck was large. But this was going to be a good morning. Ten minutes later, Williams got another chance and a second salmon was soon alongside mine in the stern of the boat. And there was still the House of Lords to come.

We should have headed there straight away instead of going ashore for lunch. We'd have got an hour at least amongst the aristos of the sea trout. But, as the minister might have said to us consolingly, "The Lord giveth, the Lord taketh away." No sooner had we brushed off the crumbs and screwed up the flask than the wind got up hard, whistling in from the Atlantic, kicking up whitecaps. A new man now, Donal pulled into the teeth of it, but by the time we crossed the loch the discoloration was already obvious in the water.

"The man who is fishing Loch Bharp this afternoon will have to have plenty of whiskey with him," said Donal meaningfully, and he meant to toast the many fish that would be coming aboard, not to keep out the cold, naturally. I'd forgotten that it was the doctor's day on Bharp. Maybe, after all, Williams and I would not be the only ones to use the weighing scales and then modestly bend over the game book to make our entries. With that thought in mind, both of us flogged the water harder than ever, even though it had taken on a pale muddiness and Donal had lapsed into sardonic silence after suggesting several times that we go home. He was right, of course. We had to admit that in the end. We left off fishing early and headed back to Lochboisdale.

There at least we could bloody the scales, although back at the hotel we had no audience. I weighed the fish, then opened the game book and wrote in the date and the weather conditions, then "Gammon and Williams. Two salmon, eight pounds and seven pounds. Fly: Goat's Toe." Williams nodded his approval. He saw the tactics. First fluster the opposition — where had we got our Goat's Toes? — then make it feel at a severe disadvantage by subtly confirming their already strong belief that it was no use trying to use anything else. It's a cruel business, hotel salmon fishing in Scotland.

In spite of Miss Morag, who turned up the Gaelic folk music program on her little radio as soon as we walked in, we took up our position in the cocktail bar which, inhospitable as it was, gave us a fine view of the hotel entrance. If the doctor came in staggering under a load of fish we would have a little time to prepare ourselves. Meantime, one by one the others arrived, passed the cocktail bar and disappeared into their rooms. Nothing to fear there. The commander, indeed, seemed to be muttering to himself as he stumped by the door. It was almost dark before we heard the doctor's car.

He parked with the car facing us, and he and his wife spent an eternity around the back, rummaging in the trunk; all we could see was a side view of the rear end of his tweed trousers as he maneuvered to lift some heavy object. A big canvas bag with six, seven, maybe eight salmon in it, I guessed fearfully.

But no. The sky seemed to lighten as he emerged burdened by an elaborate picnic basket. His wife carried home-movie equipment and a couple of camping seats. Truth dawned. Putting too much trust in the weather forecast, he had promised to take his wife on a tour of the island. Remorselessly, she had held him to it. Smiling in friendly style, Williams and I sallied out of the bar to meet them.

Negley Farson, curiously enough, once found himself in our position in a Scottish hotel. (You'll find it in Chapter IV of *Going Fishing*.) "Dammit all," he quotes an envious admiral as saying, "I'm glad to see anyone catch a salmon." Which, as Farson observed, might have been put differently. At Lochboisdale that night there was a similar degree of frigidity. The congratulations were formal. Only the minister, looking like the martyred St. Sebastian in those medieval paintings, with the Roman arrows thunking into him, insisted masochistically on a cast-by-cast description of our day. The doctor and his wife didn't seem to be on speaking terms: straight after dinner she retreated with her knitting into a corner of the lounge. The weather forecast didn't lift the temperature either. It might have been wrong the night before, but there was no way now to misinterpret the deep low drifting between Iceland and Scotland. Tomorrow there was going to be a gale of westerly wind. Bharp was going to be perfect. Williams and I were down for Bharp.

And as we'd hoped, it turned out a beautiful morning, rain lashing at the window and the wind howling in across the Atlantic. We were the first into breakfast, and we gobbled it fast and alone. We were into our foul-weather gear and away to fetch Donal before there could be any embarrassing encounter with our fellow guests. Donal himself looked in better shape than he had all week. "Have ye got them Connemara Blacks?" he enquired fiercely. "There will be slaughter today, a bloody great slaughter."

Kildonan and the other lochs had been flat, desolate places, flush with the boggy moorland. Bharp was a long black cleft in the hillside, the rocks rising high above it and the shore strewn with boulders as big as the boat. The gale was sending breakers crashing onto the stones and with cold, wet fingers it was hard to tie on the small flies. Once we were afloat, the first drift made it plain that Donal couldn't manage the boat with the two of us in it. The salmon lay on the lee shore, very close in among the stones, so that the boat had to be kept edging across the wind and held a cast's length out from the boulders. We came ashore, flipped a coin and Williams won. He said he'd go back for a quiet morning and a hot lunch. Then we'd switch and he'd fish the afternoon session.

I was into my first salmon before the noise of the car had dwindled, an eleven-pounder. In the rest of the morning I met four more fish. Two broke off on the strike, snapping the 3x leader as the fly was being retrieved fast. The others I landed, both ten-pounders.

While the last salmon was being fought, the wind shrieked even higher and drove the boat on the shore, fortunately onto soft bog between the boulders. It was a miracle getting that fish out, and I was glad to see Williams arrive, silhouetted on the hilltop against the storm. There'd been no time to shelter or toast the fish I'd caught.

Now we dragged the boat up and made up for both omissions in the lee of a low stone wall. Then, thankfully, I left Williams and Donal to it.

"Not fishing?" the minister enquired courteously as I sat in front of the fire that afternoon. He'd also come in early, dripping and fishless from Loch Roag. I explained, then confessed to my catch which I'd left in the bottom of the boat.

"Yes, I see," said the minister. He sought for some more positively cheery words but failed. I told him it was time I set off to fetch my friend. "Would you mind," he said, "if I came along with you?" I don't think he doubted my word about the salmon. He just craved to be where the action was.

And he was lucky. Theatrically, the moment we walked over the ridge of the hill and looked down onto Bharp, we saw Williams's rod bend into a fish. For almost half an hour we saw him play it in the wind and the rain until Donal stood up in the boat and bent over with the net. It was a very red fish, around nine pounds, the second for Williams, the fifth out of Bharp that day.

Farson had also had a second day of triumph when he alone brought a salmon into the hotel. "That night," he recorded, "nobody offered me a drink. The hate had set in."

And indeed I thought we might have gone a little too far ourselves. The minister had clearly signed on as one of our party, exclaiming happily as, one by one, we hoisted our fish onto the scales. But the commander, the cattle dealers, the doctor—how would they react? Farson, I'm afraid, must have run into a bad crowd. At the Lochboisdale, once the battle was over, there was a generous acceptance of the result even when, later on, I confessed about the Goat's Toe.

In truth, this was much later on after another victory had been won by the age-old method of strength in numbers. Our fellow anglers, admittedly stunned at first by the sight of five salmon laid out on the marble slab in the lobby, had rallied—though I can't recall who first suggested a move to the cocktail bar.

Until then, Miss Morag had found it all too easy to put one or two demoralized fishermen to flight. Faced with a crowd, though, she crumbled, though she held out until the singing started. Then she slipped away and one of the bright-eyed girls from the dining room took her place. "Miss Morag didn't feel well," she explained.

It was even later when the four strangers walked into the bar, just off the car ferry. At that point, I recall, Donal himself was leading the singing of "Will Ye No Come Back Again" and Williams was trying to waltz with the doctor's wife. The newcomers were clearly our successors, the new intake. I beckoned them over to join our group. "I hope," I said to them, "that you've brought plenty of Goat's Toes with you."

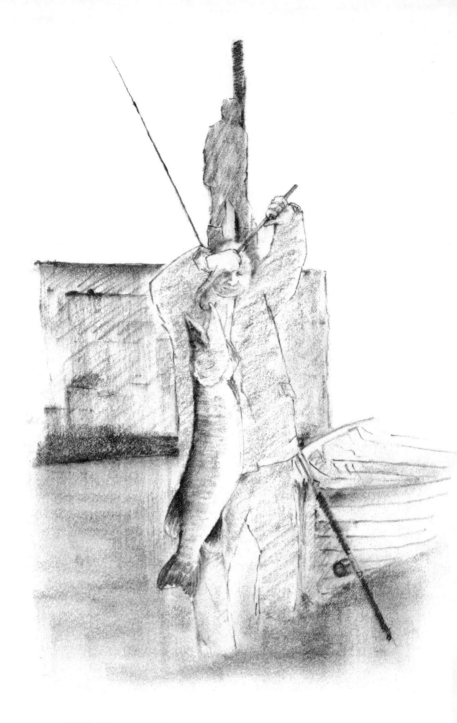

PIKE FROM LOUGH ALLEN, CO. LEITRIM, IRELAND

CHAPTER THREE

In a Land of Green, a Touch of Blue

Packy Joe Reynolds, who is the hero of this story, is also an undertaker and the inventor of a new unit of measure: the coffin lid. As in, "The big divil was a full coffin lid," meaning that the northern pike he was speaking of was truly monstrous, pushing six feet long. Packy Joe is not only the best pike man in Ireland but also the teller of the best pike stories. Nevertheless, in the depths of Lough Allen, there may swim pike of dimensions so big that they would be best measured Joe's way.

IRELAND

Joseph Mary Mooney, ex-senator of the Irish Republic, looked up from the slice of toast he was plastering with vitamin-enriched spread. "Tell him about the big fella, Pat," he said.

A turf fire flickered brightly in Mooney's kitchen, though in the west of Ireland November is a soft, mild month; outside, in the woods around Drumshanbo village, the leaves were still green on the trees.

Pat Reynolds, silver-haired and sturdy, a master of the narrative art, hitched his chair forward. "Come here till I tell you," he said, and I leaned toward him as if hypnotized, though it was only mild narcosis brought on by the turf smoke and the strong tea that Mooney brewed.

"It was back in July he hooked him," Reynolds began. "An Englishman from Derby, or someplace, and he was using one of them copper spoons with a touch of blue to it. I was just rowing him along the shore of the first island out from the pier when this huge beast of a thing grabbed hold. It was two and a half hours before we had him beat, then didn't this bloody ijjit of an angler think he'd like a movin' film of his fish lying on his side in the water, waiting for the gaff." Pat took a long suck at his tea. "I don't want to hear any more," I said, anguished.

"He was over half the length of the oar," Pat went on inexorably, "and he was lying there in the water near dead. Your man was trying to keep his head up while his missus took the pictures. He didn't jump, nor anything like that, but he just rolled over, and the wire leader broke at the swivel."

We sat in silence for a while, thinking of the great fish lost. "How big do you reckon he was, Pat?" I asked.

"I was coming to that," he said. "A week after, it would have been, I was out with this same man, and we got a good one, twenty-four pounds, and this time we went in to the shore to get the photographs. Then a farmer comes strolling down. 'Do you think that's a big one, lads?' says he.

" 'It's big enough for me,' says your man.

" 'Well, there's a bigger one nor that lying on my shore these last three or four days,' says the farmer, and off he walks.

"It was our fish, I'll swear it. When we got down to him the spoon had gone, but you could see the scar. The birds had been at him, and the smell was awful, but we shoved the lot into a plastic sack and brought it back to the village. The remains," said Pat reverently, "weighed fifty-eight pounds."

"A new world-record northern pike," I mourned.

"World record, is it?" asked Mooney from behind his late breakfast. "We'd have that broke fast enough on Lough Allen if the boys would leave the trout alone for a bit and concentrate on the pike."

From his kitchen in Drumshanbo, Joe Mooney runs the County Leitrim Local Development Association, in intervals of tending to his real-estate business. Leitrim is a small, beautiful county, very green and soft, with curlew-haunted mountains and pike-haunted lakes, but it is far away from the Killarney-Galway Bay tourist track, which troubles Joe a great deal. That was why he hadn't hesitated when I'd called him the previous evening to ask about the pike-fishing prospects on Lough Allen. Naturally, he is also secretary of the Drumshanbo Angling Club.

"What time can you get over in the morning?" he shot at me.

It was all a little difficult, really. My quest for a big Irish pike was already running into trouble. I'd had a firm tip-off about a small, hundred-acre lough below the hills of County Sligo called Templehouse Lough. Unhappily, the night before I arrived a storm in the mountains had sent down thousands of gallons of floodwater that had turned the lake so rich a brown you couldn't see a spoonbait six inches under the surface. Already I'd fished Templehouse for four days, and the biggest pike I'd had was a four-pounder. But slowly it *was* clearing. Next day it could be just right.

"I'm not sure about tomorrow yet," I told Joe.

"I'll tell you what," he said. "I'll have Pat Reynolds in to meet you. He's the finest pike man in Ireland."

"I'll have to think about it," I said.

"Right," said Joe. "Call round to me in the morning. The yellow house opposite the church. Nine-thirty."

Small, dynamic men like Joe Mooney are difficult to argue with, especially when they train on vitamin spread, and even before I'd talked with him I was half convinced that I'd have to change ground. That in itself would require a little moral courage. I had booked in for a week at the hotel in Ballymote, the village nearest to Templehouse Lough, and Jimmy Hogg, who kept it, and the locals who drank in the bar each evening were following the progress of my pike quest with the absorbed interest that Irishmen have in any sporting event. If their goodwill had had anything to do with it I'd have had a twenty-pound specimen already. Now I was going to have to tell them I would be fishing another lough thirty miles away and, worse still, in County Leitrim. But I steeled myself. It was big pike I was concerned with, not a public-relations exercise. And Lough Allen would surely have big pike. It was deep, wide and Irish.

The Irish have the biggest northern pike in the world and, with odd exceptions like Pat Reynolds, they resent it deeply. Pike are interlopers. They were introduced as recently as the Middle Ages, probably by the English. They also eat salmon and trout, which are the only freshwater fish that Irish anglers consider worth catching. Some of the more liberal-minded will concede that in winter a man may amuse himself by towing a big spoon round the lake for pike, but it's not done in the best circles. It will be a long time before I forget the shocked silence in the bar of the Sheelin Shamrock Hotel when a man came in and reported that a couple of Frenchmen were out on the lough trolling for pike. This was at the height of the mayfly season, the brilliant fortnight when the biggest trout rise from the depths of Lough Sheelin to feed on the surface, for which boats and hotel rooms have to be booked a year ahead.

I said nothing at the time, but I could understand the obsession that kept the Frenchmen systematically working their pike spoons while heavy trout rose noisily around their boat. I could understand it because I shared it.

An English fishing writer named Jack Hargreaves once came near explaining the mystery of the pike's fascination when he said that it was the only fish that looked you straight in the eyes. There is a scientific explanation: unlike most fish, a pike has binocular vision. He *does* look you in the eyes. But no zoology textbook can convey the sheer menace of a pike, its murderous streamlining, its lonely, tyrannical personality. Pike, huge smashers of tackle, attain to individual names. The Green Devil occupied a high proportion of the waking thoughts of my friends and me when I was sixteen or so. He lived under the arches of a bridge that spanned an arm of a lake we fished, and he was hooked maybe twice a year. He always broke away. Was he fifty, sixty pounds? In fact he was just under thirty. A farm worker shot him in the reeds along the shore at spawning time. But we never really believed that the once and future Green Devil had gone forever.

Trout have only a brief individual existence, from the time they are hooked until they are in the net. Trout fishermen talk about limit bags, pike men about once-in-a-lifetime monsters. And if they haven't told too many lies about the giants they have hooked, their souls finally migrate to the wild, gray acres of Irish pike loughs.

If they are lucky they may get there sooner, of course. Their tackle boxes will be crammed with expensive plugs and spoons, all of which will be condemned as useless by their ghillies, who will also fall about laughing at their ridiculously light tackle. But they are sustained by thoughts of monsters, like the fifty-three-pounder that was said to have been taken in Lough Cong in 1922. Sadly for big pike legend, the Irish Specimen Fish Committee withdrew recognition of the Lough Cong monster on January 1, 1970. It was insufficiently documented by present-day standards. But this fish existed. Its huge preserved head is still to be seen in the Natural History Museum in London.

Big Irish pike are not as numerous as they once were. Since 1957 the trout-oriented Irish have waged war on them through the agency of the Inland Fisheries Trust, whose net crews have taken almost half a million northern pike from such major trout fisheries as Mask, Corrib, Conn and Sheelin. Their catches included some huge fish, the biggest a 50½-pounder from Lough Mask. This pike was a mere eight years old. It had at least five more years of growth in it.

Nevertheless, one last great redoubt remains for the Irish northerns: the Shannon system, which is too vast and complex to be turned into a pure trout fishery. The loughs of Derg, Ree, Key and Allen and the river that connects them hold huge pike still, arguably the biggest in the world.

There are fine pike, too, in lesser strongholds, small lakes in the western hills that have never been developed for trout fishing, and the first problem the big pike hunter has to solve is whether to fish small, manageable waters, which he can read and interpret if he is experienced, or to attack the wide, anonymous waters of such a lough as Allen, which is eight miles long, three across, and deep and rocky to boot. On the big lakes, trolling is the only possible method of covering the ground. On the small waters, there is scope for the niceties of tossing a plug between lily pads or rowing silently into a promising bay in the reeds and working a big copper spoon along the shore.

Had not Templehouse Lough suddenly turned the color of drinking chocolate, maybe I would never have gone near Allen. As it was, after four bad days it was good sense to change.

"I think I'll give Templehouse a rest today," I said carefully to Jimmy Hogg, picking my words. "I might give Allen a try."

He looked at me as if I'd walked into church with my hat on.

"A lake that size wouldn't color up so easily," I explained.

"I hope," said Jimmy obscurely, "the weather holds for you."

I backed out, still apologizing, but I felt better three-quarters of an hour later, sitting in Mooney's warm kitchen, listening to sagas of the great pike fights of the past as the clock ticked the forenoon away.

"You'd better have a look at my lures," I said to Mooney, breaking the spell. I wanted to get this bit over early, having had my tackle insulted by local experts in many parts of the world. Pat wasn't too scathing, though. I had a couple of the traditional six-inch copper and silver spoons, and these were approved of. "I'll just get my Magic Marker," said Pat, "and touch them up a little." Returning with a thick, felt-tipped pen in his fist, he began daubing the undersides of my spoons. "A small bit of blue is what the big ones love," he said. "Have you anything else at all with blue in it?"

From the bottom tray of my tackle box I disentangled the pride of my collection, a long Swedish plug, blue and white with black bars. "What in the name of God is that?" said Pat, recoiling theatrically. He knew what it was, all right, but it is an article of faith among Irish boatmen that Irish pike, unlike those of any other nation, will not take plugs.

"You haven't seen anything yet," I told him, dragging out a couple of wildly colored American creations with the engaging name of Bump 'n' Grind. The main feature of these plugs was a vast silver diving lip almost half their length.

"They would go just fine on top of a bloody Christmas tree," said Pat sardonically.

I didn't rise to that one. The battle of the plugs was going to be fought out later, when the fishing started. I closed the tackle box and waited to be cross-examined on rods and reels, but Pat was more liberal in this sector. Eleven-pound-test line was acceptable, so long as I had plenty of it.

"I have scales here," said Joe Mooney, as we left the womblike coziness of his kitchen. "Call back with the big one and I'll weigh him."

The kitchen was a lot more cozy than Lough Allen. Irish lakes are usually softly beautiful, with green shores and gently wooded islands. Allen, though, is very different. The black foothills of the Ox Mountains hem it in to the west, and the eastern shore lies at the foot of Slieve Anierin (Iron Mountain). Its islands are piles of dark, slaty rock, and when the north wind is channeled down the lake, big seas run and the slim-built local boats cannot be used.

The waves were breaking white when we hauled Pat's boat into the water, but the blow was sou'westerly, a good fishing wind. "We'll head up north to start," said Pat. "There's a bit of an island up there that's a great place for a big fish." He started the motor so that I could run the trolling baits out fast without fouling the bottom of the lake. After that, though, it was going to be all oars. You can catch big trout trolling on the motor because they always like a fast, straight motion. For pike you need the slow, erratic progress of a spoon towed by oars.

It was the spoon I was trolling, naturally. The time had not yet come for independence. We came up to the island, white froth from the waves blowing across the black stones, and Pat brought the boat round so that the spoon would swing across the point. He rowed rhythmically, and the slow throb at the rod tip showed that the spoon was working well. Mallards went spluttering up from the island shore within easy shot. "Wouldn't those fellas know we haven't a gun between us?" Pat asked philosophically. If I hadn't been watching the ducks, I'd have seen the rod dip, but the first thing I registered was the reel click screaming. I grabbed the rod, and Pat stabbed the oars down in the water to check the boat. It was hard to judge the fish in the first second or two. "Is there any weight in it?" Pat shouted as he brought the boat around.

I could feel a sullen thumping deep in the water as the pike held its ground, then the line slackened. "We'll see him now," I yelled. He was going to come up. I knew I hadn't lost him and, yes, he came out of the water fifty yards away, lashing on the surface, shaking his head. A nice fish, but not a big fish. A good lively one of twelve pounds or so. "We won't write home about him," said Pat, and in five minutes he had the small, sharp gaff slipped into the V of the fish's jaw so that we could put him back uninjured. I looked at my first pike from Lough Allen — sleek, primrose-mottled flanks and the lethal jaws clenched tight, the only movement the curl of the raked-back dorsal.

I eased him back over the gunwale. A golden flash in the water, and he was gone. "It's the touch of blue that does it," said Pat. "Let out the spoon again."

But we fished back down the island shore without response, nor was there any action in the next hour until we started to cross the lake for a reef on the far shore. Then the reel screamed again, but there was no life in the rod. "Gone foul," I told Pat. The spoon, working deep, was hung up in weed. I hauled it free, then retrieved fast. I thought there was certain to be pike-repelling weed on it. Halfway to the boat, though, it was grabbed hard, and I was into a fish, not big but swimming and changing direction faster than any pike. I guessed what it was before it broke surface: a good thick trout of about three pounds — and a month out of season. Committing, as far as I know, my first offense against the fishery laws of Ireland, I got it into the boat and asked Pat to tap it on the head. "I've got plans for this one," I said.

It was time to get the big rod out, the one I'd brought for such a moment. With wire and treble hooks I rigged a formidable harness for the trout. I tried him alongside the boat, and he trolled sweetly.

We went ahead again fast, with the bait and the spoon astern. There was a good mile of barren water to cross before we reached the islands of the western shore. Though the central deeps of Allen are black and mysterious, the theory is that they hold no actively feeding pike, so we crossed on the motor, with the lures working faster and shallower than I would have allowed them to had we been fishing seriously.

If we weren't serious, though, whatever grabbed the trout was. The rod came over, and there was a three-second shriek from the reel. By the time I had the rod in my hands, though, everything had gone slack. I reeled in. No trout, and the treble hooks and wire mount dangled limply at the end of the line.

"It could have hit a log," I suggested. Pat gave me a look. He knew as well as I did that waterlogged timber floating below the surface does not have the capacity to pull a three-pound trout away from a wire mount. He said nothing, but he cut the engine and picked up the oars again. From now on even the barren water was going to be taken seriously.

When we got to the nearest island we went ashore for lunch, dragging the boat up onto the pebbles and hunting around for driftwood to make a fire. When we had it blazing, Pat filled a smoke-blackened kettle with lake water and set it on top. "I'd rather be sitting here," he said, "than over beyond." He stubbed a thumb in the direction of another small island a couple of hundred yards to the south. It looked like a perfectly normal island to me. "What's wrong with it?" I asked him.

"There's a fella living over by Drumshanbo could tell you," he said. "He went in there one time, and he thought he'd take a souvenir back with him, one of them old skulls that's lyin' there in the shallow water."

"Old what?"

"The skulls belonging to the old monks that used to be in it one time. Anyhow, the first morning after he brought it home didn't he fall downstairs and break his leg. And late that evening there was an awful rapping at the back door and nobody there when the missus went down. That went on for three nights, and then his brother-in-law put the skull in a plastic bag and he rowed over to the island and put it back where it came from. They were never disturbed after that."

For a while we sat silently, drinking the dark tea and eating home-made bread and thick slices of ham. The wind had softened, and the waves no longer broke white. "You could get your big one this afternoon," said Pat, and I had the same intuitive feeling that the water had come alive.

"I'm going to try a plug," I told him, choosing a moment when he'd be feeling mellow. I fished out the long blue Swedish job and set the lip so that it would swim deep. "Try it," said Pat magnanimously, "but keep the spoon on the other rod."

As we rowed away from the island, I let out line and watched the plug bob away in our wake like a small lighthouse. I let it go fifty yards astern, then I tightened up. It dived purposefully. I sent the spoon over the side after it, and it couldn't have traveled a hundred yards before it was firmly taken by a pike a little bigger than the one we'd had in the morning.

"Didn't I tell you?" said Pat, slipping him back a while later. "You'll never beat the good old spoon."

I was just thinking out an answer to this as we rowed along with the lines out again when there was a heavy strike on the plug. "You'll never beat the good old plug!" I shouted as Pat got the oars in fast, took up the other rod and brought the spoon in.

By then I was standing in the stern, yielding line in long bursts. I could see how it was dwindling on the spool, and I yelled at Pat to get hold of the oars as fast as he could and bring the boat round. Every few seconds came pulverizing thumps at the rod tip, more savage than either of the other fish had been able to manage. There couldn't have been much more than thirty yards of line left on the reel when Pat started to gain ground for me.

After that the fight was more sullen for a while, as the fish sounded and I thought of the tumbled black boulders and snags of the lake bed and the way the line could be taken round them. But Pat kept moving in on the fish, and I finally had him within fifty yards of the boat.

Then he exploded the water and showed himself, breaching clear, standing on his tail and shaking his great head, gill covers wide open to show the scarlet underside and the white cavern of the mouth. He sounded again, and moved fast into me as I madly recovered line to keep in touch. "He thinks the boat will give him shelter," said Pat, and he was right. For ten minutes his tactics were the same. Wild flurries at the surface that turned our hearts over as the dappled flanks showed clear, then short runs of twenty or thirty yards before he turned again and tried to get under the boat. Then the runs became shorter. The tail-lashing fury on the surface dwindled to heavy rolls. Pat laid the gaff ready across the thwarts, and soon there came the first gleam underwater of the white belly.

"You have him now," said Pat, but when he loomed out over the fish, gaff in hand, there were enough reserves left for a last despairing run in the shadow of the boat before he was on his side defeated, his great golden eyes looking up at the boat and the awful jaws unmoving. Pat slipped the gaff into the V, then used two hands to get him aboard. The fish lay quietly in the bottom of the boat, and I put the rod down. My hands were shaking. Pat got the hooks out and looked at the plug. "Didn't I tell you?" he said shamelessly. "It's the touch of blue that does it."

The Swedish plug took three more pike that afternoon, but where I wanted to be now was in Mooney's kitchen, getting the use of Mooney's scales. Any northern pike over twenty pounds is a trophy fish. Mine was certainly that, but I wanted to know precisely.

Twenty-six and a half it went, a hen fish, naturally. All big pike are, but when you are fighting one and it comes up in the water and shakes its great head at you, you can never think of it as anything but masculine.

"Look at the belly of it," said Mooney. It was loose and empty. "That fella had just started to feed when you hit him. If you'd given him half an hour you'd have had a thirty-pounder on your hands."

It was still a fine fish, though, and we took it to the convent up the road. The nuns were glad to see it. It would make a great feast for the poor children, they said. At least I hadn't killed it just for the satisfaction of weighing.

All over Drumshanbo my pike was good news. That wasn't going to be the case in Ballymote. I drove back slowly, planning my excuses. I parked quietly and took as long as I could to change upstairs. But I couldn't stay in my room all evening. I had to face them in the bar.

"Did you do any good?" Jimmy Hogg asked me, polishing a glass.

"I, uh, had one or two," I said.

"Was there any size in 'em?"

"Biggest twenty-six and a half," I muttered. "Six fish, average around fourteen."

"Is that right?" said Jimmy, flatly. "You won't be wanting the boat on Templehouse tomorrow, then?"

"Well, I thought it might be, uh, just worth taking a look at Allen again," I said. Most of that evening I watched television.

Pat and I had a small but appreciative crowd to see us off at the pier next morning. The word had got round. "If you get a nice little fella about six or seven pound would you bring it back for us, mister?" a small boy said. Next day was Friday, I remembered.

Other, slower-thinking, boys pushed round to press their claims. "No more orders," said Pat. "'Tis unlucky."

We fished the blue plug right from the beginning this time, and we took seven pike for the day, failing, however, to get one small enough to match our client's specifications. The biggest took the plug at three thirty in the afternoon, almost at the same time the big one hit the previous day. This time it was a shorter, thicker fish that fought strongly but very dourly, keeping deep and sulking a lot and not showing itself until it was almost ready for the gaff. I had a pocket scale with me this time, so we didn't kill it. A shade over twenty-five pounds.

We put back the pike with care, and it sank slowly out of sight in the dark water. "They'd have made a fine pair," said Pat.

They would have, too, set up in a trophy room. The odds against taking two twenty-pound-plus pike in two days must be very high. But I had other things on my mind.

"How the hell am I going to explain this one away back in Ballymote?" I asked Pat.

He kept a prim silence. It was not for him to comment on the shortcomings of pike fishing on the wrong side of the Sligo border.

I tried to carry it off as best I could. "Not so good as yesterday," I told them that evening. "More fish, but the biggest was twenty-five."

The shoulders of the clientele, which had relaxed over pints of black stout at my first words, stiffened again. That evening I sat through the news in Irish, then a vintage Spencer Tracy movie, before retiring early for the night.

I was up early in the morning, too, all packed and ready. When I went down to breakfast Jimmy Hogg was waiting. He had a resigned look about him. "I had your bill made out early," he said. "I thought you might be wanting to leave."

I told him truthfully that I had never eaten finer T-bone steaks than those supplied in his restaurant. Somehow that didn't seem enough.

"I suppose you'll be moving across to Drumshanbo now," he said.

Only for one day, I assured him. The Canada geese had just started to fly into Allen. From Saturday on Pat would be out shooting.

"The pike *are* there in Templehouse," Jimmy said.

"It's just that the water's colored," I told him.

"Big ones," said Jimmy.

"I'll have to come again," I said.

I didn't stop feeling guilty until I was twenty miles east and saw the first signpost for Drumshanbo. Then I realized the stupidity of apologizing for catching big pike.

As Pat and I dragged the boat down into the water, he said, "I hope you brought the plugs with you." I could see that the long process of converting the Irish had begun.

We fished blank for the first hour, then round a small complex of islands on the east shore we began to meet fish. By lunchtime we had boated seven good Allen pike. Secretly, though, I was hoping for the near impossible — a third trophy fish, to make three in three days.

Reading my thoughts, Pat said, "Wouldn't it be something to talk about if you got another big one?" I laughed deprecatingly. I was sure that voicing the wish would kill it stone dead.

Through the good hours of the afternoon we had no action, except when the smallest fish of the trip hung itself onto the Swedish plug. Slowly the light was beginning to fade, and the clouds were darkening over the Iron Mountain. "What about that funny-looking fella you showed me on Wednesday?" Pat asked.

"Is it this one?" I said, holding up the psychedelically colored Bump 'n' Grind.

"That's him," said Pat. "Give the Yankee bait a chance."

I snapped it on. We had maybe half an hour before the light went altogether. Skeins of gray geese passed over, calling like hounds in full cry. The wind had dropped. Pat picked up the dripping oars again, and we started to troll close in to the shore, where the bottom fell off steeply.

The rod tip checked, then came hard over. "This is the one," I said quite confidently to Pat. I could feel the weight in the fish.

By the time Pat got the gaff in him it was dark, and we homed in on a cottage light beside the pier. Ashore, I checked the weight by torchlight. The needle flickered just below the twenty-three. "Call him twenty-two and a half," I said. I waded in knee-deep and slid him back into the lake.

Later we sat in Joe Mooney's kitchen in the red light of a lamp hanging on the wall. "It's a shame, now," said Mooney, "that you wouldn't be going out again tomorrow."

"Pat's after geese," I said, "and I've been fishing long enough to know when to stop. You can't improve on the miraculous."

"In Drumshanbo," said Mooney firmly, "the miraculous has always been our specialty."

CHAPTER FOUR

The Shade of a Grayling

The point I am making here is: beware of wildernesses. It is the fisherman's instinct always to head to the other side of the hill but it can be a bad mistake, as Peter Williams and I found in Finland.

FINLAND

IN THE MIDDLE of the night, in the wettest birchwoods in the world, Williams and I stood soaked to the skin, waiting for the others. "Please, God," wailed Williams, "send an international airport, a five-hundred-bedroom hotel, an eight-lane highway, a *cab*." Formally, without real hope, he gave himself a burst in the face from an aerosol can of repellent, but the mosquitoes, which had at first merely probed at squadron level, were now mounting continuous command-strength attacks. "Go on, eat me, then, eat me!" Williams snarled. We glowered, full of loathing, at the Last Great Wilderness of Europe, hoping with deep sincerity that it would go away.

Endless reaches of gray-green, soaking-wet Finnish Lapland, two hundred miles north of the Arctic Circle, stretched out around us. As we stood on the soggy moss, the Kaldavsti, a beautiful, graylingless grayling river, frothed over brown boulders into a delectable-looking but barren pool. We weren't in the mood to exclaim over that, though. We just waited desolately by the long-extinguished remains of the birchwood fire to be shown the way home. Where were they, Mr. Matti Saromaa, Mr. Jorma Lappalainen, Mr. Aikio Veikko?

They had brought us here. After the first forty miles of rough road out of Utsjoki we had crossed over the frontier into Arctic Norway and then navigated Lake Polmak in a long, high-prowed

RIVER TENOJOKI, FINNISH LAPLAND

Lappish boat that tapered down to three inches of freeboard between us and the choppy water. From the shore of the lake we had tramped miles back into Finland to the banks of the Kaldavsti. "Grayling," Mr. Saromaa had promised, "and small salmon. What you call grilse." Later he amended this to, "There may be some grayling. We shall see."

It was an English fishing writer of the 1930s, Arthur Ransome, who first noted the elusive, poetic mystique of the grayling, quoting the Victorian poet Matthew Arnold, who had written more than a century ago of "Still nursing the unconquerable hope, Still clutching the inviolable shade, With a free, onward impulse brushing through, By night, the silver'd branches of the glade. . . ." To graduate students of the nineteenth-century literature, I offer the theory that Arnold was a closet grayling fisherman. There, in a few lines of *The Scholar Gypsy*, he precisely formulated the absurd, naive romanticism that had brought Williams and me to Lapland. True, our free, onward impulse had been hampered by backpacks, but still we had brushed through the birchwoods, and it was night, even though the sun was well above the horizon, and was going to stay that way for the next month. And for several hours we had nursed the unconquerable hope of a seven-pound grayling.

The grayling is a fish romantic enough to make you lose your head — a member of the *salmonidae*, an ancient, ice-haunting species left behind twelve thousand years ago when the glaciers of the Pleistocene retreated after gouging out lakes and river valleys. It is a clean, cold fish that is less tolerant of pollution than any other member of the salmon family. French ecologists classify the uppermost reaches of a river, where the water is unpolluted, as *le zone à l'ombre*, the grayling region, and the first sign of deterioration in a stream is the disappearance of grayling from the fast water that they favor. There are not many around these days.

Such a fish brings out the worst excesses of romanticism in anglers like Williams and me, especially when linked with the prospect of seeking them out in the last European wilderness, up near the Norwegian and Soviet frontiers where the map looks as if some unruly child has spattered it with light-blue paint. Lake after lake, stream after stream, almost all running from northwest to southeast, the way the glaciers drove. Water that is still icebound for eight months of the year.

We had seen much of it on the drive north to Utsjoki, the northernmost town in Arctic Finland, where we planned to base ourselves for the great grayling assault. Blue lakes bordered the road for mile on mile, and Williams and I had gazed at them as gluttonously as four-year-olds being offered thick cuts of chocolate cake. But Matti Saromaa, whom we'd met in the departure lounge at Helsinki airport and who was now riding with us, saw them through cold blue Finnish eyes. "No good," he kept saying. "All the fish here have been eaten. They made the mistake of living too close to the Lapps."

I couldn't believe it. "In *Where to Fish*," I told him, "and that's a book that has Biblical status in England, it says, 'Grayling in Lapland run large and give tremendous sport.' I am quoting directly." But Saromaa, who is editor of the Finnish national angling magazine, was far likelier to know the truth. And, as we drove north, he revealed it. The factor we had failed to reckon with was that Finnish Lapland is inhabited by Lapps. Not very many of them, perhaps no more than 3,500, a good deal fewer than one per lake, but enough.

The Lapps baffle Matti and other Finns because all they do is herd reindeer, hunt and fish. Long ago they abandoned their shamans and simple, pantheistic religion of holy birds, islands and mountains. But while they now go to the Lutheran church on Sunday mornings, they still have this lamentable attachment to catching things. In winter they hunt fur-bearing animals and the *kiiruna*, the white Arctic grouse. And in summer they fish, without mercy, using monofilament nets for scooping up whitefish, trout and grayling to be salted in barrels or shipped south to the fish markets.

No one can do anything about it, Matti told us. Finland is a liberal-minded nation unwilling to interfere with the traditional rights of the Lapps, because it might smack of discrimination. The Lapps are the last remnant of a human migration from Central Asia, with different features and a different language from the rest of the Finnish population, and they are politically hot. A committee had been formed in Helsinki, Matti said, to review the whole question of fish conservation in Lapland, but a quirky pucker of the lips indicated Saromaa's feelings about this group. "I think," he said kindly, quickly changing the subject, "when we reach Utsjoki you must come and have a sauna at my cottage. It will help you to relax." He was a very large, placid man, the product, I expect, of many a sauna. "And now," he went on, "in a few moments we will see beautiful scenery. True Lapland." Not being a scenery man, Williams squirmed impatiently and, since he was driving at the time, narrowly missed a bright yellow Volvo coming at us over a blind brow of the road.

"Norwegians," said Matti with a trace of animation. "Many are coming here for drinking holidays. Watch out for them." With the savage Finnish drunk-driving laws—three months in jail for a first offense—and the equally savage price of liquor, it seemed crazy to cross the border for the purpose Matti indicated. But he turned out to be entirely correct. Norwegians must like a challenge.

Matti was right about the scenery, too. The dark green pinewoods fell away south of us and the landscape opened up. Now it was fell country, scattered dwarf birch and little streams tumbling through rock outcrops. And lake upon lake. "Very beautiful, yes?" said Matti. "But no fish except some little trout in the brooks."

Closer to Utsjoki we dropped down from the plateau, and the road began to follow a deep, gliding river that frequently broadened out into small lakes. Across each tumultuous patch of water where the river led into a lake were stretched white plastic floats—salmon traps set by the Lapps. "You see?" said Matti. "Very few get through. But the big river is different. Plenty of netting still, but they can't stop them all."

It was the big river, the Tenojoki (which the Norwegians call the Tana), the great water course that forms the Finnish/Norwegian border in the north, that Matti himself had come to fish. When we reached Utsjoki—a wooden church, a scattering of clapboard houses and stores and a single-story hotel—we could see the river shining a quarter of a mile away. We drove down and looked at it, broad, wild, ice fed, tumbling over a stark bed of gray-and-black boulders. Historic water. A few miles downstream from where we stood, at Storfossen on the Norwegian side, a postmaster, Henrik Henriksen, tossed out a spoon one day in 1928 and found himself connected to the biggest Atlantic salmon ever caught on rod and line, a monstrous fish of seventy-nine pounds.

Only the power and strength of our grayling obsession enabled us to avoid inquiring about arrangements for salmon fishing. Matti apparently had become a little sorry for putting us down so effectively on the trip north because he said, "Jorma Lappalainen is in town. He's the police officer for the province, and he might know of some-place you'd get good grayling fishing."

Which is how Williams and I eventually found ourselves in the wilderness, dripping wet, fishless and seemingly abandoned by our companions, Matti, Mr. Lappalainen and the latter's assistant, Aikio Veikko.

It was a beautiful stream, the Kaldavsti. It was just that it contained no fish. There were broad pools at intervals, almost small lakes, but before the rain began not a single rise had dimpled their smooth surfaces. We had followed the river through swamps and along reindeer tracks, fishing a variety of wet flies. Not even a fingerling trout had snatched at them. And then the downpour started.

We lost track of the others as soon as the big rain curtains came billowing in from the north and stood uncertainly for a while where a tributary brook frothed into the main stream, a perfect place for a fish . . . in a river that had any fish. It was one o'clock in the morning and a good five-mile hike over rough country to the shore of Lake Polmak, and, after that, the boat trip and the drive back to Utsjoki. With little choice, we slogged back to camp. They couldn't be long.

They could be long. At 3:00 A.M., under heavy mosquito attack and probably running a slight temperature, Williams began to pray for a cab. Mercifully, half an hour later, Matti drove into view. "Jorma is very pleased. The Lapps have been here. I mean he's pleased he's found out that the Lapps have been here," he said. "He suspected it all the time. That was one reason why he brought us here." Well, it was nice to have taken part in a successful experiment.

"Can we start heading home now?" I asked. Jorma was coming down the trail bright-eyed as a robin with Aikio behind him carrying a very small pike, the total of the night's catch. "No, no," said Matti. "First we must build a fire to warm ourselves for the journey." I had forgotten that Jorma was a Lapp and, as I was soon to learn, the Lapp attitude to life is: If it moves, eat it. If it stands still, hack it down, chop it up and make a fire.

I'll admit it was a bravura piece of fire-making on Jorma's part to arrange the mighty blaze that he eventually achieved. And it was a rare sight to see Williams, crouching in a kind of tarpaulin tepee they had arranged at one side of it, disappear in billowing clouds of smoke to emerge from time to time like a small evil spirit. He was talking like one, too, when we finally started the long march home.

We went down to Matti's cottage after lunch next day. The wet night on the empty stream had trampled unconquerable hope deep into the mud. Now we were ready to compromise. "Matti," I said, "is it possible to arrange a little salmon fishing here?" Williams was nodding like a mechanical doll.

"Tonight you will fish for salmon," said Matti expansively.

I was glad he said nothing further about the sauna invitation. I already had made a dismaying discovery about Lapp saunas at the hotel at Rovaniemi. It is when you emerge from the sauna, pink, hot and defenseless, that you meet the death-or-glory mosquitoes in the shower room. There are never many of them, fewer than a dozen perhaps, but aces, every one. After the Rovaniemi sauna Williams had counted 134 stings on me, many of them in the most unsporting places.

And I was gladder still when Matti greeted us that evening, emerging as naked as a boiled egg from his sauna hut and waving before slithering down a steep stony bank and hurling himself into the icy Tenojoki. Matti's great head surfaced briefly from the water. "Klementi will be with you in one minute!" he yelled. Sure enough, we could hear the drone of an outboard upstream of us.

It was Klementi all right, a young Lapp in his early twenties. "Hokay!" he shouted, beaming, as he slammed his war canoe hard onto the stones. Matti surfaced alongside like a pink walrus. "I'll meet you later," he promised. "Upriver."

Klementi picked through our tackle. We had learned at the hotel that salmon fishing on the Tenojoki meant "harling." Dull as it is, it was the only way to cover such a big salmon river. Harling is a form of trolling: the rower traverses the pool, dropping downstream all the time, but so slowly that a fly or lure hangs over the salmon lies and works in the current for as long as possible. In spite of its dullness it is a very effective technique, much used in Norway and on the big Scottish rivers. But because the lure is almost stationary, you have to use a light one, a fly, a plug or an unweighted spoon of thin metal.

Klementi tied a 2/0 Thunder-and-Lightning on my line and fixed up Williams with a sulphur-yellow plug. We shrugged at each other — we were in his hands, weren't we? Afloat, we headed into the heavy current. For three-quarters of an hour we pushed upstream, and every few hundred yards a boat was pulled up on the bank and two or three men were sitting around blue smoke from a birchwood fire. The fishing night was just getting under way.

What happened to Williams and me on the Tenojoki that first evening was sheer bad fishing luck. The word around the Utsjoki hotel where the fishermen gathered had been the usual sort of thing. Snow still melting, river too high, sparse run of fish and they were traveling straight through, anyway. Nobody had caught anything for a week except for the odd grilse.

So what we needed was a civilized blank evening like everybody else had been having. Then we might have spent another night, possibly two, on the river before that good old free, onward impulse could seize us again and we'd resume our quest for what had brought us to Lapland in the first place. Seven pounds (why not eight?) of inviolable grayling shade.

But things went badly. At 11:00 P.M., as we dropped down a pool in the shadow of a high cliff on the Norwegian side, my reel screamed out and slowly, almost ponderously, thirty yards away, a thick silver fish breached clear. It was a sweet quarter of an hour, I'll admit that, before Klementi, standing perilously in the stern, got the gaff into a very handsome deep-bodied hen fish that went eighteen pounds.

What made matters much worse, however, was another incident at 3:00 A.M., when Williams' plug attracted a plainly idiotic salmon of twenty-five pounds, big enough, you'd think, to know better than to grab something that moved like a drunken banana. Furthermore, the whole of the fight, which took us half a mile downstream before it was finished, was witnessed by some people in a car on the Norwegian bank who kept pace with us along a dirt road, flashing headlights and cheering when the fish was finally boated. It was this more than anything else that turned Williams's head, though I'll admit that when we woke late and went in to lunch next day to find ourselves kings of the river, I was simpering as foolishly as he was. Again and again we had to leave our reindeer stew to accept the generous congratulations of less-fortunate anglers. That alone should have told us how thin the salmon fishing was, but we had convinced ourselves that we'd hit the beginning of a big run.

We hadn't. That ill-omened night was the first of eight we spent on the Tenojoki with Klementi, and never again did we touch a fish. Slowly our prestige grew thin at the Utsjoki hotel. Four nights later a jolly, fat lady from Rovaniemi caught a twenty-eight-pounder, and after that we slipped back into the ranks, exchanging sympathetic shrugs with the others when we saw them at lunchtime.

The fishing nights themselves took on a timeless quality. There were long breaks for coffee made over fires, in Norway or in Finland, and we became very skilled at toasting sausages impaled on sharp sticks. There were the two Lapps we called the coffee ghosts. You could look upriver or down for a quarter of a mile, and swear that there was not a living soul on it. But as soon as the kettle boiled and Klementi tipped the coffee into it, the same boat would materialize, and a beaming pair of Lapps would join us, sit politely on the stones until they were offered a cup and then wait, still politely, for Williams to reluctantly produce our dwindling liter of Scotch, irreplaceable because the nearest state monopoly—Alko shop, as the Finns starkly called their liquor stores—was a hundred miles south. Every night they came, sometimes twice a night. They never caught anything, either, as far as I could find out.

I don't know how long this would have continued had it not been for a chance meeting with a Norwegian at the hotel as we were carrying our tackle out to the car.

"You are fishink," he told us perceptively. He was very tall, his eyes were red rimmed and he swayed like a native pine. "I also am fishink," he said, "but not today. Today I am dronkink." Suddenly the spell of the Tenojoki was lifted. "Williams," I said, "do you feel like a dronk?"

Until then the social life at the Utsjoki hotel had been a closed book to us. When we abandoned the fishing and opened it, a new phase began. To start with, there was a dance every night to music by the Utsjoki Duo, drums and accordion, specialty the tango. It was a rare sight to watch a Lapp guide, unemployed by reason of the salmon shortage, executing a colorful *paso doble* in his high leather boots, solo.

Matti Saromaa had also begun to go to pieces. He had fished all week in his own boat with no success, but finally his girlfriend Lilla arrived from Helsinki, a tiny, delectable blonde half his size who, unforgivably I thought, called him PouPou. He seemed to like it, though. The four of us began to put in a lot of time at the *baari*. Outside in the birchwoods the ghost of Matthew Arnold might have been muttering something about the unconquerable hope, but we couldn't hear him. We might even have gone home at this point had it not been for the arrival of a new catalyst, a man from Washington, D.C., who was an airline pilot.

He was another romantic, only with him it was salmon. He had come all the way from Bangkok with his little daughter and his wife to fish the Tenojoki. To us, decadently toying with our Finnish Scotch, tapping our fingers to *Jealousy*, he seemed pathetically naive at first, bringing his rods into the restaurant for our approval. As old Tenojoki hands, we could have put him down easily enough, but we had the sensitivity not to do that. Instead, we passed on to him the fabled Thunder-and-Lightning and the yellow plug. "I'm meeting the guide at eight o'clock," he said eagerly. Gravely we wished him good luck. Williams languidly raised a finger to the waiter again.

But the seed of shame had been sown. Watching the American, we both agreed, had made us feel like dissolute old men looking at their bright-eyed earlier selves in a yellowing college photograph. "PouPou," I said, and Lilla gave me a hard look, "they can't have netted all the lakes, can they?" Matti's reply was more promising than I'd thought possible.

"Jorma Lappalainen did mention," he said, "that he could arrange a float-plane trip into the real wilderness for us." Just a few hours previously a seven-pound grayling would have had to come dancing into the *baari* before I'd have cared. But now things were different. Hope *is* unconquerable. I called Jorma and responded to his proposal like a stew-bred trout to a liver pellet. A one-hundred-mile flight, he suggested. We could use a hut the frontier guards slept in once a month when they patrolled that way, where Norway, Finland and the Soviet Union come together. Deep lakes, he promised, and a grayling-crammed river called the Silisjoki.

So next day, as we flew northeast from Lake Inari, a wild and mournful landscape unfolded three thousand feet below us, lake-splattered moorland, gray, green and brown with small twisting rivers connecting the open water. Half an hour later, when we slid onto the surface of a broad lake and taxied up to where the frontier guards' hut stood on the shore, the unconquerable hope was as virile and bounding as it had been when Williams and I landed at Helsinki long, long ago.

We scrambled to the top of a limestone scree behind the hut. The drab colors we had seen from the aircraft were false. The tundra was bright with yellow poppies, bloody cranesbill, windflowers, scores of mosses and lichens: a carpet of flowers. For once a cliché had come true. And the air was loud with birds—larks and sandpipers and *kohu*, the black-and-white Arctic skua with its great forked swallow-tail.

The sun was still bright and high as we brewed coffee in the hut and waited for it to sink closer to the horizon so that its rays would not be directly on the water. There was less time to wait than we thought. A pearly gray cloud front started to move in from the east, over the shadowy hills of the Kola Peninsula twenty miles distant in the Soviet Union.

We climbed the scree again and set out for the Silisjoki, walking easily over the springy moss—*dry* moss. Moreover, the breeze from

Kola had sent the mosquitoes back into the dwarf birch. And when the gurgle of the river reached us even before we could see it tumbling down its deep boulder-scattered course, the soggy disappointments of the Kaldavsti and the Tenojoki faded away.

They were totally exorcised in the next three hours as the grayling of the Silisjoki, lying in every run and glide, came generously to our small black wet flies. They were beautiful fish, silver shot with lilac and green, more subtly colored than trout. And their dorsal fins, like great banners, corkscrewed in the heavy current as soon as we hooked them. They would even grab the flies directly downstream as we started to pick up the line again for a fresh cast. They were fine, big fish for stream grayling. My best was nearly three pounds, and there were few less than two. I lost count of how many we slid back into the lovely glacial water once we had a fish apiece for supper. They stopped taking, finally, at about 11:00 P.M.

"Now we will rest," said Jorma definitively. "They will start again at about two A.M. and they will go until breakfast time. But they have to sleep even though the sun doesn't set. Like us."

I couldn't sleep. I lay on the thin mattress in the guards' hut, thinking of those lilac fish twisting in the icy water. Finally, I got up and tried a few casts, but there was no response. Jorma found me down there when he came to draw water for the breakfast coffee. He said that flies were no good for the big grayling. A spoon was what was needed. And there was a lake he had heard of that was full of big grayling, but it was a ten-mile walk.

So I never fished the Silisjoki again, which matters not at all because I will always have a perfect memory of it, but foot-slogged with Jorma to the distant lake. And there I truly met the inviolable shade. It was more than two feet long. I saw every scale on it. It *looked* at me. It was hard to believe it was a grayling at all. I was standing thigh deep in the water at the time, casting a bladed spoon that looked ludicrously big for grayling, but which Jorma had insisted I use. I'd worked maybe a quarter mile of lakeshore and was getting tired of watching the gaudy, flashing contraption winking its way back to me through the clear water when I realized that a vast, dark shadow was keeping pace with it a foot to the rear. It rolled at the bait, missed, and disappeared. I cast again. The great shadow materialized once more, but there was no roll this time. It hung in the water for half a minute, staring at me, then turned and swam slowly off. The inviolable shade in all its glory.

Oddly enough, I didn't feel as chagrined as I might have but, in an odd way, privileged. I tried to tell Williams about it on the flight back to London next day after hearing about all the two-pounders he'd caught when he'd gone back for a second session on the Silisjoki. He seemed incredulous. But some things are quite impossible to explain to the average, insensitive, *baari*-haunting angler.

CHAPTER FIVE

Red Star Salmon

To begin with, of course, Hucho hucho, *the so-called Danubian Salmon, is not a salmon at all (though it is a member of the great family of* salmonidae*) but a char, as one look at its vomerine teeth will tell you. And it is unlikely that you will encounter one in the Danube these days, since that river is simply too filthy for it to live in now. You have to travel to lesser, cleaner rivers in Austria, Yugoslavia or Czechoslovakia. It was to the last country I went, not without difficulty. But the rewards, not only in terms of fish, were great.*

CZECHOSLOVAKIA

THE BIG brass bed that the old man was lying on nearly filled the room. The pillows were bunched high behind him and his fingers were clutched tight on the pink-and-blue patchwork quilt. This was in early December 1973 in the town of Martin in Czechoslovakia, more precisely in the Slovak Socialist Republic, the eastern part of the nation. Outside it was bitter cold—rutted frozen snow in streets lined with identical drab-yellow apartment houses, the Turiec River half iced over—but in the old man's room it was warm.

His life hung on the walls in framed photographs of the long-dead, in ancient, incomprehensible certificates embossed with heavy seals, and in military mementos, the latest an award for valor in the partisan campaign of 1944 when the Germans were retreating west through Martin along the valley of the Vah. The oldest was a tinted portrait of a young cavalryman in the pre-1914 uniform of the Austro-Hungarian Empire: the same Samo Ivaska, now eighty-six years old, who was lying in the brass bed, very frail but able to speak some halting French.

RIVER DUNAJEK, CZECHOSLOVAKIA

Many of the pictures were unconnected with the complex and bitter history of Middle Europe. They showed anglers in the sporting garb of the 1920s and '30s on the banks of turbulent Slovak rivers: the Vah, the Orava, the Turiec. The tackle they held was rough-hewn — stubby rods and old-fashioned reels shaped from hardwood — but it wasn't the tackle that caught the eye, not at first. Held up for the camera, often by two anglers because one could not manage it alone, were great, beautiful fish. Some of them looked to be fifty or sixty pounds, and the adipose fins they displayed, the small, fleshy appendages between dorsal and tail fins, showed clearly that they were members of the salmon family. They were more rakishly built, though, than any trout species or seagoing salmon, with a meaner look about the head and jaws. The photographs were black and white or dull sepia that failed to show the copper-green luster of the flanks fading to pink, the peppering of tiny dark spots, the silver bellies of the living fish that I had seen in the hatchery pool earlier that morning.

They had slid from under the ice into the open patch kept clear by aerated water tumbling in from above, big brood hens around forty pounds, dark shadows until Ladislav tossed a dozen dead trout into the water. Then, as they jumped and boiled clear, the flashing colors gleamed bright, the broad-flanked power of the fish became plain. They are among the rarest of the world's great sport fish, perhaps the mightiest member of the salmon family, growing up to one hundred pounds. Perhaps also the least known: the Danube salmon, *hlavatka* in Slovak, *Hucho hucho* to ichthyologists, sometimes called the huchen in English, a salmon that never goes to sea, whose last native stronghold is in Czechoslovakia, in tributaries of the Danube flowing southward from the mountain range of the Tatras. The Danube itself is too filthy to support the huchen in most of its course.

Now from the bed, his eyes bright, Samo Ivaska spoke of the huchen like an Old Testament prophet, and a granddaughter came proudly forward with the book he had written on the species. He had done more than write a book. The hatchery I had visited that morning had been planned and built by Samo before World War II, when he had first realized that the species was threatened. Twice the hatchery had been destroyed by invading armies and twice rebuilt. The old man was vague about these happenings — "The Germans," he said. But on my homeward journey a Prague cabdriver, relishing the story in the kind of bitter way that the Czechs have, claimed that while the Germans had certainly wrecked it once, on the second occasion the buildings were burned by the Red Army while liberating Slovakia. What really tickled his fancy, though, was the entirely different, entirely characteristic way each army behaved. The Germans carefully shipped out the brood fish and fry to be placed alive in the Elbe. Then they blew up the hatchery. The Russian soldiers just set fire to everything and sat around broiling and eating the fish in the cozy warmth. The cabbie knew because his father used to take him on fishing trips to Martin, and he had once hooked a huchen so huge that the three-quarter-hour drive to the airport was not long enough to land it in.

All that was a long time ago, and Samo seemed anxious to slide over it. He called for his album of souvenirs, letters and more photographs, and handed them to Ladislav to show me, the prophetic gleam still in his eye. Or perhaps he was more like the high priest of some ancient religion passing on the emblems of his power. The symbolism was not inapt. Ladislav Skacel, as head of the Department of Flowing Waters, was now a high priest of the huchen, and its survival depended largely on his continued interest.

My own trail to Ladislav, the old man and the huchen rivers of Czechoslovakia had started in a white-tiled room reeking of Formalin, deep in the underground warren of laboratories beneath the display halls of the British Museum in London. I had reasoned that while it isn't easy for an ordinary angler to make contact with sport fishermen in countries like Czechoslovakia, there is one group of men who can jump the ideological barrier with a lot less difficulty — academics whose subjects do not involve defense considerations. Zoologists, for example.

So I started with Dr. Alwyne Wheeler, perhaps the most eminent of British ichthyologists, and a passionately committed angler to boot. He really wanted to tell me about the trout-fishing trip he was planning in Spain, but I got what I wanted in the end. "Try Dr. Holcik at the Slovak Academy of Agricultural Sciences at Bratislava," he said, "and mention my name." It worked. Dr. Holcik's reply was encouraging. "I think your desire can be realized," he wrote. And he gave me the name and address of Ladislav Skacel.

Ladislav was very slow to respond to my letter, though. Weeks passed, and I began to think that the trail had gone cold. What I hadn't realized at the time was that it is very difficult indeed for a foreigner to get permission to go huchen fishing. Only two hundred licenses are available for Slovak and Czech nationals and the bag limit for the season (now restricted to eight weeks) is just one fish. Much later, Ladislav was to say to me, "I knew from your letter you had huchen in your heart, not in your wallet." In other words, he didn't class me with the French and West German sporting agencies who constantly pestered him to arrange huchen trips for rich clients, and in the end I did hear from him, in mid-November of 1973, in a very positive way. "I recommend you to realize your visit," he wrote, "during the time for the 25th November up to the 10th December because later when it is cold and begin frosts huchen fishing is impossible. Please let me know your arrival. I shall await you in Zilina on my address. And what is concerns of huchen fishing, for this we used the shorter and harder fishing rod, nylon 0.40mm [20-pound test] and big spoons. . . ."

The style was erratic, but the message was beautiful. A shorter and harder rod was not clearly identifiable in my collection, but in the tube went a two-handed nine-footer, a veteran of spring salmon fishing on the Tweed in Scotland. It might not be short enough, but a rod that could stop a thirty-pound Atlantic in a heavy February spate certainly qualified as hard. With Ladislav's letter in my hand, I was issued a Czech visa on the spot at the London embassy. And on the last day of November 1973, in the last fading light of the winter's afternoon, I landed in Prague. A razor slash of icy wind cut into my face as I stepped onto the ground. Inside the terminal building there was more than a sufficiency of soldiers, not Czechs, with high fur collars and automatic pistols. But I was still euphoric with the thought of a huchen. At this point I saw that huchen as a trophy fish, something to chalk up on the scoreboard, to nail to the wall in triumph.

It was the simplest kind of angler's excitement. It stayed bubbling in me through the oppressive miles of high-rise apartment blocks, each precisely like its neighbor, and the dim street lamps until I was in still-magnificent old Prague, with the storybook castle sitting on a crag above it and the lights dancing on the Vltava River. The Hotel Jalta was old Prague, too, all chandeliers and red plush from a 1930s Grand Hotel movie. So was the bell captain, a courteous old man who became animated beyond the polite call of duty when he saw my rod. He retained it in his hand while he sent a colleague up with the luggage. Where was I fishing? In Slovakia? For the *hlavatka* of course? Before the war, foreigners had sometimes come for the *hla-*

vatka fishing but no one for years now. The gentleman realized, no doubt, that he was talking to a true angler, also? Not, alas, for *hlavatka*. He had never had that opportunity. But for many years his quarry had been the great northern pike of the lakes of Bohemia and Moravia. There were some interesting problems in fishing for these pike. . . .

It was a full half hour before I could follow my luggage upstairs, but when I unpacked I found I had more lures than I could possibly need on the trip, and on my way down to dinner I dropped some big Swedish pike spoons on the captain's desk, it being very difficult for Czechs to buy imported Western goods without hard currency. I didn't see him again, but in the morning the porter who brought down my luggage would not take a tip. "Those things you left gave my old comrade much pleasure," he said.

So my euphoria was still with me when I stepped out of the time machine of the Jalta into the gritty cold of Wenceslas Square. I had no clear idea of how to get to Ladislav's town of Zilina, but it looked prominent enough on the map. In Czechoslovakia you have to make travel arrangements through the state agency. "You must fly to Ostrava," the girl there said. "Then you must catch the train."

She was very positive about the itinerary — and half right. The Ostrava plane took off on time, an old prop job full of pale plump men in pale gray suits. It butted erratically into what had become a wild, whirling blizzard, and when we bumped down onto the airfield, the snow was a foot deep and still coming down.

Ostrava, on the Polish border, is no place to be in a blizzard or, probably, at any other time. The bus floundered its way into the center of the city and stopped at the airline office. Its passengers, except me, dispersed purposefully. The euphoria was shriveling in the cold and finally died when the man at the desk said that no, there was no train to Zilina. Who could have given me that idea? Outside, the main square of the small industrial city was too dimly lit for traffic safety, you would think, except that there was no traffic. The only patch of color was a long red banner with a picture of Lenin and some words in Slovak that presumably said he was a good guy. The snow melted, slid off my rod tube and formed a small pool that the office clerk studied silently for a while. It was less than fifty miles to Zilina, I reckoned. I asked the clerk if he would be kind enough to telephone for a cab.

"No taxi," he said perfunctorily. "Not this weather." He obviously wanted to close up shop and go home, but we huchen fishermen aren't put down easily, and I knew I had to stick with him because an English-speaking Czech is hard to find.

"I'll pay for the call," I offered, handing him a 20-koruna note, about $2. He took it abstractedly, called a number and spoke some rapid Slovak. Finally he said, "A man will come and he will talk to you."

There are only a few fringe areas in which private enterprise continues to flourish behind the Curtain, but cabdrivers, that sophisticated and truly international race, operate in one of them. The battered black Moskvitch that eventually drew up was driven by a small, weedy-mustached man with the world-weary air that many of them have. With the aid of the clerk, we made a deal that included an immediate supper for the driver, a supper of goulash in town. It proved necessary to accompany this with several hearty shots of Old Jellyneck — one hundred-proof Jelinek Slivovice, or plum brandy, a liquor which, my research later showed, plays an important part in Czechoslovakian life.

Under its kindly influence and the prospect of getting to Zilina that night, my euphoria returned for a while but was soon eroded again, first in a nightmare journey in the snow, a desperate four hours to cover the fifty miles, and then at my first glimpse of Zilina and the Hotel Polom, which was situated close to the clangor of the odorous chief building of the town, its railway station. Even the cabdriver excused himself from coming in for a drink at the Polom, and once inside you could see why. In my room, looking at the scabrous walls, the truckle bed, the cracked washbasin with the brass faucets rejected by some prison authority as being substandard, I touched bottom. A voice as desolate as a Kerry banshee's came howling out of the station's P.A. system and through my window announcing the departure of the 11:30 P.M. to Moscow in Slovak, Russian and German.

It was probably too late to go calling on Ladislav Skacel, but you have to be brave to be a huchen fisherman, even if it means bolstering your morale artificially. It was to counteract this kind of environment, I told myself, that the Czechs invented Old Jellyneck. I went down to the bar to see if they had any.

It is surprisingly quick-acting stuff. At 11:30 P.M. it had seemed a social error to call on Ladislav so late, but an hour later I was pointing out to myself that he would probably feel insulted if I didn't bother to show up that night. I went upstairs again, grabbed the duty-free Scotch I had carefully transported from London airport, got directions from the hotel clerk and set out into the darkness and the snow.

At first I thought my earlier instinct had been right. A lady, Mrs. Skacel clearly, answered the door after I had climbed up to the fifth floor. "Ladislav Skacel?" I inquired, in what I felt to be a smiling and urbane manner, my Scotch cradled prominently under my arm. There is no difficulty in understanding a sharp negative even if expressed in Slovak, and for perhaps three seconds I was wishing the bottle would turn into a dozen red roses. But, in fact, my timing was very near perfect, for just at that moment, whistling up the stairs came Skacel himself. Plainly he had been, as the Irish delicately put it, "visiting friends."

What is more, he still obviously conceived the night to be young. Ladislav was a small, dark, roly-poly figure of a man with an unmanagerial tendency to giggle a lot. He did as professional a job as ever I've seen in placating Mrs. S. She was all smiles in a minute, ushering me in and offering, with what I was soon to recognize as a fearsome inevitability, a glass of Jellyneck to me while Ladislav disappeared downstairs on an undisclosed errand.

It was disclosed soon enough. He had summoned up the whole apartment block. They arrive in twos and threes, comfortable-looking middle-aged ladies in curlers bearing liters of Slovak wine, teenagers, grandfathers, a fat man with Bulgarian brandy, a thin one with what he claimed to be Hungarian whiskey. They jammed into the tiny apartment until there was barely room to pass the Jellyneck. In installments, as he shouldered by with more booze and sausage that Mrs. S. was slicing in the kitchen with manic energy, Ladislav hurled confident messages at me about the next day's fishing. Sometimes he stopped with little offerings: a slice of cheese, a Czech fishing magazine with a full-page picture of himself hoisting a mighty huchen, and finally a small, redheaded girl with a very long nose—"because you are lonely," he said, giggling again. I had never been less lonely in my life.

We went back to the Hotel Polom in the morning, Ladislav and I, to collect my things. As I said, you have to be brave to be a huchen fisherman, and the greatest single act of valor I performed on that trip was to eat the breakfast Mrs. S. put in front of me after what couldn't have been more than three hours' sleep following the Jellyneck orgy. She had read somewhere that Anglo-Saxons indulged in hearty breakfasts and reasoned that I would expect one. So she had set out four boiled eggs, a good pound of sliced salami, a wedge of cheese and half an enormous loaf of bread. I ate it all with loud grunts of appreciation. A huchen fisher could do nothing less.

Ladislav and I drove out of town without talking much. The cheese, salami and eggs fought a bitter, silent war inside me, and an awful pallor that matched the snowbound landscape around us settled on Ladislav's face. After a few miles we stopped to pick up Dr. Karol Hensel, an ichthyologist from Bratislava. His colleague, Holcik, had told him of the huchen expedition and he was joining us because he had a professional interest in the species. Karol turned out to be a man you would be glad to have along on any fishing trip, charming and companionable, but, fighting my turbulent inner battle, I didn't see him that way immediately. He wore a jaunty Scotch-plaid cap and he kept telling me things about the huchen, a young, happy recruit who didn't know better than to chat away in front of veterans like Ladislav and me, who had been through so much together and even now were suffering in mutual silence. Slowly, though, he got through to me. What was killing off the huchen, he said, was not only pollution — the huchen could tolerate this better than some species, like grayling — but the destruction of the spawning beds, mainly by hydro plants. It had now reached the point where the fish had to be maintained artificially. They had tried stocking huchen in the Elbe and also in southwestern France, but the fish seemed to be doing best in Algeria, in mountain rivers.

Then, as we drove east to the corner of Slovakia where it is bordered on the north by Poland and to the south by Russia, he told me a fishing tale that broke through the fog of the night before. In 1972, he said, he had gone to Mongolia as part of a zoological team, and they camped out on the prairie on the banks of a river called the Shishhid. "In the night," Karol said, "we heard heavy splashings, and the next day I went down and threw out a small dead fish on a length of catfish line. I caught five big huchen in half an hour just putting the heavy cord line over my shoulder when they bit and walking away from the river. Each one was more than a yard long, but then I hooked one that destroyed my thick line. They were *huchen*! Not our *Hucho hucho*, but an Asian species that we hardly know anything of, *Hucho taimen*. We think they may go up to one-hundred-fifty pounds in Mongolia. Nobody tries to catch them. The nomadic tribes there are Buddhist, and killing fish is taboo. Another time we took a small net, just three meters long, and worked it down the bank for fifty meters. When we hauled it there were 270 grayling. . . ."

I was figuring out how you organized a visa for Mongolia when I realized Ladislav had stopped the car. "Look!" he said tragically.

In front of us was the Vah, the biggest of the huchen rivers. It was almost completely iced over, except for a narrow lane in the middle dotted with miniature floes. To fish was clearly impossible. The hard weather had come early—later I learned that the temperature had gone down to twenty-two degrees below. It looked as if there was no chance of my catching a huchen.

A stubborn, set look had come into Ladislav's face, though. "We will look further," he said, and so we did. That bitter day we drove two hundred miles over icy roads finding river after river icebound—the Turiec, the Orava, the Dunajec, the Poprad, the Hornad. We had moved into wilder and wilder country, the foothills of the Carpathians with goosegirls out of Grimm's Fairy Tales in the village streets. As the light started to fail, close to the Polish border, we turned off the main road onto a forestry track that ran alongside the frozen Dunajec River, past a crumbling, romantic ruin. "Cerveny Klastor," Ladislav said. "That's the Red Monastery. Or it was in the old days." It was a deep, claustrophobic valley, a cleft in jagged rocks with pines climbing into mist. In one place some freak of physics had left a patch of water clear of ice, a patch the size of a bigger-than-average bathroom. "Would you like me to take a picture," Ladislav asked, "so that you can show them at home?"

It seemed a little pointless, but I struggled into my boots and set up my tackle, tied on a spoon and cast it maybe fifteen feet to the edge of the ice as a trial while Ladislav focused his camera.

Only Karol and Ladislav believe me about what happened next. You can fish a month for huchen without seeing one. In the only clear patch of water in the whole of Slovakia a fish of about twenty pounds came slamming out from under the ice and grabbed my lure. Then it spoiled a most unlikely fishing story by jumping twice and throwing the hook.

"Next year, perhaps?" said Ladislav.

So it was the following morning that I went to the hatchery before heading for home, and Ladislav teased the big brood fish with dead trout. "If you are writing about this," he said, "will you tell people about the problem we have?"

The hatchery system, which Samo Ivaska has devoted his life to and which is now managed by the Department of Fish Ponds, has been exposed to a new threat in the last few years. Unhappily, in Czechoslovakia there is not the sensitivity to ecological problems that has grown in the West in recent years. Filling production norms is more important than *Hucho hucho*. A stone quarry is operating within fifty yards of the hatchery. The detonations are bad, but much worse is the stone dust that descends on the ponds, blinding some of the brood fish and choking fry. A new hatchery seems the only solution, but state aid cannot be counted on and the cost might be 20 million Czech koruna—about $2 million. "Do you think there's a chance that the World Wildlife Fund might help us? Or UNESCO?" Ladislav asked. I couldn't give him an answer to that.

My own huchen story didn't end at this point, though. During 1974 Ladislav and I exchanged letters in a desultory way, and I was hopeful that he would make a firm invitation again. He did better than that. In September one of his bombshell letters arrived. "Hearty greetings," it said. "The best time for new attempt to catch *Hucho hucho* is before beginning of official season. I have planned the term from 29th October to 1st November. Karol agrees . . . please write to me by return mail if you agree with this term." *Write*? I had a wire off to him before breakfast. It might be cheating a little, but who was I to argue with the head of the Department of Flowing Waters?

In the end, for all Ladislav's helpfulness, I wasn't allowed to cheat. Forty-eight hours before my flight came an international telegram. "Do not to Zilina," it said woefully. "Here are terrible inundations." Weeks of torrential rain in Central Europe had sent the huchen rivers spilling over their banks. There was nothing to be done about it. In frustration, I slammed a lot of surf-casting tackle into the car, got on the ferry to Ireland and took out my feelings on the beaches of Kerry. I was still there when new word came from Ladislav. The rivers had gone down, though they weren't exactly right yet. We could try if I didn't mind risking the weather, for by now we were almost into December again.

Yes, I wanted to try, I wired him. The salmon rod went into the tube again. The same bell captain was still behind the desk of the Hotel Jalta, and he had caught a fifteen-pound pike on one of the Swedish spoons. This time, though, I caught the Moscow Express from Prague, seven hours to Zilina and no dining car. You still had to be brave to be a huchen fisher. It was snowing in

Zilina—probably it had never stopped—and nobody had spent any money on the Hotel Polom in the interval. This time, however, I thought it wiser not to disturb Ladislav late at night.

It seemed to be a more sober occasion altogether, possibly because my feelings about *Hucho hucho* were somewhat more ambivalent than they had been. They didn't seem to be just trophy fish anymore. I still wanted to catch one, but only because I wanted to know the species better. I wanted the experience of a take and I wanted to look at one closely, enjoy the sight of it.

Next morning we went straight to the Turiec. The snow was deep and it still came down spasmodically, but the river was clear, nearly bank-high.

Maybe fittingly, no huchen came to my rod that first day. Ladislav and a friend he had brought took one apiece, but we were widely separated and the fish were released before I could see them.

That night Karol arrived from Bratislava and he had a surprise for us. He was finished with catfish lines. He had invested in a rod and reel. The rod was bright blue and telescoped down to eighteen inches. When Ladislav saw it, he said something devastating in Slovak, but Karol smiled beatifically and no longer pretended he was with us purely out of scientific interest. There was a certain amount of Jellyneck in the evening's reunion but we went to bed early. Next morning we were to fish the Orava.

The Orava was a much bigger river than the Turiec, but it seemingly had its disadvantages. "You must be careful," Ladislav said. "Sometimes they release water from the dam and the river shoots up one meter. That upsets the huchen and perhaps you as well."

I waded shallow and cast long all morning, glancing upstream occasionally, looking out for such indicators as twigs and leaves suddenly swirling down or maybe a wall of white water. But nothing happened. We worked downstream, and after a few hours I was casting my bait, a small dead cyprinid fish mounted to wobble, as mechanically as a tired gambler pulling the handle of a slot machine. And then I became a lucky tired gambler; I won the jackpot.

I had dropped down to a bend in the river where a big gravel bank was exposed in midstream, and here, discouragingly in effect if not in logic, the Orava ran close to some kind of factory. I dropped the bait into the swirl at the tail of the bank. It traveled a couple of feet and was stopped hard. It would be pleasant but dishonest to write that the reel screamed and that fifty yards away a living bar of silver clawed its way skyward, as they say.

But this was a small huchen, about eight pounds, and I was loaded for a possible fifty-pounder. In fact it surprised me by buzzing off a few yards against a fairly tight drag, but all it could do after that was splash in a frenzy until I got it into the shallows and beached it.

That was not how I won the jackpot, though. I unhooked and released my huchen and immediately caught another a couple of pounds larger. I let him go, cast again and caught a third, twelve pounds I reckoned. Three huchen in ten minutes, and you can go a season without seeing one. That was certainly jackpot standard, and I was glad I had an audience for the last two. Ladislav had arrived. That evening rather more Jellyneck was drunk and this was when Ladislav made his remark about me having huchen in my heart, not my wallet, so I hope he meant it.

We went back to the Turiec next day, the last for fishing, and I caught two more huchen. Lying in the snow they were beautiful fish. It would have been good to catch a fifty-pounder, but, oddly, I was perfectly happy with my small fish, with seeing them swim away in the dark, cold water. We went back to Martin before I left the country. Samo Ivaska was still propped up in his bed, still wanting to talk about the great salmon of the Danube system. The hatchery had deteriorated. There were only three brood fish left. Maybe it would have been good, after all, to have caught a big hen huchen just to get it safely to the hatchery.

It was still snowing in Zilina when Karol and Ladislav saw me off on the night train to Prague. "You'll write about our fish, then?" Ladislav called after me.

Well, so I have. But it might be worth saying again that *Hucho hucho*, one of the world's great, if least-known sport fish, is seriously imperiled, a fish that, given a solid base of recovery, could stock and enhance rivers in temperate climates all over the world. We don't have so many of them that a species can be lightly discarded.

BROWN TROUT FROM RIVER TARN, FRANCE

CHAPTER SIX

Trout & Truffles on the Tarn

I think that the most delightful phone call I ever got from my office came when the late Andre Laguerre, then editor of Sports Illustrated, *rang to enquire whether I would like to head to southwestern France and, as he put it, "try the trout fishing and the food. No hurry," he went on. "Take a few weeks over it." The result you see here.*

FRANCE

THE BROWN hairy forearm of M. Louis Bugarel cast an imaginary lure with an imaginary rod at the far bank of the Tarn, where a heavy glide of water slid along a cliff still pearly with the morning rain.

"Cloc!" explained M. Bugarel, "tic . . . tic . . . tic . . . Bop!" He no longer held the phantom rod. Now his arm was a well-hooked two-pounder, leaping just once before lunging toward some dangerous midstream rocks.

"Don't try to horse him!" I shouted, entering into the spirit of things, forgetting momentarily that we were conversing in Angler's International, that curious language of gesture and onomatopoeia. We had no alternative; as bad as my French was, Louis's English was worse, consisting of the single word Glasgow accompanied by signs and eyerollings indicating improbable quantities of drink and women. The mystery was eventually explained by the multilingual wine waiter at the Château de la Caze where Louis was janitor and I was a guest. He'd had a few days ashore in the gray Scottish city before sailing in a French destroyer to the Norwegian Campaign of 1940. The five years in a German POW camp that followed must have added a touch of bright pink to his memories of that last shore leave. Glasgow shimmered as romantically for Louis as Peiping or Samarkand.

Other differences of culture held us apart also at the beginning. As every Anglo-Saxon knows, thigh waders for trout fishing are green, a tasteful, drab green. When I first met Louis he was rolling along in this unspeakable shiny pair, the color of milk chocolate, and I knew I could have nothing in common with this evidently non-serious fisherman, though I was glad enough to see him since I was dripping wet, chattering with cold and in deep need of being instantly guided to a large cognac.

That was because I had just emerged from the Tarn, a beautiful, spiteful, glacial trout river in southern France that falls steeply from the mountains of the Massif Central in the department of Lozère and dashes through wild gorges before it levels off and joins the Garonne. The water is green glass broadening out into wide riffles with deep runs under the bank that you instantly recognize as perfect wet-fly water.

I had come across such a run on the afternoon I arrived at the château and I couldn't wait to put a team of flies across it. I waded in calf deep at first, covering the near water in case the trout were lying in the rough shallows, but I hurried over that section, certain that most of the fish would be lying beneath the deeply undercut far bank. As I waded further, the pull of the stream got heavier but I could see that for twenty yards ahead there was no great depth.

I was quite wrong. The Tarn is treacherously clear. The water was deeper than it looked and, snow-fed from high altitude, its power increased with every inch of depth. As soon as it was over my knees I knew I had to turn back and that it was also necessary to turn upstream. I had waded bad rivers before, notably the Wye in Wales with its rock gutters, but I had always had a steel-tipped wading staff. I hadn't thought it necessary to bring a staff to the Tarn.

The water took me when I was halfway around and swept me very quickly into the deep run I had been trying to reach. Then I was merrily away downstream in deep, icy water, my boots full and holding me down. For the record, I did not see my past life unroll before me. Outraged disbelief, as if a total stranger had shouldered me to the ground in the street, was my first reaction. But a calmer part of my mind recalled clearly what I had once read in a book on Scottish salmon fishing. If you are swept away by the river, the author said, don't try to swim ashore, just concentrate on keeping upright by dog-paddling. Fast, rocky rivers being what they are, you will keep going in spite of your boots and eventually you will be cast upon a pebble bank or a shallow shore.

He was entirely right about going along with the river, but the haven I found was a willow bough that I grabbed in one of my brief shoreward excursions. For a short time I streamed out from it, gathering strength, then I got a better grip, hauled myself some way along it until I could grab some bank. It was a little longer before I could drag my great dropsical boots up on the grass and lie there panting, having traveled roughly three hundred yards, an all-time record, I would bet, for boatless navigation of the Tarn. I was also rodless, the delicate little Hardy Riccardi split cane having disappeared in the early stages.

I emptied my boots, then my canvas fishing bag (I had wondered what was dragging me back as my boots tried to drag me under) and squished back to the château, in the gardens of which I first made the acquaintance of M. Bugarel in his unsuitable boots. He was sniggering, too, and holding a spinning rod. Only a man in boots like those, I remember thinking, would have the lack of taste to throw hardware across a perfect fly river like the Tarn. Our relationship might have deteriorated further had he not replaced his grin with a sympathetic "tsk, tsk" and escorted me to the bar for immediate treatment. As the cognac lit its small fires through my body I recalled what a similarly saturated Irishman had said to me as he drained his flask on the banks of the Bandon. "Inside and out," I told the uncomprehending Louis, "I'm as wet as a trout."

A fine beginning, and nearly a quick ending to the long, devious journey that had brought me to the Tarn, one that had begun in the elegant tackle shop of Hardy Brothers in Pall Mall, London, very handy for the club members of St. James—the kind of shop where you can arrive only by taxi. By a stroke of luck, the manager, Mr. Lee, was free, having just dealt, so he said, with the needs of the Duke of Devonshire. "The Tarn," I said, ignoring his name-dropping, "in southern France. Suitable flies and tackle."

Mr. Lee came back fighting. "The French folio," he ordered, snapping his fingers. A young assistant shimmered away and returned with a leather-bound volume. It proved to contain letters from several generations of Hardy customers recounting their findings in France. Astonishingly, though, not one of them seemed to have fished the Tarn. The chalk streams of Normandy, certainly.

The fast rivers of the Pyrenees and the Savoy Alps, by all means. Also the southern lakes. But not a word of the Tarn.

This did not faze Mr. Lee. When in doubt, apply general principles. Dry flies, wet flies and nymphs for all seasons built up on the counter. "You'll need a fast-sinking line for the mountain torrents, sir," said Mr. Lee and immediately an assistant was tying one hundred yards of backing on a No. 6 sinker. I seemed to have a new rod also and a lightweight landing net. Drifts of leaders accumulated. With a pair of studded waders over my arm I found myself out on the sidewalk. Game, set and match to Mr. Lee.

In Paris the equivalent of Hardy's is St. Hubert. Surprisingly, there also the Tarn was a mystery, but a gentleman with a thin mustache whom I would have matched against Mr. Lee any day was able to suggest some fly patterns that would undoubtedly meet my needs. I left with these and a superb fishing vest with twelve pockets finished in kid leather, without which I could not possibly manage. (For sportsmen who might fish the Tarn in future, I feel I should point out here that I was eventually able to purchase the correct Tarn patterns in the post office at Ste-Enimie on the banks of the river. But don't expect any style.)

There were further delays. Heading south on the Autoroute, it seemed a sin and a shame not to break the journey at Vienne, not far from Lyons, for a visit to La Pyramide, one of only sixteen restaurants in France considered worthy of three rosettes in the *Guide Michelin*. Unhappily there was no possibility of a reservation until lunch next day. But such experiences come rarely. I decided to wait, booking a room at Valence nearby.

That meant killing an evening somehow, and Valence seemed to have few resources until I saw a neon sign in the main street. LE PUB TWICKENHAM it said. I should have remembered that south of Lyons is one of the great strongholds of rugby football in France. In the provincial glumness of Valence that sign beckoned like a harbor light. Twickenham is the big rugby stadium in London where international games are played. Undoubtedly, this was where the fans gathered and I was entirely right. Inside, any space left over from framed team photographs was hung with international rugby shirts. The blue, with thistle, of Scotland; the red, with ostrich feathers, of Wales; the white, with red rose, of England; the Irish shirt with a shamrock; the South African with a springbok; the New Zealand with a fern; the Australian with a wallaby; and, naturally, the light blue of France with the cockerel superimposed. A true Valhalla and presiding over it a man I immediately recognized, Elie Cester, until two years ago a first choice front row forward of the French International XV. Around him, poring over copies of *L'Equipe*, were lesser but still imposing figures. I knew exactly what to say and as I went up to the bar to order a *pastis* I said it. "Barry John . . . *c'est terrible, hein?*"

That opened the floodgates all right. I knew they would not have heard about it. Barry John of Wales is the greatest rugby player in the world. And on the day I left home for my trout-fishing trip he had announced his retirement from the game at the ridiculous age of twenty-seven. Once the shock was over, those gallant Frenchmen assisted me to mourn, even though the news meant that in 1973 the chances of France beating Wales were greatly enhanced. (She did, last month, twelve to three.) We mourned steadily through the night and the people who switched on their bedroom lights at 4:00 A.M. in the main street of Valence as my new friends escorted me back to my hotel probably didn't even realize that our voices, upraised in *O'Reilly's Daughter*, were simultaneously paying tribute to the departure of a great one and to the cross-pollination of cultures that meant that such a classic song was known wherever rugby is played.

Twelve noon was the time set for my lunch at La Pyramide and it says much for the stamina of us trout-fishing rugby men that I was there on time. There to greet me was *la patronne*, Mme. Point, an old lady with piercing eyes who has been known to refuse to admit naive English and Americans for lunch because they have asked not only for aperitifs but *gin-based* ones. I myself, this morning after, had no wish for an aperitif, not ever, not for the rest of my life.

The mousse of trout, with which the meal started, was delicate and light enough to master. I might have managed the *pâté de grives* also had I not been foolish enough to ask the waiter what *grives* meant.

"I do not know the English word for them," he said, "but they are the little birds that are always flying around the olive trees." Mercifully, I did not learn until later that they were thrushes. But I was able to take a little of the turbot poached in white wine and was only shown up in my true colors while trying to hide my portion of *poulet de Bresse* under my *dauphinois* potatoes. Madame and the headwaiter were desolate. What was wrong? I couldn't tell them what was wrong. How can you tell the proprietress of a restaurant with three stars in *Michelin* that everything tastes of *pastis*?

It was clearly time that I headed south for the Tarn, to the Château de la Caze, a fifteenth-century turreted castle, now a hotel set with absurd romanticism on a cliff above the river. The lobby was cool and stone-flagged. Stone steps, worn hollow, led up to my turret room and even inside it I could hear the roar of the Tarn. How much better, how much more life-enhancing this was than that seedy rugby pub in Valence and its coarsened customers, I thought, taking a generous chestful of mountain air. I grabbed my boots and tackle, slipped on my new fishing vest and with the flies of Hardy's and St. Hubert went to make closer acquaintance with the Tarn.

An all-too-close acquaintance. But so magical was the look of the Tarn, so clearly demanding to be fly-fished that I was dry and back on the river within the hour with a spare rod.

This time I stayed dry, but that was the limit of my achievement. I fished down run after run of entirely responseless water. I knew that I was covering the right places. I went through the gamut of flies that I had brought from London and Paris and later in the evening I tried the locally tied ones also. Not a rise, not a pluck. There was no insect life showing either, but I'd fished plenty of streams where this was the case. There, if anything, the trout were easier to catch. The only other fishermen I saw were a couple of tourists tossing spoons across the water. They weren't having any success either, which would not have been surprising in any circumstances.

I went back to the château, defeated but willing to be consoled by the *spécialité de la maison, la truffe entière*, a complete truffle to myself, cooked in pastry. At least I'd recovered from that temporary setback of appetite at Valence. When I'd finished, the waiter leaned over. "The pastry cook would like to have a word with you," he said. *He* couldn't have any complaints, I thought. I'd made short work of the strawberry *gâteau*, hadn't I?

The *pâtissier*, though, had no complaint. He merely wished to show me his catch, which he had kept alive in a tank. It was a splendid five-pounder, a native trout, since the Tarn is not stocked. It had fallen, he told me, to a paste concocted there in that very kitchen. He took me out to show me his tackle. The *pâtissier* had his own special pitch, much trodden down, at the foot of the cliff on which the château was built. There, as a permanency, leaned his rod, twenty feet of bamboo. There was no reel, just a few yards of stout cord tied to a ring at the top like an illustration in a seventeenth-century edition of *The Compleat Angler*. Mr. Lee would have fainted, but as for me, anybody who can catch a wild river trout of that size gets my immediate and close attention. "This paste," I asked as carelessly as I could, "was it simply a flour-and-water dough? Was anything added?"

The *pâtissier* smiled apologetically. As an angler, one had one's secrets. As an angler himself, Monsieur would understand. Monsieur understood, all right. It was already becoming plain that the entire staff of the château was fishing crazy: all through the days that followed I was to see them, singly or in pairs, sneaking down to the water in the off-duty hours, still in their blue-checked trousers and their white coats. The kitchen, probably, was a hissing stewpot of piscatorial competition and intrigue. As an outsider I couldn't expect any privileges.

So next day it was the fly rod again, and in the morning I fished my way down through perfect glides and riffles until the sun was high and the most responsive of streams would not have yielded a trout anyway. Not a twitch. And not a fish showing on the surface though you could see them well enough if you climbed one of the cliffs and looked down into the deeps. The trout hung there unmoving and nothing short of a harpoon gun was going to shift them. It was time to seek further aid.

That evening I drove fifty kilometers to Millau where, if every French trout-fishing story I'd ever read was correct in detail, I would find the members of the Club de la Pêche Sportive gathered for the hour of the aperitif. The stories were entirely correct. A brief inquiry at the Syndicat d'Initiative, the town tourist bureau, confirmed that the Café Moderne was the place. Within minutes I was in the presence of M. le Président of the club and his committee colleagues. They admired my fishing vest, picked through my fly box and exclaimed politely at the creations of Hardy Brothers and St. Hubert. And then the president broke the news. There was, naturally, no sport to compare with fly-fishing. Had not he himself been honored to appear on internationally distributed posters of the French Tourist Board, thigh-wadered, casting a line across a pleasant reach of the Tarn? Did he not, in fact, *live* for fly-fishing? But, alas, Monsieur was a month too early. In May the Tarn was still too cold, there was no insect life, the trout would not move up in the water. There were small tributary streams, certainly, where Monsieur could fish fly but the trout were insignificant. It was a shame to have come such a long way. Was Monsieur staying at Millau?

No, I told them. At the Château de la Caze. At the château? Mild consternation. Then perhaps Monsieur has encountered Louis Bugarel, the janitor? I admitted this. But what good fortune! I recalled the short, thickset man with the sailor's gait and the chocolate-brown waders. I couldn't see any reason for the excitement.

"But, Monsieur," said the president, continuing in the somewhat literary style he favored in English, "Louis is king of the river. His catches are the greatest. Three, four kilos of trout he brings in after an hour's fishing. He speaks to the fish in their own language!"

And so it was that next day, as soon as Louis had finished carrying in the olive boughs that would fuel the great open fire in the restaurant of the château, he took me to the banks of the Tarn for a demonstration of his methods.

"Cloc!" His imaginary lure plopped into the water a foot from the edge of the far cliff. "Tic . . . tic . . . tic. . . ." He made three turns of the handle of his invisible spinning reel. "BOP!" and the trout was hooked, twisting in the green current. His face split in a Fernandel-like grin and he pulled from his pocket an old tobacco tin. Inside was the device that had made him king of the Tarn.

It looked like the hollow head of a bullet. Two holes were drilled through it and two tiny treble hooks each on an inch of fine nylon hung from the swivel built into the top of the contraption. "*Attendez!*" exclaimed Louis. His hand dived into another capacious jacket pocket and came up with a white plastic bottle. Opening it with the loving care a *sommelier* gives to a Château Lafite, he thrust it forward. Within it were swimming half a dozen little gray fish. "*Les vairons!*" he said reverently. Minnows. I might have guessed. Louis was a drop-minnow king. He did not have to explain any more. Years before I had learned how deadly for trout was a dead minnow mounted with plenty of lead at its head so that it dived like a plummet as soon as it hit the water. You retrieved sink-and-reel and if you didn't take trout this way you could hand in your rod. It all came back to me, the memory of easing the rod tip, with the minnow reeled right up to the top ring, through a jungle of brambles and sally bush that lined the Taff in Wales and, when it was clear, flicking the minnow out to the far bank. If a trout was there you'd get it in the first two turns of the reel.

I made signals to Louis that now, instantly, we would go back to the château for the rods. He sent back a soothing, no-hurry gesture, pointed to the sun and imitated, successively and with surprising skill, first heavy sleep and then an alarm clock going off. He pointed to five o'clock on my watch face, and I got the full message. Louis and I would make a dawn start. Meanwhile we retired to the bar for a cementing *pastis*. "Glasgow!" I said, raising my glass. "Glasgow!" responded Louis. The word had achieved a new semantic level. It now meant "Death to trout!"

At first light next morning I raised the heavy iron bar that secured the mighty oak door of the château and, skidding a little on the cobblestones in my nailed boots, rendezvoused with Louis. We brushed between tamarisks heavy with dew and scrambled over boulders until the Tarn, as gleaming with promise as ever, slid before us. Under Louis's watchful eye I mounted a minnow, threading copper wires through the holes in the lead cap to secure it. He stood back, arms folded to see if I had absorbed the lesson. I let the minnow swing at the rod tip for the moment to judge its weight, then let it go.

"Cloc!" I said as it dropped in close to the far bank. "Tic . . . tic . . . tic" went the reel. And "BOP!" The rod went over, the drag was buzzing and out there, rolling in the current, flashing gold and silver, was my first Tarn trout. A bit over one pound, which sounds better than a demi-kilo. "Bravo!" said Louis, netting it out. "Glasgow!" I said.

We split up, Louis going downstream and I heading toward a spot half a mile up where the gorge closed in completely and prevented further progress. I didn't get as far as that, though. By the time I had basketed my fourteenth trout the minnows had run out. The best fish would go a pound and a half but there wasn't one under a pound. The fish were not as plump as they would be in July and you could see why they had not been interested in the olives and duns I'd been wafting over them for two days. Meat hungry, they had no time to waste on trivia. I walked back, the creel strap cutting nicely into my shoulder, to join Louis for breakfast. He had caught eighteen, being more expert than I was at remounting a damaged minnow.

We took them down to the kitchen and tipped them out to annoy the *pâtissier*, who caught his very large trout at very long intervals on unnatural, still-fished bait. This day there would be no need for me to carry out the shameful task I had undertaken the previous morning. Around the château was a moat crammed with indolent, hand-fed rainbows bred to figure on the restaurant menu. And, taking pity on my fishlessness, the *chef de cuisine* had invited me to catch the day's rations for him (for the information of those who might one day fish the château moat, they come readily to a No. 14 Butcher, lightly dressed with a gold-tinseled body. Or to anything else). "Tonight," I told him, "you can serve the real thing."

Now I was eager to get to grips with a fish that at least would beat the pastry cook and his paste out of sight, if not anything like the vast 18½-pounder that held the Tarn record. Besides, that was taken at Ste-Enimie before World War I. No, a simple six- or seven-pounder would be fine. "*Plus de vairons!*" I said to Louis. Let's get more minnows.

It was now that Louis raised Catch-22. It was a lot easier to catch trout than minnows. At this time of year, he explained through willing kitchen interpreters, they were exceedingly hard to come by. In fact, on our dawn session we had squandered them like a sailor's payroll—in Glasgow. The day could not be devoted to fishing. Instead every effort would have to go into minnow collecting.

We walked over to Louis's private fishing shack in the château grounds and examined his minnow equipment. A trap made of a corked burgundy bottle with the glass knocked out from the end of the cone in its base. A miniature trap net that could be staked in the shallows. Hand nets as well. A little rod set up with a tiny hook to take a fragment of worm. Louis had clearly been in this predicament before.

Back to the river again, but this time to a backwater that was less than knee-deep. Louis examined it with care and rejected it. "Bah!" he exclaimed and we walked another quarter mile. This time we found a pool that must have had possibilities, though not for instant fishing with rod and line. Instead Louis set the burgundy trap and we left. "Poop! poop!" he said mysteriously. I figured this out for a while then realized he wanted to be driven somewhere.

On his directions we motored downstream to the village of La Malène and went into the café. Louis seemed to be well-known there. There was a lot of handshaking and we settled down with a couple of brandies until maybe ten minutes later a small boy burst in with a plastic bottle. Two *vairons*, by heaven! It was only courteous to take another brandy before we proceeded to our next stop, the café at Les Vignes, where a similar drama was enacted. It was several cafés later, by which time the situation was becoming distinctly Glasgow, that we made our last stop at Le Rozier. That brought us up to two dozen *vairons* and a diminishing chance of getting back to the château that evening. It was only the thought of a repeat order of the entire truffle for starters and a promised cassoulet de Toulouse that got me over the last twenty kilometers and home for dinner. That and hauling the trap net. It contained one minnow.

To describe the rest of the week would merely be repetitious. Each day Louis and I followed the same routine. An early-morning massacre of the trout (we both turned out to be quantity, not quality, men, for we never topped two pounds) followed by a bibulous patrol of the cafés of the Tarn valley and a restful, well-fed evening. The last morning I recall well, though. I was returning to the château for breakfast, Louis alongside, when a big, new 4.2-liter Jaguar swirled the gravel as it pulled up on the drive. I scratched my head. Maybe I should have combed my hair that morning or at least shaved off the three-day growth. I had put on four pounds by way of cassoulet, truffles, pâté of guinea fowl, red wine and cognac, my fishing vest was losing its leather binding and a large stain of raspberry liqueur discolored the place where you are supposed to clip on the little pair of scissors. But I had caught many a trout

From the Jaguar stepped a large, silver-haired gentleman and I could see the Hardy labels on the rods lying across the back seat. He addressed me politely in Anglo-French. "Est-il possible, Monsieur," he said, "to attraper les trouts round here?" I indicated my friend with a graceful gesture.

"Mon cher colleague, Monsieur Glasgow here, will tell you all about it," I said. "He is the king of the Tarn."

HALIBUT TAKEN OFF STIKKISHOLMUR, ICELAND

CHAPTER SEVEN

Pushed to the Icy Brink

Iceland, in my fishing life, was a kind of half-way house. Soon after this trip I would be heading across the Atlantic to make my home in the United States. And so, I thought, a story about this mid-Atlantic island might be appropriate here.

ICELAND

H E'S GOING to call it off, I told myself comfortingly. Any moment good old Konrad Juliusson is going to come clattering down the companionway and tell us with polite regret that sea conditions are impossible. My groan of disappointment was already prepared. I reckoned we could be back in Reykjavik by early evening. A long hot bath with the water setting adjusted to 120°F., slip into the dark gray mohair and the Chelsea boots, a touch of Monsieur Rochas After-Shave and straight into the second-floor restaurant of the Saga Hotel where they still do the twist. Saturday night in the Saga. The most beautiful girls in the world, bored out of their minds with clodhopping Icelandic trawlermen. . . .

"Shove up!" said my huge, discourteous friend Leslie Moncrieff, breaking into my reverie. Aboard the sixty-ton scallop dredger *Gisli Magnusson* the belowdecks accommodations were very cramped and certainly not designed for Moncrieff, 270 pounds and 6′5″ in the woolen sea-boot stockings, knitted for him with loving care by Mrs. Dora Moncrieff, that he now was aggressively thrusting between me and the galley stove.

I shoved up at the expense of Haldur Snorrason, Peter Collins, Tom Hutchinson and Johann Sigurdsson, the other members of the Anglo-Icelandic Giant Arctic Halibut Expedition, as the *Gisli Magnusson*, yawing like a drunken pig, butted its bow into a freezing southwesterly gale straight off the ice of the Snaefells Glacier. Not only was Moncrieff bigger than the rest of us, he was also our leader. You had to make allowances. "Excuse me," I said politely and he eased his great bulk out of the way long enough for me to get at the pot of tarry black coffee bubbling on the hot plate. I filled our mugs and then ritually, with great attention to handing out a fair ration, Collins added the hard stuff, the last of the Dufftown-Glenlivet malt whiskey, the last liquor we were likely to see for days. Inadequate research, characteristic of this expedition, had failed to reveal that Stikkisholmur, the little harbor town that was our port, was totally, remorselessly dry.

I took a deep suck of the black mixture. Unless Skipper Juliusson came soon on his errand of mercy, we were going to have to clamber up onto that wild, lurching deck again, into the soaking, freezing sleet. I closed my eyes and let the lush pastures of the Saga Hotel swim into my inner vision. I'd gotten as far as catching the eye of the tall dark one who sold me the sweater in the shop on Hafnarstraeti—she was bound to be there, wasn't she?—when I was cruelly thumped on the shoulder by Moncrieff. "Let's have you on deck!" he shouted.

I dragged myself into my soaking parka, realizing that the engine note of the *Gisli Magnusson* had changed. The absurdly intrepid Juliusson had swung her round broadside to the weather, setting us up for yet another drift over the lava gullies that lay twenty fathoms below. I clambered up on deck behind the other idiots and took the wind full in the teeth.

It was an impressive scene, though in my state of mind one better viewed on a color telly. Black crags to shoreward standing in mad, jagged silhouettes against the glacier. Rags of cloud scudding northward. The sea a patternless jumble of breaking crests with brown, eagle-beaked skuas screaming over them. The gale was off the land. We could not have stayed out in it otherwise, but it was enough to send the boat skidding along as if she were under power. Which, as I repeatedly tried to explain to Moncrieff, made the pursuit of the giant halibut impossible. They lie in the lava gullies, lunging up a fathom or so to take a bait. Our drift was so fast that even three pounds of lead streamed out near the surface as if we were trolling—or so it had proved all morning. "We can't fish in this!" I yelled at him over the wind.

"Yes we can," he shouted back. "I've brought my parachute." As if to prove how obstinate he could be, Moncrieff tried to light a cigar, wasted six matches and flung it over the rail. "Down below," he ordered, "and fetch it."

The expedition has gotten too much for him, I told myself, he's cracking up. I knew that Moncrieff wanted a big halibut even more than I did. Possibly those huge unattainable fish, so close to us yet so impossible to catch, had forced him over the edge. "The, er, parachute," I said, gaining time.

"In the big canvas pack," he elaborated, "stowed under the for'ard bunk." Obediently I went below. There was a brown pack there. I dragged it up behind me as the boat pitched and tossed.

"What do you want a parachute for, Leslie?" I asked him as lightly as I could. "You aren't *going* anywhere, are you?"

He gave me a cold look. "To counteract a fast drift, what we need is a sea anchor. I foresaw this problem before we left London. That is why I have brought along my parachute."

What he had not foreseen in London was the difficulty of getting it into the water. "We'll stream it out over the bow," he said, as we began unwrapping the chute into a long sausage shape, the two Icelanders holding on to one end. From the wheelhouse, Konrad Juliusson looked on with fascinated awe.

"I'm going to ease it into the sea," Moncrieff said confidently. "Let it out slow and stop as soon as I give the word. Stand by," he told me, "with the big gaff. As soon as the end of the chute is in the sea, prod it down. Understand? PROD IT DOWN!"

He should have realized that by the time the crown of his ridiculous device was wet, the wind would have taken it a couple of yards from the boat. I prodded hard but couldn't reach it, and it began to billow. I was just trying to damp down the middle section when Moncrieff made his big mistake. "Leave it," he yelled. "I'll do it."

Both Snorrason and Sigurdsson speak very good English. It was the howling of the wind that must have carried away Moncrieff's last phrase. Later they strongly maintained that they heard him yell "Leave it go," ungrammatical, certainly, but excusable in the circumstances. So they let it go.

Moncrieff now showed a remarkable turn of speed for a large man. As the parachute burst forth in its full glory he grabbed the harness. For a moment it seemed likely that the last we would see of him would be as a figure bestriding the clouds, a triumphant Jove in some vast Renaissance painting. But we reached him in time, clutching the mad chute and overcoming its dying struggles on deck.

I knelt on it in the driving sleet, thinking what an absurd pass I had been brought to by this obsession with a giant flatfish, an obsession shared by the others. For them, as for me, it probably started a long time ago, as small boys dangling a handline over the end of a jetty, hooks baited with sandworms and hoping for a rattling bite from a fat flounder. You could take cod or pollack home and just get polite acknowledgment, but a stringer of flounders, brown above, pearly white beneath, frying-pan-sized, ensured a proper welcome. You could be as late as you liked with flounders.

I've always thought those adults had a coarse attitude, evaluating fish in terms of their edible qualities. I loved flounders for themselves alone, for the delicate, undulating way they swam, the heroic dives they tried to make as you hauled them up, your line rasping on the rail. Above all, it was their extraordinary and wonderful *flatness*. My own son produced a poem on the subject, clearly responding to their mystery as I did at his age. *Little flatfish, little flatfish*, it began, *Where is your nest in the depths of the sea?* Only a vague notion of ichthyology, you'll observe, but the right kind of wonder. He gave up poetry after this, but is still keen on flounders.

I, too, would probably have been happy with flounders for many more years but for a film deemed educational that I saw at school. It was about the commercial line fishermen who sailed out of Aberdeen on the east coast of Scotland. They went north to the White Sea and the film showed them shooting ten-mile-long lines marked by huge orange Dan buoys. There was some irrelevant scenic stuff but the real thing started when they began to haul the line. A big gaping cod came up first, then some unfamiliar Arctic species — blue-striped torsk and fanged wolffish. Then the winch began to labor. The camera was focused over the lurching rail and there in the clear cold water was a breath-stopping sight. It was a vast flounder, or so I thought, bigger than the dining table at home, a huge and mighty flounder that must have weighed two hundred pounds. Amazingly, the commentator's voice did not rise to a hysterical screech. Instead, it noted calmly, "The great halibut of northern waters fetches top prices on the Aberdeen fish market. . . ."

It was the best afternoon I ever spent at school. I was in a dream for days, muttering, "Halibut, fetches top prices, northern waters, Aberdeen. . . ." I would have shipped there and then as an Aberdeen deckie if I could, but other, more powerful persons had different plans. Instead, I read all I could about the species. It grew to six hundred pounds or more, said the book. Known to smash the gunwales of small craft when brought on board. Immensely powerful predator, largest member of the order *Heterosomata*. That was the good news. Then came the bad. An occasional straggler southward to British waters. An extremely rare catch on rod and line. . . .

Fair enough. I filed the halibut away in my mind, next to the fifty-pound salmon and the lunker rainbow trout of New Zealand. I had plenty of time, I reckoned.

It was twenty years, in fact, before the curtain went up on my halibut search. Act One was set in Stavanger, Norway, on my way back from a salmon trip that had failed to produce the fifty-pounder. I found a man who claimed to know where the halibut were and was willing to take me to sea for a few hours. We steamed out after lunch and caught some bait-sized cod in the shallows — two- and three-pounders. With infinite care I mounted one on a marlin hook and sank it in seventy fathoms.

After three hours something formidable happened. My rod tip was dragged down with huge force and I slammed back hard. No resistance. I reeled up. The cod was smashed. "This was the halibut!" said the Norwegian brightly as I tremblingly mounted another bait. When I was finally ready, though, there seemed to be some misunderstanding. The skipper had lit a cigar and was heading back to port. He was still smiling. "In Norway," he announced, "we eat dinner very early so that we can have it with the children when they come home from school." End of Act One.

Act Two. Another part of the Norwegian coast, two years later. It was Kristiansund, said to be the halibut capital of Norway. On my first evening I went down to the quay to see about a boat.

"Yes, many halibuts are coming into Kristiansund!" said the first skipper I met.

"You catch them here in the fjord?" I asked.

"No, no," he said helpfully. "Mostly we are catching them off the Shetland Islands, off Scotland. We stay out for three weeks."

Act Three. The Shetland Islands. "No sir, you'll not take a halibut here in September. April is the month. There's a man fishes down at Sumburgh Head, he's a grand wee man for the big 'buts. Come back next spring and he'll take you out."

No time for that. Straight into Act Four. Belmullet, County Mayo, on the northwest coast of Ireland. Pretty far south for halibut, but they had been caught there and at least I knew that in Belmullet nobody was going to tell me I couldn't catch one. At any time of day or year.

"Paddy Lynch's father caught one of them horrorbuts back in the old days in the race off Achill Island," said the first man I met in Edmund Walshe's bar, "on a bit of green crab for bait."

"That's right," I said. "It was as big as a little horse and they had to bring the ass-cart down for it and the tail was dragging the ground all the way back to Belmullet."

"You've been talking to Paddy already," said my informant, but I hadn't. I was just well acquainted with poetic convention west of the Shannon.

The odd thing was that I did hit into a halibut in the Achill Race on my first day out. I wasn't even seriously trying. There was a run of big pollack, twenty-five-pounders and better, and I was using a Norwegian "pilk," a very heavy stainless-steel jig designed for commercial cod fishing.

The pollack kept coming but then, with the pilk on the retrieve and a fathom off the bottom, the rod was wrenched hard again, just as it had been off Stavanger. It was no pollack. It thumped sullenly under the rod point for a while, certainly a fish of more than one hundred pounds. Nothing of that size but a halibut would take an unbaited lure in those waters.

It kept sulking for a while and with surprising ease I gained five or six fathoms of line. Then, slowly at first, but with an increasing rhythm, came a series of heavy blows at the rod. The fish was arching its back, undulating just like those little flounders had long ago, building its strength for a crash dive.

I weathered the powerful plunge that followed and two more like it and I was beginning to feel that I had the fish mastered when the split ring that joined the treble hook to the lure snapped. Some flaw in the metal, I suppose.

I babbled all this out that evening in Walshe's bar. "I was telling you, wasn't I?" said the man I'd first met. "There's platoons of them down there. Regiments." But, though I fished for two more weeks, I never touched another Irish halibut.

And so to Act Five and the Anglo-Icelandic Giant Arctic Halibut Expedition. It would be the final act, I was convinced. Collins was the man who started it off by meeting Johann Sigurdsson in a London pub and getting into an argument with him over the Cod War that had broken out when Iceland declared she was extending her fishing limits to fifty miles. What with British trawlers thumping Icelandic gunboats, cut nets and violent feelings, it was the stuff of stern dispute. To forever prove some point, Johann flourished a copy of the Reykjavik daily, *Morgunbladid*. Collins gaped at it silently.

"So I am right, then," said Sigurdsson, taking this as a concession of defeat. But Collins had forgotten the Cod War. He was looking at a picture of a burly Icelander, rod in hand, beaming beside a noble halibut. "A 152-pounder," marveled Collins. "It looks bigger."

"Kilos, not pounds," corrected Johann. "Now you can see the quality of fish we are trying to protect from the ruthless British fish exploiters." Collins was not listening. Already he had begun to plan.

What he did was call up some other ruthless British fish exploiters; Moncrieff, a hard man from Dover, called Tom Hutchinson and me. Sigurdsson, when he learned what was afoot, insisted on coming, too, together with Haldur Snorrason of Reykjavik. The Expedition was born.

Naturally, Moncrieff made a major production of the preparations since he is that sort of man. He was a plastics engineer until Dora Moncrieff opened a baby-wear store in the London commuter town of Merstham, Surrey. In Merstham, babies are a bigger industry than plastics. Now they have three shops and very occasionally Moncrieff can be seen displaying pink angora pram sets to fond grandmothers. But certainly not in the weeks preceding the Iceland trip. He migrated permanently to his workshop. There, slowly gestating, he came up with such concepts as the parachute. Three or four times a week he would call me up after anguished periods of doubt. Should it be nylon wire or straight monofilament for the leader? How sharp were halibut's teeth? Would the crew speak English?

"Go to sleep, Leslie," I would tell him gently, for these calls were often late at night. "We'll catch halibut. There's platoons of them out there. Regiments."

I was pretty confident that there would be. After patient investigation Sigurdsson and Snorrason had discovered the ultimate home of the halibut — inside an island-studded bay called Breidafjordur on the west coast. It was said just one boat fished halibut, operating only two days a week, and in the month of August it had landed more than two hundred halibut of one hundred pounds or more.

"We will not take this boat though," announced Sigurdsson. "Too small, only twelve tons. Instead we will have the *Gisli Magnusson*, sixty tons with room for us all. And we will take along the skipper of the small halibut boat to show us the places."

From Reykjavik to Stikkisholmur was a five-hour, bone-jarring night ride by bus (we had rented one to take ourselves and our gear), with Moncrieff snoring sonorously much of the time. But the Expedition's morale was high when the bus jolted into Stikkisholmur in the small hours, fortified by endless nipping — actually extravagant nipping — on the duty-free booze we had carried from Heath Row. It was blowing hard with a lashing rain turning the dirt surface of the main street into a shallow yellow stream. "There is no hotel," announced Sigurdsson. "We are staying in houses." He turned to me. "You are sharing a room with Mr. Moncrieff," he said.

The rest of the night was hideous, but thankfully short. By 9:00 A.M. the next morning, moving as slowly and laboriously as astronauts in our parkas, jerseys and oilskins, we boarded *Gisli Magnusson*. When she rounded the big rocks that sheltered the harbor she started to dip to the first of the swell and soon we were thrashing through it. The rain turned to sleet as we set up our gear, bracing ourselves to the heave, and my fingers turned numb mounting the frozen herring bait. But none of us cared. This was the end of a long journey. The ultimate flatfish were out there. Platoons and regiments of them. The rain and the wind could do their worst.

It took about three hours for both elements to achieve this, by which time the weather side of my face felt frozen solid. The boat was bucketing along and Haldur Snorrason came out from a long conference with the halibut skipper, a small, wizened man with two teeth. "He says you will not catch anything as things are here," said Snorrason. The gnome grinned in delighted confirmation. "But he will look for another place where there is more shelter from an island."

That was when we crawled below for coffee and Highland comfort and it came upon me that maybe there were better things in life than giant halibut, such as the cocktail bar of the Saga Hotel, a heresy that would have been unthinkable a few hours earlier and one that, even now, I would not dare to voice aloud.

But fishing was still impossible when we tried again, even if the limit of farce had not already been reached with Moncrieff's parachute. The crew offered to put out their longline, but in spite of our tribulations we were not yet so demoralized as to take part in a commercial operation. "No longlines," said Moncrieff magisterially. "We stand or fall by the rods."

We fell, naturally. Back at Stikkisholmur that night all we could do was pray for the wind to drop. And it had to drop at once for it was now explained to us that our vessel would only be available for one more day since it could earn $2,500 a week dredging scallops. But we got the concession that we could put to sea two hours earlier the next morning.

It was a better day, but not by much. The wind came round to the southeast, still hard, but with more shelter from the land the drift was slower. All through the morning we worked our baits, though the skipper was still pessimistic. "They are moving too fast still," he said. But at 12:45 A.M., just as we were ready to go below for another break, my rod stuttered, then curved over.

I stood and clobbered whatever was down there as hard as I could. A huge resistance, then nothing. When I reeled up I found that my herring, hooked through the eyes, had been filleted. There was just a head and a backbone. Up in the command module the skipper was shrieking in Icelandic, a difficult language to follow. "He says you are pulling your line too soon. He says that this was a big fish, more than two hundred pounds." I didn't think that was all he was saying. "This halibut," continued Mr. Snorrason, "you must give him much time." That must have been why I had lost the Stavanger fish, I thought. I felt sick and sorry.

"I'd have done the same," said Tom Hutchinson, fishing alongside me. But the encounter had done us good. From fishing like frozen automata, without hope, we began to work hard and at 5:00 P.M. the second chance came, to Peter Collins. "Let him take it right back!" I yelled. Peter spooled line back and then struck. The fish was on and all of us were shouting and dancing and cheering on deck.

Collins worked that fish for twenty minutes before the hookhold gave. Two hard-won opportunities and two disasters. It was too much. When the Icelanders dragged out the big basket around which the longline was coiled, nobody objected. There was only an hour or so of fishing left anyway. We went below for sad inquests while they shot the line, and we sat around liquorless in the warm cabin until they yelled from the deck that they were ready to haul.

The empty hooks came in, one after the other. There were sixty of them altogether, and we must have been about three-quarters of the way through when the skipper gave a yell and started to throw coils of line back into the sea. "Now the halibut is there!" shouted Snorrason. "He is letting him eat the herring!" The old Icelander bent over the line, then started to haul positively. Then we were all helping him haul and deep in the water a great moonshape of pearly white showed. Two gaffs went in a moment later and, shouting and cursing, we dragged our halibut over the gunwale. It thundered on the deck with its mighty tail until one of the Icelanders slid his knife in under the pectoral fin. "To bleed it," said Mr. Sigurdsson. "To make the flesh white for the market."

We looked at the great brown fish with reverence. It was just over 120 pounds. The hook had fallen out as soon as it was on board and I could see now why Peter had lost his fish and quite probably why I had lost mine. The jaws were like an old-fashioned bellows camera, the extensible membrane that joined them paper thin. We were lucky to get this one. It explained all the insistence on giving the fish plenty of time.

And that seemed to be that. The end of the Expedition. An ill-fated Expedition. But that would not be quite accurate. Wound licking was the next, obvious move, and I suggested to the others that many wound-licking facilities existed at the Saga Hotel. My information was certainly secondhand, it having come from certain Fleet Street acquaintances who were covering the Cod War from there. And I think I might actually have gotten to the hotel but for the fact that the only hot dog stand in Reykjavik is run by a Mr. Kristmundur, a devoted saltwater angler. Since he has no competition in the hot dog trade, Mr. Kristmundur has made a lot of money, enough to buy a fancy sport-fishing boat.

On the afternoon of our return from Stikkisholmur we met Kristmundur slapping the mustard on his hot dogs since, with a population of only 210,000, there is a labor shortage in Iceland. Reykjavik is a small town and Mr. Kristmundur had already heard of our tribulations. He might, he thought, be able to help. He was leaving for Copenhagen on the weekend. By the time he returned winter would have set in so that this would be the last opportunity for a project he had in mind, which was to fill his Deepfreeze with halibut. Perhaps we would like to help him do this.

Heavy-handed joshing is permissible sometimes. At others it can be sadistic, and I was ready to call Mr. Kristmundur to order for a moment. But then I realized that he was entirely sincere. "Give me half an hour," he said, "and I'll close down the stand. I'll see you at the quay. Look for the *Jan Sulimsson*." He wrote the name down carefully on a piece of greaseproof paper.

I don't know if the others counted their catch that afternoon and evening, but mine was fifty-four halibut taken in twenty feet of water close to Reykjavik harbor and I would imagine that the others took roughly the same number. What Mr. Kristmundur had not revealed to us beforehand was that these were very junior halibut. They averaged five pounds apiece. I hope they were not the same species, but they looked very much like it and now I wake up nights thinking of what my friends and I have done to the Icelandic halibut run. All I can say, contritely, is that we could not help it. As our frustrations were released, we filled Mr. Kristmundur's Deepfreeze with a savage joy. Then we changed and swaggered off to the Saga Hotel.

It's a fine place, elegant and evidently well run. No one had chosen to tell us, though, that in Iceland hotels are not permitted to serve drinks on Wednesdays—except wine with meals. This, naturally, was Wednesday.

AMERICA'S FISH: NANTUCKET ISLAND

CHAPTER EIGHT

A Date with Nemesis

Long before I'd gone to live in the U.S., I'd been a touch obsessed with what, not without justification, has been called America's Fish — the striped bass. And once I was established in the country, I made swift arrangements to make acquaintance with the species. I was doubly fortunate as it turned out, for I was able to arrange for Desmond Brennan, over the years my closest angling companion, to head over from Dublin and fish with me.

NANTUCKET

THE JOKE was twenty years old and weak enough, even when it was first hatched aboard Brennan's old Hillman wagon as we trundled south through Ireland, along County Wexford hedges creamy with meadowsweet and richly entangled with July honeysuckle. For a while he had been silent, polishing the words, no doubt. Then he came out with it. "Nemesis approaches at forty miles per hour," he announced. Half a mile back we had nearly hit a nun who was dreamily cycling along on the wrong side of the road, missing her by a rosary width. I naturally thought Brennan had this in mind. I should have known better. What Brennan had in mind was fish. Unknown to the schools of bass hanging in the slack water, waiting to feed over Splaugh Reef when the tide started to run, Nemesis Brennan was sneaking up on them.

Twenty years later here I was, ready and waiting to bang the ball back at him, outside U.S. Customs at JFK. "Nemesis approaches, hey?" I said to the disheveled figure with the rod tubes. "By way of Dublin, Shannon and New York. At 500 miles per hour and 33,000 feet. . . ." If I hadn't said it first, Brennan would have; no score had been kept, but one of us had come out with some sort of variation on the greeting since that first trip in 1958. Each year since then we had met to go fishing. Not a single year had we missed. In the early days, Nemesis traveled slowly enough, at around twenty knots aboard the old *St. David*, the ferryboat that plied between Wales and Ireland. The trips to our home-and-home meetings on the surf beaches of the two countries had speeded up when a regular air service started and really began to move when the first short-haul jets came in. But this was the first time that Nemesis had crossed the Atlantic.

By necessity. You do not toss away a twenty-year-old fishing partnership just because one of its members has migrated three thousand miles west. The 1977 Annual Outing would not be held in County Wexford or County Kerry or on the coast of west Wales. Instead, it was going to be in Massachusetts, *terra incognita* for both of us, like a country on one of those old maps inscribed "Here be dragons" when the cartographer could think of nothing better.

Well, perhaps that was a slight exaggeration. For a very long time, out there on the Celtic fringe, Brennan and I had thought longingly of going after striped bass, those fish that looked so similar to our own sea bass except in two particulars. Ours were pure silver, with no lateral stripes. And they were very much smaller than stripers. In Kerry, a seven-pound bass was more than acceptable, a ten-pounder a more-than-viable reason for a late night at Tom Fitzgerald's bar. It was hard to believe in forty- and fifty-pounders. The fever to catch one had grown strong enough to turn both of us into propagandists, trying to persuade our respective Ministries of Fisheries that striped bass should be introduced to the eastern side of the Atlantic. No chance. Who could tell the effect stripers would have on our native Atlantic salmon—invading the estuaries, maybe, to feast on smolts migrating to the sea.

So, possibly, even if I had not crossed the Atlantic to live and speeded up the process, Brennan and I would have made the trip someday. As it was, as I stood there relieving Brennan of his duty-free Scotch and cramming him into a cab, it seemed to me that it might have been better had we made that east-west trip together. I had been in the U.S. for several months and so I felt responsible for the weather, for the time of year I had picked, for the guide. From what I had heard and read, the place seemed right: Nantucket was classic ground. I was remembering, though, how critical weather could be. The saddest words in the English language, Brennan once claimed, were in the sentence found all too frequently in the weather section of the *Irish Times* on the morning we started a trip: A NORTH-EASTERLY AIRSTREAM COVERS IRELAND, a wind that would flatten the surf, making it fit only for water skiers. We would drive away from Shannon, and a little south of Limerick we would start to look for a particular tall factory chimney, for the plume of white vapor that would tell us whether or not the wind was the sou'westerly we wanted, not too gentle, not too strong. We were lucky about one time in five.

We flew to Boston and then out across Cape Cod. I didn't even know what weather you *needed* in Nantucket, or at least which way you needed the wind to blow, but we could see that there was a lot of it. Below, whitecaps flecked the sea, and when we saw the island, lines of surf were curling in, how high we couldn't tell. "Nemesis arriving by air," I told Brennan, "without a single clue." In Kerry we would know what to do. We could go to Tom Fitzgerald's and be told that the surf was great last Wednesday and there was this woman down from Dublin on holiday, never had a rod in her hand before, and you wouldn't believe it but that evening she walks into the bar with the biggest. . . . We wouldn't be *happy*, but we'd feel at home.

That was the shape we were in when Bob Francis found us, bewildered, disoriented and, in Brennan's case, jetlagged. Francis was a small man, lean, with an elfish look enhanced by a woolly cap and red flannel shirt worn outside his trousers, his machine-gun speech and rapid movement. It was with no surprise that I later learned he had been the master barber of Nantucket for twenty years. Snip! The rod holders were in the back of his wagon. Snap! So were the tackle boxes, the bags and ourselves. No time to take in the island, a pattern of small hills and scrub woodland in fall colors, little weathered houses and then, incongruously, a cobbled street. "Stones came from England," Francis rapped out. "Come back as ballast on the whalers." He pulled up at a tree-shaded house. On the sidewalk was a hitching post surmounted by the head of a horse in cast iron. "Not genuine," he snapped. "Put there for show. Come on in."

A long time ago Brennan and I decided that on the Annual Outing, hotels were not for us. Or at least hotels built since, say, 1930. At one time we used to patronize Benner's Hotel in Dingle, County Kerry, where a thirty-pound salmon from Castle Island glowered down on the tiny lobby, and the manageress, Miss Maloney, didn't believe you could register until she had brought you a full and gratis glass of Powers whiskey. But when Miss Maloney retired they put down a new carpet and tricked out the bar with a lot of plastic and chrome, so we migrated to Mrs. MacNamara's on the far side of the Connor Pass where we felt at home again, even after her son bought her the color TV.

So I had made no hotel reservation for the Nantucket trip, relying on Francis's telephone promise. "Best food on the island, in my place," he had claimed. That might be so. Meantime, I reasoned, if we stayed at his house we wouldn't have problems like securing a box lunch at 4:00 A.M.

That afternoon I was pleased to notice that at least the infrastructure of our trip was in good shape. For lunch there was homemade chowder at the Francises', and the significant fact soon emerged that the kitchen was going to be the social center. And later we found that even if Tom Fitzgerald's bar was three thousand miles away, the Nantucket Anglers' Club, a short walk from Francis's house, was no mean substitute.

By then we needed solace. We stood out on the deck of the club and listened to a northeaster rattle the rigging of the yachts in the marina and howl through the little town. It didn't look good for the next morning. Francis hung moodily over the rail and wondered aloud if he could charter one of the big boats to use instead of his own twenty-six-footer. We went back inside to stare at the sixty-pound striper set up on the wall, until I sensed that Brennan was getting homesick for Miss Maloney's salmon.

Next morning we woke early, well before the 4:30 A.M. call that Francis had promised us, mainly because Brennan was still operating on Dublin time, five hours ahead of EST. We listened for wind but we couldn't hear it, maybe because the town was sheltered. We also lacked an indicator, like the skeleton of an old apple tree in Mrs. MacNamara's yard on which rooks would settle if the wind was not too hard; you could pick them out black against the false dawn. But in Nantucket we had no such guide. We had to wait until Francis appeared and be content with his "We'll go and take a look."

The street still black, we lumbered out of the door bundled up like Michelin men and saw the stars fade as we drove out to the dock, white tails of rabbits bobbing out of the headlights, the profile of the low hills beginning to show and then the sea. Sheltered here, of course, but a sharp ripple over the gray showing that the outside would be rough going. It was the same low, gray seascape that you see in protected water from the Baltic to County Wexford and on west, the same skeins of geese arrowing through the growing light, the same ribs of old hulks showing through the muddy grass.

We were going to head out. The sea would be up, Francis shouted over the engine noise, but that meant good fishing if we could get to the right rips. The wind was easier than the previous day and the forecast said it would go on dropping. He was steering the McKenzie bass boat straight for a line of breakers that had to be the sandbar that protected the harbor. As we closed on it, though, we saw a gap, fully big enough for Brennan's old station wagon. "Nemesis is about to get a wet rear," I told him.

Another correct prediction. Two wild minutes, though, and we were through, punching into a steep chop that was manageable enough. Ahead of us was the first of the tide rips, but we turned from it and ran close under the land until we were in the lee of a sand pit that cut across the weather, forming a small area of comparative calm. Francis stopped the engine. "Now cast," he said.

Striper experts Brennan and I were not. But a minimum of research had taught us that this was not the kind of locale where bass might be expected. We looked at one another, shrugged and did as he asked. "All wrong!" Francis yelled. Brennan bridled, as well he might. The poppers had gone out straight and true, a good fifty yards or thereabouts. For thirty years, ever since he caught his first mackerel off the end of the North Wall dock in Dublin, Brennan had reckoned he could cast. And Gaelic football players active in that same city less than twenty years since would have recognized the full red flush now rising up to his cheekbones. "How do you mean, wrong?" he said. It seemed like a full three-second pause before he pronounced the last word.

You don't practice the barber's art for long without learning a little tact. Francis saw his error. "Let me tell you," he said, somewhat dramatically. "Every time I turn my motor off at the end of a trip, I say, 'Thank you, God!' No matter how smart you are, no matter how educated you are, you can make a mistake with a plug. In the excitement. Lose an eye. Both eyes. Had one up my *nose* once. Bunch of men from Maryland. So now I have this drill. First man goes into the stern, backs up, watching his plug all the time. Casts overhead. Moves up. Second man into the stern, backs up, casts. Soon as his plug gets within eighteen yards of the boat, caster drops his rod tip to stop the plug's action. If a fish hits a plug that close to the boat, then comes loose, that thing is going to fly back like a bullet. I'm sorry," he said. "I spoke rough."

Brennan's flush had died away. After all, what Francis had said was reasonable. Except, possibly, for that eighteen-yard bit. Wouldn't it be natural to say twenty yards, or fifteen? Francis had either conducted a series of controlled experiments with some physicist from MIT, or there was something just a touch obsessional in his makeup. Not that *that* would be very unusual in a fishing guide.

But for the moment we seemed to have satisfied him. We swung away from the sheltered water and bounced out toward the nearest rip, a quartering sea lashing us with spray. As Francis worked the boat into range, Brennan and I lined up the casts like jets at O'Hare in the rush hour, moving up slowly until the tower gave us clearance. "Rod down!" I snarled at Brennan before Francis had a chance, thereby failing to spot soon enough the heavy brown swirl at my own popper. "See that?" I roared at Brennan.

"I was watching my own plug," he said virtuously. I cast again. So did he. No results. No results, either, for the next ten minutes as we drifted parallel with the rip. I've blown it, I thought. All those miles of travel, all those months of making arrangements, and the one chance I would get to show Brennan a striper had gone. The way I was feeling, even the weather would deteriorate and keep us from trying the next rip, and my natural pessimism interpreted the fact that Francis kept heading out as a sign that he probably didn't know what to do next.

But he did. "Miles and miles of rips off this island," he shouted suddenly over the engine roar, "and only about one in ten of them holds the bass. Don't know why. They all look the same, a lot of them have the right depth, between eight feet and twelve feet, but they never have a fish on 'em. Maybe it's the way the sand eels bunch. Maybe they can't hear the motor so good in some places."

We hung on in a sea that was still wild, heading toward yet another confused area of white water. "Don't cast yet," Francis called as we came in close. We patrolled it slowly, bunched in the shelter of the wheelhouse as the McKenzie rolled and bucked eccentrically. "Can you see them?" Francis shouted.

In a moment we saw them. The rip was not a regular pattern of breaking waves. Close up, it had almost as much variation in it as a salmon river: an area of boiling water that heaved and eddied, but where there was no break, perhaps because the tide had scoured a deeper hole there. It was like a salmon pool between shallow, stony runs. Only this was a striper pool and the fish were as thick in it as salmon in the Junction Pool at Kelso on the Scottish Tweed at the height of the spring run. They were there like chunks of brown driftwood, more than we could count, breaking the surface sometimes, head-and-tailing like salmon.

Brennan was very moved. "Janey Mac!" he roared, lapsing into Dublinese. "Didja ever see the like of them fellas!" Francis got the anchor down and killed the motor. Fleetingly I hoped it would hold in the sea that was running, but there was no time to worry long about that. Brennan's plug flew out, he took half a turn of the reel and he was into a fish. Seconds later so was I and so was Francis. We stumbled to keep balance as we fought the fish, ducking under arms, passing rods around bodies, in a kind of wild, intoxicated square dance. "Keep your rod tips *low!*" Francis took time to scream. His own was high in the air. Then, somehow, he gaffed his fish and swung it aboard. The maniacal scene in the cockpit was resolved somewhat, with just two stripers left to land. They fought hard and doggedly, but we were downtide from them and we had all the advantage. It was still ten minutes, though, before Brennan had his at the side of the boat.

Once it was aboard, he knelt beside it. "Meet Nemesis," I said as I still struggled with my own, but Brennan was rapt. "Striper, eh?" he was murmuring. "So that's a striper. . . ." Soon, I was looking at mine, also. So similar to our own bass, the same outline, the same look of brutal power and greed. But so much bigger. Twenty, twenty-five pounds, Francis guessed, average for him, one supposed, but to us magnificent. "Wait, now, till I get a picture," said Brennan.

Francis was shocked. "Pictures on the way home," he yelled. "Get out at those fish again!" Dutifully we obliged. Coming out, we had been heavily wrapped in sweaters, parkas and slickers. Now, as the fish kept coming and we fought them, we peeled off our outer skins one by one, ignoring the spray. For two hours, barely a cast went to waste. At no time were all three rods unemployed. The two fish boxes we had brought filled fast; soon stripers were being stacked in a hastily contrived corral of fuel tanks and buckets. The average size of the fish was twenty pounds; the best, caught by Brennan, weighed thirty-seven pounds, we found later. Total catch, more than four hundred pounds.

And then, as suddenly as it began, the action stopped. "Tide has eased," Francis said. "Fish moved off." We hauled anchor and turned for home.

That evening we celebrated by looking at the Muppets on TV. So far as we were concerned, we could have been in Paris on Bastille night instead of Nantucket and it would have made no difference. We weren't going out. The hard-fighting fish, the beating we'd taken at sea had put us into that cozy, unquestioning lotus-eater's mood in which you sit, with the ice slowly melting in your drink, and watch midevening TV, about your intellectual limit. There was also the warm feeling that the 1977 Annual Outing was already a success. Certainly we had caught more and bigger fish than on any previous one. If we had any doubts at all, they were overlaid very effectively that evening. We retired early; another predawn call lay ahead.

The wind had shifted; that was the first discovery we made next morning. It had gone around to the south, and the significance of that, as we found when we went to sea, was that instead of being able to anchor downtide of that fertile rip we would have to look for holding ground uptide—otherwise, with the wind hard against us, we would have to move so close to put the fish within casting range that we would probably spook them. The stripers proved to be still there in strength. They hit plugs with as much avidity as they had done the previous day. The difference now was that we had to bring them in against the tide.

Landing every striper was a war of attrition as the fish hung in the strong current and the line sang dangerously. Well, fishing can be like that at times. But this was the Annual Outing. Brennan and I had not fished together for twenty years without learning that there are times when, if you feel like it, you pause for a while. So, after an hour, we paused.

It was not a popular move. "Let's get those fish in, hey?" said our guide. Brennan looked at me. He was making the same connection as I was. Neither of us knew much about the mores of bass fishing on this side of the Atlantic, and the previous day we had been too intoxicated with instant success to worry much about the ritual thumping over the head of each striper as it was landed. For years we had released almost every one of our own bass, taking home a couple apiece, maybe, at the end of the trip. Possibly it would be different in Massachusetts, but I suspected that not every striper angler would approve of what we were doing.

"John Ferguson," I said to Brennan. He knew who I meant. John Ferguson, the best bass guide on Splaugh Reef, County Wexford, Ireland, wind-reddened face, collarless flannel shirt, in one of those cloth caps they call "ratters" shouting, "Haul 'em!" as small war parties of bass detached themselves from the main school and hit the long, twinkling spoons we used there. Ferguson, hating the six-pound-test line we used, closing his eyes in frustration as the reel drags buzzed and added a minute or two to the time elapsed before the bass would be safely flapping in the fish box that would be shipped to market in Dublin that evening. It looked very much as if Brennan and I were still in the business of filling fish boxes for other people.

As I have suggested, though, Bob Francis could pick up a hint. One reason why we had had to opt for the downtide position was that balsa swimming plugs had proved more effective than poppers and you could cast them nowhere near as far as the latter against the wind. Poppers were more fun, though. You might not get as many strikes, but you got some, and they were visual strikes. Ferguson never gave his clients priority over the fish box, but now Francis proved that he was capable of rising above the price of bass. "We'll haul and go round," he said. "Try poppers."

"You know something?" he went on. "I'm about the only guide left here who would take you casting. Everybody else, it's all wire-line trolling. Can't stand to do that." On the Annual Outing, Brennan and I don't care for too much tension. An olive branch offered is an olive branch received. We have also been at it long enough to know when to give a really good opening to a guide.

"Uh, how does the fishing here compare with, what's the other island? Martha's Vineyard? Cuttyhunk?" I asked him.

Francis savored the moment before replying. "Cuttyhunk?" he said. "Well, now, most of them Cuttyhunk bass are down deep. I went over there with three fellers from Nantucket one time, fished two nights. Fished them Sows and Pigs, whatever they call 'em. We did fairly well, but the bass were down deep. Like in North Truro. 'Course, they catch a lot of bass in them places. . . ." He paused to give emphasis to the payoff. "Only, there, a lot of bass means about five."

We made a long detour around the rip, came up on the other side and started to throw poppers into the wind. The scoring rate dropped but the bass still came steadily. Then I hit one far out, so that I didn't see the fish strike. It behaved like the others for a moment or two, giving that solid old brick wall imitation, then moved irresistibly to the left, taking line.

"You may have Bosco," Francis said.

The fifteen-pound outfit made no impression. The bass moved back, almost to the place where it had been hooked, then swung right. "Who's Bosco?" I asked. I should have known better. Wherever there are fishermen there are Boscos, though they have different names. I once knew of a fifty-pound northern pike called the Green Devil that was thirty-one pounds when it was caught. What I should have asked was, "How big is Bosco?" But I got the answer anyway.

"Big bass. Eighty pounds. Could be more. Passes this way every year, busts two or three people up. So take it easy on him."

Bosco, if it was Bosco, would not let me take it easy. It was twenty minutes before I had him coming toward the boat. "Bosco meets Nemesis," Brennan said, predictably, I thought.

It was not to be. "Not Bosco," yelled Francis, peering into the water from the bow. " 'Bout a thirty-pounder, foul-hooked in the shoulder. . . ." No wonder it had been able to take command. Every time I had tried to shift him he was broadside to me.

But Bosco made our trip. Brennan and I fished two more days. We caught three-quarters of a ton of bass, a total somewhat shameful to our essentially puritanical natures. But the fishing was no longer mechanical. Every cast was aimed at Bosco.

We failed to catch him. No harm in that. Bosco lives! Nemesis Brennan and I will continue, God willing, to search him out in future years: sometimes he will be a striper, sometimes, maybe, a channel bass, sometimes a silver bass from an Irish beach. On the whole, I hope we never catch him.

CHAPTER NINE

Alaska! Welcome to the Chocolate Factory . . .

Sometime in the mid-nineteenth century, when the Oregon Territory was still in dispute between Great Britain and the U.S.A., a Royal Commission headed out from London to inspect the damn place, see if it was worth having. It reported back to Parliament in a strongly negative style, the nobleman who was its chairman having been disgusted to discover that the salmon in the Columbia River did not rise to the fly like those of the Tweed. This, conceivably, altered the history of North America. It was also a slander on noble fish as you will see.

ALASKA

OVER THE Shelikof Strait the morning sky had the iridescent sheen of the shell of a freshly shucked oyster, steel gray suffused with pink and blue lights that took fire on the snows of the Valley of Ten Thousand Smokes and on Mount Katmai, a 6,700-foot-high volcano forty-five miles away on mainland Alaska.

The sea was an oyster shell, too, blue with rose highlights, calm, barely moving until it broke lazily against the monolithic cliff of Tanglefoot, stirring the kelp, pushing by Mary's Creek until the water swirling out of the Karluk River checked and roiled it. This was slack tide, with the water as idle as the fur seals riding the little swells, immobile as the three bald eagles settled on a stony spit in the river.

The Karluk itself, on the west coast of Kodiak Island in the Gulf of Alaska, looked barren; empty, translucent water slid fast over gray stones until it met the Shelikof in an acre or two of confused chop.

RIVER KARLUK, KODIAK ISLAND, ALASKA

On a ridge above, I watched the water for a sign that the ocean was starting to bully its way in again. The seals had vanished, the eagles taken to the air before my senses picked up the change and the daily miracle that would come with it, foreshadowed now by a fretting of the calm water and the silver reflections in it, like the sun catching the shields of an ancient army's vanguard.

And now, though this is my seventh morning on the Karluk, the fly rod shakes in my hand as I scramble up the loose pebbles to watch the army that's surging into the Karluk's mouth—the day's new wave of coho salmon streams out of the Pacific on the turn of the tide, thousands of bright-struck fish leaping, cavorting like circus clowns.

Stripping line as I go, slithering down the stones, I wade clumsily out into the river, launch the garish green and purple streamer fly, flashy with tinsel, into the thick of them. My right hand, gripping the rod butt, is wrapped with half a dozen Band-Aids covering cuts of a week's worth of salmon battles. The past seven days have seen this fly rod bend into more than one hundred cohos. Still, I tremble. I am in the finest salmon river in the world, no matter what the people in the rustic lodges along Canada's Restigouche or the tweedy inns on Scotland's Tay or Spey or Dee might think. The Karluk is salmon fishing as known in heaven.

The great fly-fisherman G.E.M. Skues, father of modern nymph fishing, once unbent enough to write a little fiction concerning the late Mr. Castwell, a somewhat bumptious dry fly purist who, as he thought, had ended up in heaven and been provided with a perfect streamside cottage, the finest tackle and an attendant water keeper. And perfect trout fishing, it seemed, until Mr. Castwell began to grow uneasy after catching fish after splendid fish from the same spot. Skues concluded his tale with this bit of dialogue:

"How long is this confounded rise going to last?" inquired Mr. Castwell.
"I suppose it will stop soon?"
"No, sir," said the keeper.
"What, isn't there a slack hour in the afternoon?"
"No afternoon, sir."
"What? Then what about the evening rise?"
"No evening rise, sir," said the keeper.
"Well, I shall knock off now. I must have had about thirty brace from that corner."

"Beg pardon, sir, but his Holiness would not like that."

"What," said Mr. Castwell. "Mayn't I even stop at night?"

"No night here, sir," said the keeper.

"Then do you mean I have to go on catching these damned two-and-a-half-pounders at this corner for ever and ever?"

The keeper nodded.

"Hell!" said Mr. Castwell.

"Yes," said his keeper.

Mr. Castwell's hell, though, was confinement to a corner. There was no infinite variety of flies, of techniques, of locations, as there was on the Karluk. Nevertheless, the reports of the spectacular fishing on the Karluk over the past year or two had seemed to suggest a kind of drawback that might best be summarized as the Chocolate Factory Syndrome. It's said that chocolate factories have no pilfering problem because employees are free to eat all they want. After a couple of days few of them retain a taste for sweets. Could salmon, then, turn out to be like chocolate? Was it possible to fish until success became satiety?

Journeying to Alaska in midsummer, that seemed unlikely. No fishing could be that good. There would be someone, you could bet your chest waders, who'd greet you at camp with such time-honored words as, "You should have been here last week." And, indeed, during a stopover at Anchorage, there came a foretaste of such a put-down.

That was in Northwest Outfitter's, the city's major tackle store, aglitter with trays of salmon flies. The salesclerk was confidently buoyant about the patterns as such men always are — the Polar Shrimps, the Skykomish Sunrises, the Bosses, the Skunks. "Figure on one fly for every hour you fish," he said alarmingly, scooping up a dozen Purple Fishairs with Mylar. "You'll want a box for all these and . . ."

"Did you hear how the silvers are running?" I interrupted him — cohos are often called silvers.

"And you'll need something in green and orange," he said.

The silvers, he was reminded. "Uh, I didn't get word yet," he said offhandedly.

From a tackle salesman, this was the equivalent of a cynical laugh, an indication that the fish were still offshore. I got the same message at the departure lounge for Kodiak, where people were lugging rod cases around as they do garment bags in other airports. "Early for silvers," a rod-bearer said to me. "Where are you heading?" I told him the Karluk. He'd never heard of it.

I needn't have worried. The next morning, forty-five minutes after the light airplane headed out of Kodiak, over Women's Bay and across the hills and tundra, I looked down onto the thread of the Karluk as it broadened into a lagoon, down onto fish erupting everywhere on its placid surface. Hello, chocolate factory, I said to myself as we landed.

And a factory, it turned out, where there was no need to report for work unconscionably early. The lagoon fish, well, they were sort of semipermanent residents, said Robin Sikes, the elderly Alaskan (elderly at twenty-eight, that's to say, in a state where twenty-six is the median age) who greeted the group of which I was now one. Better to breakfast at leisure, wait for fresh fish to run in from the sea on the tide and enjoy the balmy summer's morning with the temperature in the sixties.

So there was time to make acquaintance with the other anglers in my charter: Drs. Hamada, Habu, Hatasaka and Inouye and Mr. Okazaki, all Japanese-Americans, all from northern California, all but one dentists; more California dentists, Drs. Cosca, Wagner and Angel, with his son Jacob; and the odd men out, Mr. Channing, a physical therapist, once a trainer with the 49ers, Mr. Sopwith from his Sacramento rice farm, and Mr. Lindner and Mr. Miley, retirees.

Later they would become Teds, Stans and Leos, et al. Now, as they assembled their gear on the grassy slope in front of the lodge, they divided neatly into two groups—the fly-fishers and the men with, well, the hardware, the spinning gear, the heavy spoons. I was no fishing snob, I told myself, but I knew which group I would go to if it came to an emergency root canal job during the week.

We strolled down to the river together to clock in. Salmon were breaking everywhere in the lower pools, and before I'd even made a first cast I could see one of the spin fishermen with his rod bent into a fish. I took my time, made a short throw or two to get the feel of a new graphite rod, then put out a long cast at the classic angle, across and downstream. The Skykomish Sunrise must have swung by a whole school of leaping fish.

An hour later the silvers were still passing it by, as they had the Purple Fishair I substituted later, and later again the Polar Shrimp. There was a moving belt of salmon, but I hadn't sampled one; nor, so far as I could judge, had the other fly-fishermen. Mortifyingly, the spinning rods were enjoying heavy action. Jacob, eleven years old, was just about keeping his foothold on the pebble bank as a thick-bodied silver, fifteen pounds maybe, tried surging for the volcanoes on the far side of the strait.

When it was clear the run had ended for the morning, I walked back with Jacob to the lodge.

"He was kind of big," Jacob said. "I couldn't reel him in. I thought he was going to win."

"Oh, really," I said.

"I was kind of relieved when I had him on the shore."

"Oh, you landed him, then," I said.

"I wanted to keep him," said Jacob. "Very much. But, see, there's an Eskimo legend that if you kiss the first fish you catch and then you throw it back, it tells its buddies and you can catch more fish."

"And did you kiss it?" I asked Jacob.

"Yeah," he said.

I told him that was terrific as I glanced at the fat spoon now clipped to the keeper-ring on his spinning rod. I tried to smile, but I'm fairly certain it came out like one of those tortured Humphrey Bogart grimaces.

Sikes had said there was a good chance of taking salmon that afternoon in the big lagoon higher up on the Karluk, but the prospect of blind casting into the deep holes up there was unappealing to one nurtured in the white turbulence of northern Atlantic rivers. So I hiked yet farther upstream where the Karluk became a river again.

And a different river, the obverse of the tidal water downstream through which the bright battalions of cohos from the sea had poured in the morning. This was a battlefield in its hideous aftermath. Salmon, dead and dying, leprously white, patchworked in virulent yellows and reds, lolled and drifted in the slack water close to the banks. Fish, sockeyes and humpbacks, that had spawned and were now spent, finished. And hanging on the flanks of this broken salmon army were river guerillas, Dolly Varden char, pink flecked on their sides, predacious, vicious-hitting, in character absurdly unlike Dickens's delicate heroine of *Barnaby Rudge*, for whose pink-spotted gown the species is named. They gobbled now on the profusion of ripe salmon eggs that dribbled from the stony redds, as four weeks later they would gobble salmon fry. They gobbled also any small bright fly I threw at them, like Mr. Castwell's trout, two- and three-pounders hitting on every cast. I had released maybe thirty of them, and

I was ready to admit that this wasn't even a chocolate factory. It was a peanut farm.

That evening after supper there were no dentists to be seen, for a seminar was in progress. In businesslike style they had chosen the Karluk River for a convention. Left in the clubroom, among a few others, was a gentle-featured man of sixty-five, Bob Miley from Red Bluff, California, a retired telephone company repairman, who said he had saved for two years for this trip. Now he was hunched over a vise in a corner, under a reading lamp, tying flies, notwithstanding the fact that he'd brought two hundred or so with him.

It was a mild emollient to one's self-esteem to discover that Miley, almost fifty years a fly-fisherman, had also found the Karluk no chocolate factory, at least on the first day. "What are we doing wrong?" I asked him.

Miley gave his answer some thought. "Don't believe it's the pattern," he said. "Just tying these 'cause I like tying flies." He thought again. "We've got to go deeper," he said. "Those fish we're casting to, the ones leaping and slashing on top? They're not the hitters. Hitting fish are underneath. Those men got 'em on heavy spoons, right? We got to get our flies scratching the bottom. Reckon that's the way they want it."

What I'd been doing, what *we'd* been doing, was fishing conventionally downstream, forgetting that the cohos and the mighty chinook salmon of the Pacific were a different kettle of fish from Atlantics. At this moment I couldn't help feeling nostalgia for the fish of that other ocean, the ones the Romans, in admiration, had named *salar*, the leaper. "Trouble is," I said, suddenly, petulantly and illogically, "these damn silvers have no history."

Robin Sikes overheard me and said, "Come with me a minute."

This August evening there was light to spare. We walked away from the lodge to a steep earth bank. He took out a knife and started to probe at its side. Soon he had worked free a small, smooth oval stone, flat with a broad groove at each end. He handed it to me.

"Fishing equipment," Sikes said. "A sinker—six thousand years old maybe." He pointed at the cutaway bank. "See the layers?" he asked. "That's a kitchen midden. We had five anthropologists up here this summer from Bryn Mawr. They found slate knives, axheads and sinkers. They reckoned the early people, the Koniags, moved in here right after the first glaciers had gone through, found the big fish run and stayed." Sikes took some string from his pocket and hitched it around the stone. A sinker, self-evidently. "No history?" he asked. "Man, this has been one of the hottest fishing areas in the entire world for hundreds of years now."

Thousands, more precisely. Sikes warmed to his lecture. The native people had had it to themselves, he said, for most of those six thousand years, until the Russians came in the eighteenth century, pushing the empire forged by Peter the Great to its ultimate eastern frontier. In particular, it was Alexander Baranov who first swashbuckled onto Kodiak Island and the Karluk, seeking fur-bearing sea otters. What he found was perhaps the mightiest salmon run in the world—chinooks, sockeyes, humpbacks (pink salmon), dogs (chum salmon) and cohos—that lasted from May until September. "There must have been twenty million fish moving into the river," said Sikes. "And there were no laws."

Massacring many of the Koniags as a prologue, the Russians salted salmon in barrels, then shipped them west. Later they were joined by freebooting Americans, and then came two events that almost destroyed the most prolific salmon resource on earth. The canning process was invented in the 1790s, and in 1867 the U.S. purchased Alaska.

When that purchase became known, men fought with crowbars on the spit across the Karluk River, for favored netting locations. "At the peak, in the 1890s," Sikes said, "there were seven canneries working at the mouth of the river, and they shipped in around five thousand Chinese laborers, paid them something like $125 for working the entire summer, five months of hard labor, eighteen hours a day, six days a week. The beach gangs would stretch the nets across the river and when one was full they'd set another. All day long, for five months. They threw away the humpbacks. For the sockeyes, the reds, they got a penny a fish. They'd catch so many the canneries would clog."

Later I would read in a report on Alaskan fisheries published in 1899 by the Government Printing Office in Washington, "The waters surrounding the outlet to the Karluk Lagoon are probably the most remarkable in salmon production in Alaska, not only in numbers but the length of the run."

It couldn't last: The real miracle was that it continued as long as it did. But 1901 saw the last huge harvest, four million sockeye. By then the demeaningly named Iron Chink was in operation, a machine that automated the gutting process, making many laborers redundant. It only enhanced the dramatic decline. "Boomtown to ghost town in fifty years," Sikes said of Karluk. The White Act of 1924, one of the first federal laws to concern freshwater fisheries in this country, was enacted specifically to protect the Karluk and other Kodiak rivers; it required that only half the run could be taken commercially, and it may well have saved the salmon run from extinction. The last cannery closed down in the late 1920s. Still, by 1938 a big run numbered just over two million sockeye. By the time of Alaska's statehood in 1959, the run was down to 666,000 sockeye—the nadir had come in 1956, when the run numbered only 229,000.

And now the slow climb back, the river nurtured again by the Alaska Department of Fish and Game. Last year 2.6 million—including all species—had come up the river. "It's taken them fifty years," Sikes said, "but we're on our way. The state is limiting the commercial fishing until at least 250,000 reds have gone up the river. Even out in the ocean here, from Cape Karluk to Rocky Point, they've stopped the netting."

The valiant efforts of the Department of Fish and Game, though, couldn't persuade those silver salmon that if they wanted to be considered truly aristocratic, like the Atlantic's *Salmo salar*, then they'd better start thinking about hitting flies. The next morning, this was still an unsolved problem.

We even had discovered a potential defector in the fly-fisher ranks. Dennis Cosca, a Sacramento dentist, had already confessed to heretical, revisionist practices committed the previous day. "I became convinced that if I used a spoon I'd get a fish," he said. "I went down to the river mouth. My very first cast I hooked a salmon on a spoon. I . . . I landed it."

He was heard without comment. "I was so frustrated," Cosca continued. "I caught several, in fact. But then it lost all its luster. The excitement went. No skill was involved, so I trudged up and rejoined you. I knew I wouldn't be spinfishing anymore."

He'd fallen from grace, all right, but the tribunal felt able to overlook the lapse—the man clearly had the right stuff in him and he rejoined our group of purists as we followed Miley, the Golden Gate Club veteran, who now made for a narrower, smoother stretch of river than we'd fished the previous day. Then it hadn't looked deep enough to hold fish, but the clarity of the water had deceived us. It was five feet deep there, and there were silvers, too, unperceived until they slashed open the glassy surface.

This time I sent my cast ten degrees upstream and deliberately snaky, so that I could strip off an extra yard of fly line. I flicked the rod top over and downstream and fed out the extra line — with the high-density weight-forward line I was using the fly would sink fast and swim down close to the bottom.

I missed my first silver hit because I was expecting the sudden wrenching pull of an Atlantic. Instead, there came a faint pluck, like the touch of bottom grass, and I let go. It was my last mistake, though. Casting again, I saw that Miley was playing a salmon thirty yards downstream from me. "They're taking very soft," he shouted — and the next time I touched "grass" I tightened up hard.

And there was my silver, holding position for the first seconds, jagging its head, then breaking loose, screaming away downstream with the devil on its tail as I scrambled to shorten the line, stumbling to get below it, Miley burying his line in the water to let me get by. All ninety feet of my fly line was out and a lot of the backing, and the fish was rolling on the far side of the river. That was fine by me because now I could get pressure on it from downstream, convincing it that it had to go up the river to escape danger, thus forcing it to use up its strength heading against the current.

After that it was pure attrition, the side strain pulling the salmon off balance, working it by degrees into shallower, slower water where its strength ebbed as it fought air, found no purchase for muscles and tail, until I could slide it easily over the wet stones and into my element.

My first silver, first coho salmon, *Oncorhynchus kisutch*, thicker in the body than an Atlantic, with the same iridescent silver sides but without the neat black "x" marks of *salar*, instead, a dusting of small black spots; surely, though, the *salar*'s equal in power. I removed the hook and cradled it in the shallows again, head upstream, swinging it slowly so that water forced its way through its gills. The fish had given much. Five minutes passed and then, with a sudden muscular spasm, it shrugged free and sped into the dappled water. In this chocolate factory, I thought, you had to work hard for your candy.

After that the fly rods could more than match the spinning sticks and bring into play all the fascinating complexity of skills that the latter didn't require. I had ten fish that morning.

The tide eased and the run with it. We straggled back, the sun catching the spire of the old Russian Orthodox church. It had been built by ships' carpenters in 1888, the last building left from the old cannery days when the great stone spit, from which the nets were set, stretched almost across the lagoon.

Years ago an expansion bridge had linked the spit to the far side, but in 1977 a three-day, 130-mph blow had swept away the bridge, most of the spit and all the detritus of the old cannery buildings. Now a new Karluk village of two hundred people is built upstream from the church. Today only the old people speak Suqcestun, or more properly, a Suqcestun-Russian patois, and few even bother to fish for the sixty salmon, a year's subsistence, that are theirs by federal right. "Nobody heads up the valley to trap anymore," Herman Malutin told me one evening. He's in his eighties, remembers the canneries and still relishes the *ukala*, the wind-dried salmon that had been his people's staple winter fare for centuries, fare despised by the younger generation. "Hamburgers," he said expressively. "*Monday Night Football.*" He'd look curiously at the rods laid out in racks. "Never saw one of those until six, seven years ago," he said. He himself favored a spear, he told us.

It would be repetitious to describe the minutiae of the rest of the week's sport, once the secret of the chocolate factory had been revealed. Probably all of us, spinners and fly-fishers alike, realized that nothing like this would ever happen in our angling lives again. We gorged ourselves on sport. Twelve, maybe fifteen salmon could be expected to each rod each morning tide. If not sated by then, an angler could head up to the lagoon and continue to fish from a boat.

Oddly, few were sated, even though our party's total catch, we estimated at the end, was in the neighborhood of fifteen hundred silvers averaging about fourteen pounds each, better than ten tons. If you like to visit the wilder shores of statistics, that would cut up maybe into fifteen thousand generous steaks, which, in turn, a posh Manhattan restaurant would convert to about a quarter of a million dollars — including sauce, but not veggies.

But for six days, except for an unfortunate few that Dr. Stan Inouye, orthodontist, had sliced up into sashimi, all the landed, beaten salmon had been nursed and eased back into their river alive. The chocolate had been admired, not consumed, which probably accounted for the fact that satiety had never been reached, that Mr. Castwell's hell had been turned into a salmon fisher's heaven. Even Day Seven, billed as the Black Friday (because it was the last morning and it would've been less than human not to take a few fish home), turned out to be no massacre.

Even though the generous possession rule was twelve salmon per angler, we'd learned the chocolate factory lesson. A decorous cooler full of coho fillets suited everyone and scarcely scratched the surface of the world's greatest salmon river. Next morning, scarred veterans all, we lined up at the Kodiak airstrip as the bush plane dropped off a new group of anglers. "Are the silvers running?" called an eager voice.

"The chocolate factory," I said, "is down the hill and to your right."

CHAPTER TEN

Sea-trout Heaven

Little did I think that in April of 1982, for a
few short days I would achieve such fame. Word first got out in
the Time-Life Building, then spread to other media offices in
New York, that, right in town, *there existed a man who had*
actually been to these obscure Falkland Islands that had just sprung
into the news by getting themselves invaded. I did my best in the
interviews. I told everybody that those little islands had the best
sea-trout fishing I'd ever come across. But it didn't seem to be
what those interviewers wanted.

THE FALKLAND ISLANDS

THE FALKLAND Islands had seen plenty of violent death long before the Anglo-Argentine War of 1982. On a stony ridge above Skull Pass in the Mount Maria range, the bones of a sailor still lie, picked clean a century ago by foxes and buzzards. Scraps of navy blue serge are clues enough to his occupation and his lonely death. Three hundred and fifty miles to the southwest lies Cape Horn. Ship after ship, a hundred years ago, was beaten back from the Cape or, weathering it, made a desperate landfall on the Falklands, only to be smashed on its reefs and headlands. From such a wreck, this poor man had somehow got ashore and scrambled as high as he could, searching for some sign of habitation. Finding none, he had died from cold and despair.

On the blue-sky morning that Syd Lee told me the story, he was wrestling his Land Rover across stone outcrops, through peat bogs and over high tussocks of grass to the Warrah River, which we could see shining beyond Skull Pass. It was so benign a day that it was

MALO RIVER, FALKLAND ISLANDS

hard to believe the islands could be so cruel. The hills around us were surely the Big Rock Candy Mountains. Small flocks of Upland Geese, instead of skyrocketing out of sight on our approach, waddled away. They are peculiar fowl, so easily shot or brought down by a stone that they offer no sporting challenge whatsoever. In the grass there were the wild Falkland strawberries that looked like double-sized raspberries and tasted like neither fruit, but had a delicious flavor of their own. There were also delicate pink-and-white tea-berries. And, as I had already discovered, the streams and rivers of the island held magnificent trout, in particular some of the finest sea-run brown trout in the world.

Even if he had the means or the strength to catch them though, the unlucky sailor commemorated in the name of Skull Pass could not have saved himself that way, for trout are comparatively recent immigrants to the Falklands. Precisely when they established themselves is not known: an implantation of eyed ova from Chilean stock was made in the early 1940s and another batch, a gift of the Chilean government, arrived in 1947. There were further consignments from Scotland and England in the early 1950s, but it was not until 1954 that Falklanders, fishing in traditional style for a small, indigenous perch-like fish, with mutton for bait, started to catch trout.

At first, they were not especially impressive trout. They were slow-growing and not very well nourished. A nine-incher, it proved, took four years to achieve that size. The Falkland rivers are acid and peaty, without much natural food. Altogether it looked as if the trout were going to prove a bad bargain.

Then, on February 25, 1956, Norman Cameron, wet-fly fishing in the Malo River, caught a three-pound trout. The barriers were down. Within two years, trout of up to fifteen pounds were being taken. In the cautious words of an ichthyologist who came out from England to investigate the fishing, "These fish . . . appeared to have been feeding in the sea, and resembled sea trout." Well, yes indeed. Sea-run brown trout, brilliant silver, dappled with small black "x" markings that made them resemble Atlantic salmon.

The Falkland Islands are surrounded by dense concentrations of krill, as well as immense schools of smelt-like fish. The small trout that local anglers had been catching before 1956 were unambitious stay-at-homes. But others had dropped downstream to the estuaries and the inshore waters around the islands, where a rich food supply, hard to match anywhere else in the world, awaited them. The same ichthyologist who had been so tentative in labeling the fish sea trout found that their condition was far better than that of sea-run browns in Britain. The word was slow, very slow, to emerge in the world of angling. That was understandable. The Falklands, which consist of 202 islands with a total area of 4,700 square miles are, of course, extremely remote, and before that remoteness was shattered by war, fewer than two thousand people lived there, mostly of Scottish and English stock, who made their living raising sheep. To some, the Falklands might seem forbiddingly lonely. "An undulating land, with a wretched and desolate aspect," Charles Darwin called the islands in 1834. In the same year, Captain Robert Fitzroy, Royal Navy, commented tersely, "Admirably suited for a penal colony."

It is certainly true that the Falklands are not the Costa del Sol. Fronts build up over the Andes, then cross Patagonia and three hundred miles of cold South Atlantic to give the islands a kind of manic-depressive climate of sunshine and cloud that alternates bewilderingly. It is almost always windy, sometimes ferociously windy. There are exceedingly few trees, and those have been planted and carefully nurtured. But the islands have a fragile, delicate beauty that is very hard to put into concrete terms. The colors are muted greens and browns; the sky is constantly changing; the settlements are brilliant patches of red roofs and white walls. From them, faintly, comes the reek of peat smoke: this is the West of Ireland or the Scottish Hebrides transported eight thousand miles into the Southern Hemisphere. With, however, much bigger trout. No angling magazine, then or now, carries advertisements for fishing in the Falklands. My own journey began, in unlikely fashion, at the Flyfishers' Club in London, appropriately enough over a lunch of lamb chops. "Three sixty-five," said Sir Edwin Arrowsmith, an ex-Governor of the Falklands, indicating my plate. "That's what they call lamb in the Falklands," he explained. "Because, you understand, they eat a great deal of it. Pretty much every day."

He told me further that I would have to travel there via Buenos Aires. Until 1971, the only way to get to the islands was by sea, via Montevideo, but in that year an airlink had been set up between Comodoro Rivadavia in the South of Argentina and Port Stanley, the capital (and only town) of the Falklands.

Before you could get on the plane though, the Argentinians insisted on your obtaining a special visa from their Foreign Ministry in Buenos Aires. Now the plane flew just once a week, on a Monday, and you had to get your visa on a Friday. Which meant arriving in B.A. on the Thursday. Which meant leaving New York on the Wednesday . . . the trip was not made easy and, in my case, complicated by an odd interview I had at the Foreign Ministry when I went there for my visa. Suffering from whatever strange delusions the Argentinians harbored in those days, a naval officer in a comic opera uniform took me aside and suggested that I should report back to him on my return concerning the islanders. Their wish was to be liberated by Argentina. . . .

A couple of years later would come the invasion and the end of that particular air service. In the meantime, though, it took me six days to reach Port Stanley where, naturally, the wind was blowing hard from the southwest. Stanley has one hotel, the Upland Goose, where I had planned to stay, having meditated also on the problem of getting to the rivers. Land Rovers were the chief means of travel, I'd been told, and since there were no roads outside of Stanley, this meant proceeding at an average speed of around five miles per hour over the wickedly rough terrain. It seemed as if the number of rivers I would be able to visit would be very limited.

There at the airport, though, was Terry Spruce, chairman of the Falklands Angling Club and fourteen years out of Liverpool. "You're on the Beaver in the morning," he said. "West Falkland Island, Chartres River." We drove right past the Upland Goose. "No point in your checking in there," Spruce said. "Joan has dinner waiting for you and your room is ready." There it was: the classic hospitality of remote places.

At that time, the Falkland Government Air Service consisted of two Canadian Beaver floatplanes that worked their way around the settlements on an ad hoc basis, depending on demand. The plan was that, using the Beavers, I'd be passed on from sheep farm to sheep farm, wherever the fishing was good. "You'll be staying with Bill and Pat Luxton at Chartres, then June and Syd Lee at Port Howard," Spruce said. "After that, it's the Millers at Port San Carlos. Then I'll meet you myself for the last weekend on the Malo River. The club has a fishing hut there."

I boarded the Beaver next morning and told the pilot that I had no ticket. "I'll bill you later," he said. He might also have told me that, en route, he would be dive-bombing the settlement at Port Darwin with a mailbag. Suddenly losing altitude, roaring in at sea level, then shooting over the roofs so tightly that you could see where the shingles needed attention, was in no way conducive to a calm start for a fishing trip. My heart was still pounding when we landed on the Chartres estuary. The pilot got out on the starboard float and paddled the plane over to where a man in hip boots was waiting to throw us a line. "Try not to frighten the trout when you take off," was the best parting shot I could muster.

Bill Luxton was waiting for me there. A couple of years later I would read in the papers how Bill, a member of the islands' governing council, had been imprisoned by the Argentinians as a "troublemaker," and then deported to England. In the meantime, though, a different sort of problem, one which seemed serious at the time, had arisen for him. Long before, on the advice of Sir Edwin, I had arranged my trip to coincide with the end of sheep-shearing on the islands, the busiest time of year. But there had been two weeks of constant rain, and since it is impossible to shear wet sheep, Luxton still had three days' work ahead in the sheds. "But don't worry," he said. "My wife Pat will take you up to the river after lunch."

I wasn't immediately worried myself. I had already seen what was unmistakeably a sea trout leaping in the estuary, fifty yards off a rocky point. There was still time to fish before lunch. So at the risk of looking a little over-eager, I set up a spinning rod and I very nearly caught a sea trout with the first cast I made in Falkland waters, when a bright little fish of a couple of pounds hit the small silver spoon and shot high in the air, only to throw the lure. I was just going to cast again when I heard, "Hey, mister! Mister! Over here!" A boy was shouting at me. I looked to my left and the water was boiling with fish, well out of the tide run, in a small bay. I clambered over the rocks and threw the spoon across them, but even as I did the sleek black shoulders and great cowled head of a sea elephant broke surface. He had a big school of trout well corralled, and it was pointless for me to fish on. The sight itself was well worth the lost fishing time. The sea elephant ripped through the school again and came up with a broken-backed five-pounder.

"You're not allowed to shoot 'em," said the boy from behind me, a smallish boy, I saw now, who told me in swift succession that his name was Trevor, that he had broken the handle of his own reel or he would be fishing now, but that he would be eleven on the thirteenth of the month and he was hoping for a replacement. He would have liked to have taken me fishing, he said, but for the trouble with his reel. However, if he were to borrow mine, he would be able to show me how to catch a few. "I'm here every morning," he said courteously.

There is one pool on every sea-trout river that, through the season, is more productive than any other. Often it is called "The Sea Pool" though it is not tidal but rather the first pool above the tide's influence. Here the fish will be fresh in from the sea, their saltwater instinct to hit a fly or a lure unabated. And it was the Sea Pool on the Chartres to which Pat Luxton drove me after lunch.

I was quite settled in my mind that we were wasting our time. The wind had dropped and the sun come blazing out. Any sea trout in the pool was going to be cowering under whatever shade it could find. "I'll try the head and you can work up from the tail," Pat said. There was possibly one hundred yards of fishing between the two points. The water was dark and peaty, the river running full after the two weeks of rain. I had hoped to flyfish, but this was spoon water. The trout would not be able to see the fly from more than a few feet away.

I cast. In that smooth water the quarter-ounce spoon hit like an artillery shell, a gross insult to any trout. Two turns of the reel and my rod was pulled over hard. A sea trout erupted. Three pounds, he turned out to be. Twenty minutes later I had made no progress at all in making my way upstream towards Pat. I stood, cast—and most times a sea trout hit. I landed four and lost as many again. It dawned on me what was happening. Fish were running up into the pool. But it was too bright and hot for trout to behave like this. They should wait for dusk or full dark, like sea trout everywhere else. I stopped fishing and walked up to join Pat. She had a brace of three-pounders on the bank. All the fish seemed to run to a size—fish of the same year-class, presumably, coming in from the salt.

"How often do you fish this pool?" I asked Pat.

"Oh, I think we came up here twice last year," she said brightly. I was fishing, plainly, over the least sophisticated sea trout in the world. When Pat explained that soon we would have to set out on the hour-long Land Rover trip home so that she could get dinner under way, it was not too much of a hardship to consider that we would have spent about twice as long in traveling as we had fishing. Tomorrow we would have more time, she said, enough to work upstream to the livelier water where flyfishing might come into its own.

It didn't happen like that. As we walked in through the door at

Chartres, Pat heard her name on the radio which supplements the telephone in the islands and prattles away all day. "Four more for tomorrow night, is that all right, Mrs. Luxton?" The settlements in the Falklands fulfill one of the functions of the medieval monasteries: they shelter the traveler without question. Pat finished her radio chat. "We've got a professor of geese, or something, coming in from Aberdeen, and his assistant, and two grass experts. I'll have to defrost the beef . . ." She trailed off into one of those silent, lip-moving feminine trances that signify complex arrangements are being worked out. It would be difficult to cope, I suggested respectfully. "No, no," she said. "When we finish shearing we have Sports Week. I've got twenty-nine staying; they'll be sleeping in the kitchen, the bathrooms, everywhere." Outside, the wind had picked up again, howling around the settlement. "Forty knots," Pat said. It seemed a precise estimate. "The living room carpet," she explained, "lifts at forty knots." And, indeed, it was shifting fitfully. "It only takes twenty knots for the kitchen linoleum," she added.

In the light of all this domestic pressure, it was understandable that the next day's fishing would also be short; there were rooms to be readied in the morning, and a mighty piece of beef to go in the oven early. And so next day on the Chartres River turned out almost a carbon copy of the first—a short assault on the Sea Pool and nine trout this time, the best a little better than four pounds. That evening, naturally, we talked mostly about grass and geese, but Bill Luxton spoke once of the mighty runs of sea trout that had hit the Chartres from the late 1950s on. "Even some of the small feeder streams were choked with trout," he said. "There was a little pool the size of this dining room with fish of eleven and twelve pounds milling about with hardly room to turn. It was pointless to fish. We could pull them out by hand. Maybe that's why we don't fish that much now. Just take a picnic up the river once or twice a year, fish for an hour or two, maybe, fill the freezer." The size of the fish had gone down, by rapid natural selection. The Chartres was a small river; an average size of three pounds suited it better. And perhaps after the twelve pounders they were anticlimatic.

In one soul in the Chartres settlement, though, the Waltonian flame still burned brightly. Next afternoon the Beaver was to pick me up and fly me to Port Howard. In the morning I took a walk along the estuary shore. Young Trevor was there, as promised. "Where's your stuff?" he asked. When I told him it was at the Luxton house, he was away like the wind and back in moments with my tackle. "Need some bait," he announced, and he was off again. "Here you go, mister," he said, returning in seconds it seemed with a small, bloody package. "Bits of mutton. You got a hook?" I had to concede that the only ones I had were attached to flies or lures. Resignedly he dug into his jeans. "Tie this one on, mister," he said. "You'll want a float as well, I suppose." From his other pocket he produced a giant, egg-sized bobber. "I'll tie that on myself," he said. "It's the only one I've got."

When the gear was rigged, he told me to cast about twenty yards out. Almost immediately the bobber jiggled and darted away. I tightened up and missed. "What's your name, mister?" Trevor asked. I told him. "All right, Clive," he said, "you better let me do it." Trevor took over. Inside a minute the spinning rod was dancing and shortly he was beaching a golden fish of a pound or so. "Plenty of mullet here today, Clive," he said. Apparently abstracted, he rebaited and cast again himself.

I looked at the fish on the beach. There was something mullet-like about its head, but it has a dorsal fin that ran almost its full length and very large, fan-like pectorals. This was, I was in no doubt, *Eleginus falklandicus*, of which Leslie Stewart, the English ichthyologist who had investigated the sea trout, had written that specimens of up to twenty pounds had been recorded and that "the larger fish, when caught on rod and line, fight as well as Atlantic salmon." A big claim and one that the little fish that Trevor and I caught for the next hour could scarcely prove. The biggest Trevor had ever caught, he said, was a five-pounder.

"Got to go for smoko now," he said, ending the session and recovering his hook and his bobber. Smoko? Trevor wasn't even eleven yet. Only later did I learn that this was the Australian-derived Falkland word for any kind of mid-morning break, smoking being forbidden in the shearing sheds.

Trevor walked off, a diminutive, reel-less fisherman. I hoped things would go well for him on the thirteenth and it was hard not to leave one of my own reels with him. But I had more than a week of fishing ahead, and only a single spare if anything went wrong.

At Port Howard, later in the day, Syd Lee's son was waiting for the Beaver in a dinghy—the jetty on wheels that they normally ran out for the plane had been carried away on a high tide. There were the same red roofs and the same white houses as in Chartres and, as in all the settlements, the gardens ablaze with the familiar flowers of England. "And so, Syd, how is the fishing going?" I asked him when we got to the house. Well, truthfully, it seemed that it had been quite a few months since he'd been up on the Warrah, he admitted. We'd just have to go up there and find out.

It was another jouncing, rocking Land Rover trip, two hours to the lower reaches of the Warrah, over wild country and across Skull Pass to the river. While he drove, Syd told the story of the sailor on the mountain and of an eighty-five-year-old man who lived alone down on the estuary of the Warrah, and who had lived in the same shepherd's house for fifty years. It was four years since he had been in the settlement, nearly forty years since he had been in Port Stanley. He was entirely self-sufficient except for tea and sugar and oddments that Syd brought him now and then. So self-sufficient, indeed, that a few years earlier, catching the flu and deciding that his last day had come, he had got rid of all the food in the house and laid himself neatly on his bed, arms folded over his chest, reasoning that when he didn't answer the phone, in the next day or two somebody would be out to look. In the morning, however, he felt much better and very hungry. There being no food, he went out and shot a sheep. The Falklanders are a pragmatic race.

Naturally enough, Syd had headed the Land Rover towards the sea pool of the Warrah. In a situation where you have an enormous plenty of fish and virtually no angling pressure, it is difficult for sophisticated fishing methods to develop, and for that day, certainly, it was necessary to go along again with spin casting. The Warrah was a bigger river than the Chartres, admittedly, and with the wind getting up and blowing straight into your face it was impossible to cover more than a small fraction of the water with a fly.

And sea trout were running, it was clear, under the far bank. Both Syd and I were into fish as soon as the thin, lightly dished spoons hit. Back at the settlement that evening, my best fish went eight pounds, Syd's a little under that weight. And there had been still bigger fish around. The eight-pound test line that both of us were using should have been strong enough to hold them but in one short spell both Syd and I were broken by fish that ran strongly to the tail of the pool and sounded. Not until the last fish had been lost did either of us notice that the last foot of line was perceptibly abraded. The bottom of that pool was pure glacial boulder, and it was virtually impossible to stop the bigger fish from getting down amongst the stones.

I had one more day left on the Warrah, which is named for an extinct mammal, the Falkland wolf-fox, the last of which was shot hereabouts in 1876. It was shearing time again, which meant that Syd could not fish, though he spared a man to drive me. No sea pool this time, I thought, and on this occasion we made an even longer journey to a place Syd had told me of higher up the river. It turned out to be at least four hundred yards of trout-holding water, falling away at the end into a series of bubbling pots in which the fish would naturally rest on their way upstream. At last I had come upon excellent fly water.

At the head of the stretch the water came down in a smooth glide and for the first hour I took nothing but small brown trout on an orthodox Black Spider ribbed with silver. I had the nagging feeling that I was a fool to have risked everything on the flyrod. Maybe the fish were just too big to concern themselves with a few fibers of black hackle. But then, as I worked down to where the river narrowed, there came the classic violent strike and a five-pounder was catapulting out of the water so wildly that for the first thirty seconds it would be idle to pretend I had any serious contact with it. And so downstream: I took nothing as big as I had done the previous day, but the best was no mean seven-pounder and the whole bag went more than thirty-five pounds—a magnificent day's trouting.

Next day I crossed the Falklands Sound to East Falkland, landing in the sheltered inlet of San Carlos Water. It was beyond my—or anybody's—wildest fantasy that in a short time that utterly peaceful bay would be the bloody scene of the first electronic battle in history, the biggest air-sea battle since World War II. The fiercest fighting in the Anglo-Argentine war would take place there, and British Marine Commandos would establish a bridgehead, leading to the expulsion of the Argentine troops from the islands.

This day, though, the sky that would be riven by the screaming of Harrier jets and reddened by the burning HMS *Antelope* and HMS *Ardent*, was a calm and pearly gray. It was a day also when I played truant and headed out to Paloma Beach—to white sand, gray mist, white breakers—to the surrealist scene of thousands of penguins, a straggling army, marching from the sands to their rookery. As if to upbraid me, the San Carlos River yielded me precisely nothing on the following day when I went there to fish.

It was disappointing, but I was not particularly disturbed, for I still had in reserve the Malo, which had the reputation of being the finest sea-trout river in the islands. On my first day in Stanley, Terry Spruce had shown me photographs of a brace of Malo trout, each of which went over fifteen pounds, taken on fly the previous season. And it was near where the fishing club had its lodge that one of the islands' then-small garrison of Marines had taken the current record, a twenty-pounder. The plan that Terry and I had made was simple. He would drive up to the fishing lodge from Stanley, a racking three-hour trip covering some of the roughest country in the Falklands. Meantime the floatplane would put me down, as close to shore and as high up as possible, on the estuary of the Malo. I would wade ashore in hip boots, leave my baggage to be picked up later, then walk the mile or so to the lodge.

The pilot, I learned later, was meant first to have flown low over the fishing lodge to show me its location. This slipped his mind. He was also several degrees off when he pointed out the direction to me when we had landed on the water. At this time, it was the middle of a day of burnished sunshine. I kept my high boots on, and took a rod and fishing bag in case I was at the lodge ahead of Terry and could steal a march on him.

A march is what I got. It was an hour before I began to suspect that anything was wrong. I must have traveled a mile in an hour, I reasoned, even though the going was slow over rocky, uneven ground and high clumps of grass. The watercourse where I had been landed was part of a delta-like complex, and obviously, now, not the single mouth of a river. There were two distinct ranges of hills on the horizon, and under one of them the Malo had to flow. Because the Malo was the biggest of the island's rivers it seemed logical to head for the higher range. It appeared a long way off, but I reasoned that the undulating ground probably hid the river from me. I calculated I would hit it long before I came to the hills. So I pressed on.

After two hours of walking and changing course in case I was headed too far upstream, I was fairly certain that I was lost, and at this stage I should have back-tracked to where I had been left and sat on my luggage until the Land Rover came. But maybe, I told myself, that was a little timorous. The Malo had to be under those big hills. Once I hit it I could walk downstream until I found the lodge, which was just above the tideline.

Four times I thought I had found the river. Each time it proved to be a broad, blind creek with the tide running up it so strongly that I had to make a wide detour to cross. I was beginning to appreciate the wildness of these islands, to have a different perspective than the one gained from a Beaver or even riding a Land Rover back to the safety of the settlement.

The sun was hot at first, and the hip boots were proving a curse, but there was plenty of water to drink in the brooks I crossed, although bitter-tasting and peaty. I tried not to consider the chance of a dead sheep upstream. I crossed emerald green bogholes and curious plateaux of peat, climbing ridges of a couple of hundred feet, hoping to get a glimpse of the river, then descending again. I had been carrying my jacket so far. Now, after the sun had begun to lower and my watch showed that I had been walking for about five hours, the Falkland sou'westerly sprang up and I put my jacket on.

In the clear air, the mountains seemed no nearer. About then, for the first time, I thought of the sailor above Skull Pass. Absurd, of course. But when I reached the next creek I went well above it rather than wade. If I had to stay out all night, then I didn't want wet feet. It was already getting cold. Later, I twice fell into holes in the peat and the second time I thought I'd torn a muscle in my left thigh. It became painful to walk and I was now looking round for a sheltered place to spend the night. The two previous nights, after a bright day, there had been sharp frosts.

I made it to the top of the next rise and then, not entirely believing it, I saw a telephone pole and heard the wire whistling in the wind. In the Falklands, God bless them, they paint the poles white, and now I could see them, marching away across the next hill. They might be leading to Stanley, for all I knew, thirty miles away, but for the moment I was well content to stay in touch with an artifact. I stayed with the poles over the next two hills, going more and more slowly, stopping to rest more frequently now. And then across the next valley I saw the white walls of a house glowing pink in the evening sun.

It took me almost an hour to reach it, and long before that I had realized that no smoke was coming from its chimney. But when I reached it I found that the door hung open and inside was a stove and a pile of cut peat. It was a shelter for the shepherds who came that way occasionally when the sheep were being gathered in. I was luckier than the Skull Pass sailor. Oddly, it was only after several minutes that the thought came to me that, if there were telephone poles, probably there would be a telephone here. Not that it would be connected, of course. It was on the wall, an antique instrument with a handle to twist. I picked it up and twisted. Nothing. I twisted again, more violently. "What number are you calling?" a voice said brightly.

Much later, I would discover the name of the building — Top Malo House, where in the last days of the Falklands war, British and Argentine marines would fight out a bloody little skirmish which ended with the house being burned down.

Now, though, it was intact and a perfect refuge. I had the stove going well by the time that Terry picked me up, around 10:00 P.M. In the darkness it took us two hours to drive to the fishing lodge, and when I awoke in the morning my left knee was football-sized. Later we figured I had covered close to fourteen miles, and for the first time in my life I had a record dedicated to me on a radio program, *These Boots Were Made For Walking*, and the request, the local radio said, had come from "numerous" sources.

Now, the best fishing on the Malo, where the fifteen-pounders were caught on the fly, is in a steep, rocky gorge. With my knee, there would clearly be no gorge fishing for me, and it looked as if my Falklands trip would end on a low note. I could haul myself as far as a shingle beach along which trout might run with the tide, but the prospects didn't seem good. Unlike the Chartres and the Warrah, there was little fresh water coming down the Malo, and few fish coming in from the sea. Oddly enough, I did almost catch one of the Malo monsters, though. It jumped three times before it threw the spoon, and both Terry and I had a good look at it. A conservative twelve pounds, we reckoned. I took two small trout later, and that seemed to be the end of it.

But it wasn't. We toiled back to the lodge, and when we reached the pool below it we could see the swirls of heavy fish and the bow waves they were putting up in the shallow water. "Mullet," said Terry. "We take a lot of them here. You want to try?"

"No mutton," I responded. I hadn't forgotten my fishing lesson from Trevor.

"No mutton needed," said Terry. "Just a small spoon and a couple of diddle-dee berries."

The silver diddle-dee bush grows everywhere in the Falklands. It has small red berries. Terry now proceeded to adorn each point of my treble hook with diddle-dee berries. "Mullet love anything red," he said. The bow waves of big fish followed my lure several times before one hit. And then there was a solid, massive resistance, just like a salmon's, a huge golden swirl on top of the water, a crashing leap, and then, quite suddenly, my fish seemed to be fifty yards downstream of me. It was twenty minutes before it was close enough to beach, and it went fifteen pounds on the club scales. To completely endorse the salmon comparison I would have to catch more. But they are very hard fish to land.

"I hate this drive back to Stanley," Terry said, as we were climbing a scarp of loose stone on the way back.

I looked at him incredulously. "It beats walking," I said.

RAINBOW TROUT FROM DON LAKE, BRITISH COLUMBIA

CHAPTER ELEVEN

Royal Red Setter

In a perfect world, I'd have caught the very big native rainbow trout you'll hear about in a moment on the fly that the next king of England presented to my friend Mike. But it would have been too much to expect in this one.

BRITISH COLUMBIA

I'D WADED through the frigid shallows in jeans and sneakers as far as the southwest corner of the lake, where a high yellow cliff blocked my way. Then I looked down into the water, and a wave of vertigo grasped and shook me as if I had been climbing the face of the cliff itself.

There was a touch of sharp fear also. How far down into that lapping, bottlegreen water could I see? Fifty feet, a hundred? Those white and fibrous ghosts of ancient spruces that the refracted light made shift and roll, how deep were they? And what could live under the ledges, in the gouged-out caverns of the underwater cliff that fell away close to vertically?

It was a far less rational fear than the one I was entitled to feel, that suddenly the willows behind me would snap and crash and a bear materialize. There were grizzlies enough in the snow slides around the lake, those verdant lanes down the mountainsides where spring avalanches had smashed through the trees and cleared the way for the sweet young growth the bears relish.

If I tossed out the little Swedish spoon again, something Jungian was asking me, what aqueous horror, unknown to biologists, would slide from its lair and absorb it as it twinkled through the depths? Until now I had waded across a broad, knee-deep shelf. But here the drop-off was almost immediate. I had a couple of feet of standing room at the most.

I shook off the foolishness. Away at the far end of the lake I could see a patch of bright red, the little inflatable boat we had packed into the lake and which could only take two. Even now, I reckoned, Cranston, the guide, would be unloading Begg and the fly-fishing gear at the stream mouth, and then he would be heading back for me. Any moment now I would hear the motor start up. Then I would take off the small, slim, silver and brass spoon and head for the landing place, but meanwhile there was time for a cast or two. The vertigo, the chill of fear had gone. All there was in front of me was deep water with some dead trees and rocks in it. I swung the spoon back over my shoulder, flipped it out, let it sink a touch and started a slow, fluttering retrieve. It must have traveled two-thirds of the way home when it was hit with a violence that made my fantasy thin-blooded.

The reel sang its high, screeching obbligato, on and on, and then this marvelous silver and rose beauty was breaching clear of the water once, twice, three times, and I could see the plastic of the reel spool showing through. That meant almost two hundred yards of line had been ripped away and the smash would come any second. Still I yelled across the sounding board of the lake for a landing net — not that anything we carried would have encompassed the biggest trout I had ever seen. And, shaking as I was, there was time for a fleeting thought: This was the Balmoral Trout, the one that should have been for Charlie.

This story, it should be understood, had its real beginning in London, in Buckingham Palace if you are willing to stretch a point, but more properly in the Flyfishers' Club on Brooke Street, where, earlier in the year, I was lunching with an old friend, Michael Begg. He is a TV producer for the BBC and he was looking more haggard than usual. He was not reticent about the reason. Upon his shoulders, he had just learned, had been put the responsibility of covering the wedding of the Prince of Wales in July. The way he talked, it was like being granted the honor of being the first man to try to climb Everest in tennis shoes. "Sixty-eight cameras," he was saying, "and me in the middle." He could be knighted, I suggested lightheartedly, if all went well.

"Or unemployed," he said, moodily pushing his Dover sole around the plate. A silence fell. Then — a man seeing the first crack of light at the end of the tunnel — he thought of something. "You got any plans for Afterward?" he asked me. "Fishing plans?" Time, for Begg, was clearly divided between the gray Now and the rosy Afterward.

It happened that I did. I had been in touch with a Vancouver lawyer by the name of Greg Cranston who was running an operation in northern British Columbia which he hoped would be different from the fly-in, booze-it-up, fly-out deal that so many wilderness fishing camps too often turn out to be. I told Begg about the packhorse train that we would be taking into the mountains, the mighty Dolly Vardens, the incredible grayling and the secret lake with the giant rainbows. "Can I come?" Begg asked pitifully.

The man had to have something to live for. "Sure," I said. We left it that we would meet in Vancouver, not the day after the wedding, as Begg urged, but very soon afterward. We would iron out the details then; Begg, I reasoned, would be incapable of coherent plans before that. I was mistaken.

A week before the wedding he called me. He had been at Buckingham Palace, he said, taping an interview with the Prince of Wales. It had gone well enough, but he hadn't called to tell me that. The interview over, Charles had relaxed. He seemed to realize that Begg was under some strain also, and had asked him if he planned to take time off once the wedding was over. So Mike told him about our B.C. trip.

At the mention of fishing, Begg said, Charles became considerably animated and pulled out his desk drawer, which proved to be crammed full of fishing tackle.

"Try this one," he said, selecting a fly. "Got it from New Zealand."

"Red Setter," Mike said, recognizing the pattern. "They make 'em from the tail hairs."

"Looks like the whole damn dog to me," said the future monarch, and that was that.

"Do you realize," Mike now said to me on the phone, "if one of us catches a huge rainbow on that, I'll report back and maybe we'll get invited to fish Balmoral." The royal stretch of the River Dee at Balmoral is perhaps the most delectable beat on one of the most delectable of Scottish salmon rivers.

"Look after it," I told him.

And indeed the fly was the first thing he produced when I met him, eventually, late at night in a Vancouver hotel room. He was jet-lagged, his body clock was eight hours adrift, but he was wedding-free at last and he had the Red Setter scotch-taped to the inside of his passport. Naturally, we couldn't keep calling it that. The Prince of Wales's Feathers? Too formal. Charlie's Angel? Too flip. In the end we settled for just Charlie. "Should I put it in the hotel safe?" Mike asked.

He was only twenty-five percent joking, though, and Charlie was kept under tight security when, later, we headed north to Fort Saint John. In Vancouver we had bought other flies, local patterns, but Charlie was not expected to mingle with them in the fly box. We had bought a heavy, sinking No. 9 fly line also, to get Charlie down deep to where the big trout might be. Would a big Dolly Varden, which is really a char, or a trophy grayling count as a Balmoral fish? Possibly, it was decided, but a mighty rainbow had to be the true target.

On the 450-mile flight to Fort Saint John, Begg had his first opportunity to study the fishing prospectus that Cranston put out.

"This is not a drinking camp," he read starkly from the sheet, and went on to quote a prim phrase about a glass of wine at dinner being permissible. "Thank you *very* much," cried Begg, whose family name is an honored one among Scotch whiskey distillers.

Not altogether oddly, a couple of months earlier I had myself quoted the same words to Cranston over the phone. He had never intended them to be taken literally, Cranston said. They were there to put off the sort of outdoorsmen, common in hunting camps, who fly in with cases of the hard stuff, get their moose the first day and spend the rest of the week stumbling from stupor to stupor. I could see the point. In particular I recalled a week in a Costa Rican fishing camp made miserable by a crowd from Macon, Georgia, who caught two fish all week and breakfasted on vodka.

So I was able to calm Begg, who was pointing out that he had not flown six thousand miles to vacation at a health farm. "A couple or three stiff ones after fishing have been cleared with the management," I told him. "And if Charlie scores, the bar stays open late. We have time to stock up in Fort Saint John."

There seemed to be plenty of time indeed. This was August 3, and the floatplane that would take us to Cranston's base camp, deep in the Canadian Rockies, was not scheduled to ferry us out until the following morning. It even seemed possible that the local liquor store might have a bottle or two of the appropriate thing, genuine twelve-year-old Begg's Scotch whiskey.

If it did, we didn't come near it. Let future travelers to the Far North be advised that August 3 is British Columbia Day, whereon every shop in Fort Saint John is locked up tight. Short of constructing our own camp distillery, it looked as if any victory of Charlie's would have to go untoasted. We might have had a shot at stocking liquor the following morning, but, as if by inexorable fate, we had been in our hotel for only an hour when the floatplane pilot called up to say he wanted to ship us out to camp immediately.

And so, boozeless, a couple of hours later we were bounding in the thermals over the high peaks, and the small deprivation dissolved as we projected into the green-glass lakes and the cotton-thread rivers below the grayling, trout and char that dreams are made of. And then we were sliding low through a pass and slapping down on the water. Home Lake, Cranston calls it. "Call it that when you write about it," he had told me. "The real name would bring the meat fishermen in."

Cranston was just coming in from fishing when we landed, a short, plump man of thirty-three, who, it turned out, had plotted for a year and a half for his two months' guiding in the bush. "I didn't book any trials from June to September," he told us later. Which may account for the fact that he is probably the only criminal lawyer in Vancouver who drives a '66 GMC pickup.

The floatplane left and the silence settled in. We were two hundred miles from a road, as the golden eagle flies, and the evening air was just taking on its first chill. The greetings over, Cranston left us for some unnamed mission, which gave Begg the chance for a swift survey of the cabin shelves. "Only sherry," he reported, "and not even dry."

It would be good for Charlie, though. We'd be putting in a lot of fishing hours. A small creek ran alongside the cabin and emptied into the lake not fifty yards away. It looked a perfect spot for a fish and maybe for the baptizing of Charlie. I suggested this.

"What do you reckon?" Begg asked sardonically. "Twelve-pound leader?"

"Fifteen," I bid.

"Wire," raised Begg. Clearly we had hit on a problem we should have anticipated. It would be anticlimactic to lose Charlie on the first evening, indeed on any evening, to a weed bed or a sunken branch. So how to fish it then without taking out absurd insurance in the way of heavy tackle?

The problem stayed unsolved because now Cranston was back. "Sauna before supper?" he asked. And, by heaven, he led us to the back of the cabin—which had no plumbing or electricity—where stood an improvised hot room sealed off with plastic sheeting, with a massive wood stove burning. "How about the cold bit?" I asked, though I had guessed the answer before Cranston pointed to the turbulent, glacier-fed stream.

"Pass," I said.

"I had a shower in the hotel this morning," said Begg. You have to put your foot down, or before you know it you *are* on a health farm. In such institutions, though, they rarely serve up moose steaks and fried potatoes, such as Cranston now had sizzling, nor is the after-dinner entertainment rich and gaudy fish talk such as followed this meal.

In the morning, Cranston said, we would fish Home Lake, on our doorstep. We would not look for monsters, though there were very big Dolly Vardens and who-knows-what in the lake depths should we wish to haul a heavy spoon around on a down-rigger. That would be a shame, though, for the shallows were full of free-rising native rainbows, up to three pounds, mainly.

It would be the right kind of workout for us, he went on, before the serious fishing started, the long horse trek over the mountains to what we should be careful to refer to as Don Lake, though that was not the name it was known by. There we might find such fish that would spoil us, cause us to put our rods away forever, because we would never hope to find their equal.

Or it was something like that he was saying because by now, moose-satiated, I was dozing at the table and great, heraldic trout, all rose, mauve and silver, rolled at a bountiful hatch of flies. The next thing I clearly recollect was the morning light pouring into the cabin and Cranston with coffee. "No hurry," he said. "The fish are gentlemen here. They start to rise around 10:00 A.M." It figured, of course. The nights were very cold and the sun would have to warm the lake shallows before flies would hatch and cause the trout to move in.

The weather was gentlemanly, too, with no more than a wisp or two of cumulus hanging over the snowy cap of Cloud Maker, the peak that towered above the cabin. We pushed the boat out from the creek mouth and headed for the western end of the lake. Long before we reached it we could see the rings of rising fish.

"There's one for Charlie there," I said to Mike, but already in his eye was the fanatic gleam of the far-gone dry-fly junkie. Royal as it might be, Charlie was still a wet fly, a lure if the truth be known, to be fished subsurface. As Cranston cut the engine and we drifted closer to the trout, it was plain to see that they were taking surface insects.

It was a benign moment for dry-fly fishing and for Begg, who had learned his angling on the classic chalk streams of southern England, on the Kennet and the Test, where the art of the dry fly had been born and nurtured to its ultimate sophistication.

Not that much sophistication was needed on Home Lake. The hatch itself was a raucous parade of mayflies and sedges led in its various stages by an occasional, enormous, silver-winged salmon fly. And the rainbows loved all of them. They loved our imitations, too, in particular Begg's big Yellow Sally, a mayfly tied for those English chalk streams, and, though there were pauses, the action went on until the sun was low.

The fish were extraordinary fighters, even for rainbows, the true Kamloops strain that are almost pure silver, very late in developing the pink flush along the lateral line. Each pound-and-a-half fish was three pounds until you saw it, each two-pounder fought like a trout twice its size. We kept the first three fish, an adequate supper, and lost count of the releases.

In one of the pauses I urged Mike to give Charlie a shot. Although it was somewhat flamboyant, sunk deep and inched back it might draw a fish larger than the two-pounders which we had been catching in indecent numbers. "I put it in my wet-fly box," he confessed, hauling that article from his fishing vest and opening it carelessly.

At that very moment, from the sides of Cloud Maker far above us, came a puff of wind. The boat swung at its anchor. Mike's arm jerked and about half the contents of the compartmented fly box flipped into the lake and sank out of reach. "My God, it's gone!" he shouted.

For a moment, as we scrabbled through the flies left in the box, it seemed as if Charlie had indeed been lost untested. But then I looked down to my feet and saw that some of the missing flies were in the bottom of the boat, swilling about in that little pool of muddy water that collects in every fishing craft. I put my hand in and dredged up Charlie. It was locked in a close embrace with a Connemara Black.

We had both been fishing long enough to recognize an omen. The old Indian gods up on Cloud Maker were telling us to hold Charlie for another time, and we obeyed them. Charlie was destined for Don Lake.

That night, Don Lake was all we talked of. It had been named for Don Peck, Cranston said, a respected Fort Saint John hunting out-fitter who had died a couple of years before. Peck, it seemed, had ridden by the lake on hunting trips. It was one thousand feet higher than Home Lake and barren of fish, for the simple reason that its outflowing stream spilled over the mountainside in a waterfall so spectacular that no trout had ever been able to push up from the Peace River system and populate it.

Which seemed a shame to Peck. So much so that one day, around ten years ago as far as Cranston could recollect, Peck horse-packed in a water container with a dozen Home Lake rainbows swimming around in it. The trail he took was the one along which we would be heading the following morning—the Bedaux trail.

Which led the conversation to Monsieur Bedaux, who, it seemed, was a latter-day *voyageur* who in 1930 conceived the outlandish notion of leading a caravan of Citroën half-tracks from the Alaska Highway across the Rockies to the Pacific. Naturally enough, he ground to a halt, somewhere in Peck country, and among many other things he abandoned were several copper-bottomed metal panniers filled with gas that he had loaded on the ponies that accompanied his expedition. Fittingly, it was one of those old containers that Peck had used for his rainbow-seeding operation.

"Can't recall who caught the first fish up there," Cranston said as he served up a Waldorf salad to go with the trout. "Could have been Don himself. But it was big, how big I don't know. That lake up there proved to be full up with *Gammarus*, freshwater shrimp, and all those twelve lucky trout had to do was open their mouths and browse. They reproduced fine, too.

"There's a drawback, of course," he went on. "The Don Lake fish are very hard to catch. Too well fed. We got nothing the last time I was up there, and just two the time before. *But one of those measured twenty-eight inches long.*"

"A Charlie fish," I said.

"Right on!" said Mike. "Tomorrow we hit him!"

But Cloud Maker vetoed that. We awoke to gray curtains of rain sweeping in from the Pacific and the entirely credible information from Cranston that a four- or five-hour horse trek in that would be misery. We headed up to the far end of Home Lake and there was no hatch. In the afternoon we were reduced to trolling for the supper fish and Begg dropped his Swiss Army knife in fifty feet of water.

We hit our lowest point when we hung strips of bacon fat on the hooks of our spoons and hauled Dolly Varden out of the creek mouth. But even at this low ebb, no one suggested similarly adorning Charlie's hook point.

The gray, wet night was what Scotch had been invented for, but we could look for no consolation there, either. "I was going to give you fellas lemon meringue pie tonight," said Cranston, who was beginning to prove that if he hadn't two professions already, he might well hire out as a five-star chef. "I had two lemons saved for tonight but somebody must have been in here and used them."

In the end, it was the radio that saved the evening, when we tuned in to the forecast. The front was going through, it said: tomorrow would be blue skies. If we'd had the means we'd have drunk to the weatherman.

And toasted him again in the morning, because he was absolutely right. We loaded up the boat and headed down to the foot of the lake, where Ray Watkins, the wrangler, and his wife, Mickey, had their corral of horses, and where I met Switches, my mount. She was a sorrel Appaloosa, ugly as a mud fence, as Watkins rightly said, and she began our relationship with a sneer. Begg's four-legged friend seemed no improvement, a big, pale, lazy horse named Buckskin Jesus for reasons that were explained but remained obscure. "They stay out here all winter," Watkins said proudly, "feed with the moose and the caribou, fight off the wolves and the grizzlies."

"I *thought* they looked tired," Begg said, *sotto voce*, but aside from us dudes everybody was busy with the intricate and highly skilled business of loading up the horses so that the panniers balanced perfectly and the ropes never slackened.

It was two hours before they had the loads right, and then the trek to Don Lake began, at first through swampy, gently rising ground, through thickets of stunted willow enclosing the mouth of a small valley, where, Watkins now lightly informed us, a grizzly had chased an Indian boy and him a couple of weeks earlier. Until the wrangler described it, I'd had no notion of the terrifying speed of such a huge animal over the ground, hind legs reaching forward like a greyhound's to overtake the front pair. Taking his word for it, I kicked on Switches until her nose bumped Buckskin Jesus's rear end.

Later, under the high midday sun, we began climbing steeply through the silent, birdless spruce woods, gigantic dun and mahogany fungi sprouting from the tree roots. Then we were over a crest and dismounting, leading the horses down steep wet rocks and hearing, ever so faintly, the distant roar of the river in the valley.

It was another hour before we reached it, though, and right away all thoughts of stopping to fish went from our minds. Grayling we'd hoped for, but this river was opaque white from snow melt and silt. For three miles we followed it, crisscrossing it, fording as deep as the horses' shoulders sometimes.

Then there was another mountainside to climb and another long descent, the horses picking their way over endless tree roots, down miry slides. Altogether we had been going more than four hours when suddenly we were out of the trees and into a sunlit alpine meadow with long sweet grass and an extravaganza of wildflowers—the blue of larkspur, the bold red of Indian paintbrush. And beyond the meadow, under the still unmelted snow of the mountain slope, gleamed Don Lake.

Something else gleamed also, though, and our hearts sank. The sun flashed on a lurid red never seen in nature, on white and on silvery chrome. We rode on. Yes, there was a floatplane moored by the far shore of the secret lake, and I thought ironically of something that Cranston had said the previous evening: "Twenty years from now, not many people will be able to say they ran a pack train. There'll be airstrips cut out everywhere in the bush, floatplanes on every lake."

He also had explained his own hope that he could keep fishing in the old way. "I could easily put a gasoline stove, a propane fridge, a generator in camp," he said. "Hell, you can arrive in the wilderness these days and there's a TV blaring—there's a diesel generator in camp." He liked hot cakes over the fire, he had said, and the satisfaction of catching trout that you had paid for with the aching muscles of a five-hour ride over rough country. Cruelly, it seemed now, he was being shown how anachronistic his notions were.

At the lakeside, though, the conflict faded from my mind. I sat on a tree stump knowing that I would never fish again. Or possibly even walk. Switches, I was convinced, had permanently shifted the lie of my pelvis. Also, there seemed something gravely wrong with my knees. The Watkinses and Cranston got the fire going and rigged the bivouacs as if they had been on a half-mile stroll. Even Begg was actually moving around, putting his fishing gear together.

The inflatable we had packed in, I knew, would only hold two. It was no self-sacrifice to say to Mike, "You go down the lake with Greg first while I put a few things together."

They were gone a long time, though. I got the glass on them and saw that they were stopping to investigate each little bay they passed. Then, little by little, I realized I could walk again. I might just as well pass the time, I thought, tossing a spoon around in the deeps close to camp until Cranston came back to me.

And that was how I came to encounter the biggest trout of my life, and why, a half-hour later, I was standing deep in freezing water, all aches vanished, and freely cursing the smart-aleck clerk in the Vancouver tackle shop who had sold me what proved to be the wrong-sized spool as a spare for my spinning reel, the spare I had intended to fill with twelve-pound test for such an encounter as this.

Instead I had had to use the regular one with the arbor clipped on it so that it held barely two hundred yards of wispy eight-pound test. That arbor was showing through right now, and I was all set to lose the fish of a lifetime. With my rod held high, I scrambled back along the ledge, trying to reach the broader shallows and to put a little bit of sidestrain on the trout.

When it turned, I don't think there were more than five yards of line remaining on the spool. I was trembling all over and I kept up the yelling, "Net! Net!" though I knew that I would have to play that fish until it was close on dead so that I could slide it onto the pebbles and get a hand under its gills.

It was more than thirty minutes before I saw it clearly again. In the interval there were three more major runs, though none as far as the first, each ending in a heavy surface roll instead of a jump. Later the fish sounded, going for the deep logs, bulldogging it like a big tuna. I felt no obstruction, but later, just four inches up from the spoon I could see how the monofilament had abraded shockingly.

It was lucky I had no idea of that at the time. Otherwise I would never have had the confidence, in the end, to put pressure on the fish and see him come up and roll five yards out in a way that said he was hard up, nearly gone. And then, with infinite care, to slide its head and shoulders out of the water.

I was still shaking when Greg arrived. By then I had given the great trout its quietus with a heavy stick. At that point, there was no way in the world that I was going to return him to the lake: it was pure atavism which made me hold him aloft and grin like a wolf as the inflatable approached shore.

Cranston was awed also. It was the biggest rainbow he had seen. For the record it was thirty inches long, seventeen inches in girth and weighed—in three sections because our scales were inadequate — a little under fifteen pounds. The odd ounces we granted it for the blood it lost in the cutting-up process, so we called it fifteen — I had no plans to enter any trophy competitions. It was a cock fish, crammed with shrimp and, for heaven's sake, chironomid pupae, smaller fish food than which can hardly be found until you get down to the diatom league. It cut as red as a salmon, and it was delicious.

It was quite a time before the weighing was done: we had waited for Mike to be ferried back first, and I could see that the same unworthy thought was crossing his mind as it was mine. So easy, it would be, to stick Charlie into the jaws of the great trout and snap the picture. Then, heigh-ho for Balmoral on the Dee! Unspoken, though, the unworthy thought passed, and then Begg was reporting on his fishing.

At the far end of the lake, he said, where the stream tumbled out, the trout were as crazy for the dry fly as they had been on Home Lake, only they were bigger. "The finest dry-fly fishing I have ever experienced!" he was babbling — but he in his turn was cut short by Greg. "Look!" he said, and there, heading toward us across the lake at taxiing speed was the floatplane. "They had binoculars on you all the time you were playing the big one," he said. "I know, because I had my glasses on them."

So we walked down to the shore, the three of us, as if it were High Noon, except that I was wearing a fishing cap with a piece chewed out of the bill by a Labrador I once owned. Then the floats were touching shore and two men got out. "Must be a pretty proud fisherman," one of them said to me. "How much did he weigh?"

From the corner of my eye, I could see Cranston glaring at me. "Five pounds," I said brassily. I got a long, cool stare. That evening, the hospitality code of the wilderness was broken: no invitation to camp was issued, no viewing of the trout permitted. The confrontation ended awkwardly and the plane left. "It'll be all over Vancouver by the weekend," Cranston mourned.

But Begg and I were already thinking of other things. We had one more full day at Don Lake and it had to be dedicated to Charlie. We would spend it, we decided, at the stream mouth rather than under the menacing cliff where the monster had hit. You could fish a week there and not see another fish like it.

Next morning it took a lot of resolution to ignore the free-rising rainbows and put on the sinking line and use Charlie, but it was done, and it worked fine. Those marvelous cold-water two- and three-pound British Columbia rainbows loved it, ate it, leapt high in the water with it, and dutifully we snapped them as they were netted and released.

It was well after midday, indeed, when the Balmoral Trout came along and hit it so hard that the rod stopped in Begg's hand as if a grizzly had come out of the willows and grabbed his wrist. A heavy, deepwater take.

There might, you think, be only two endings to the story here—the triumphant landing of Charlie's Rainbow or the tragic loss of the royal fly as the big fish parted the leader.

But neither actually happened. The reel screamed as the trout surged away. Then, suddenly, the line was slack. Begg reeled in. Charlie was still there, but he had no barb. Somehow, probably on a careless back cast, the line had dropped low and the barb must have snicked off on a stone.

In a way, though, it was an acceptable ending. Begg had a story to tell back in London. He could even present the somewhat tattered remains of Charlie to the Flyfishers' Club.

As it happened, that turned out to be impossible. Nowhere on the hallowed walls of the Flyfishers' Club will Charlie be mounted as part of the club's imposing collection of angling memorabilia, which includes the leather creel that Izaak Walton carried his catch home in. For there is a sad postscript to the story.

Mike flew back to London, picked up his car at Heathrow and drove home. He went inside for a moment, then returned to the street to unload his baggage. No baggage, no rods, no reels, *no Charlie*. London, they say, is getting as bad as New York.

So Charlie's fate will never be known. Tossed away contemptuously in some garbage can, no doubt, with other unsalable items.

I have a better theory, though, just within the realm of possibility. Charlie was thrown into a gutter, was flushed down a storm drain and fetched up in the Thames estuary where a salmon — yes, salmon are coming back to the Thames — caught the glint of its tinsel, swirled, grabbed it. . . .

Well, stranger things, indeed, have happened.

SEA-RUN ARCTIC CHAR, CRESSWELL OUTPOST,
NORTHWEST TERRITORIES

CHAPTER TWELVE

The Lady in Pink

More Canada, but much farther north now, close to the Pole, where the angler's biggest challenge is the journey itself.

ARCTIC CANADA

T HE HIGH arctic northwest of Baffin Island is a land without color. It consists mostly of gray whaleback hills rising out of a gray moraine, and the only highlights to draw the eye are the patches of snow and the occasional ice boulders, still present even in this midsummer landscape. "Canada's gulag," I told myself. "First they deep-froze it, then they photographed it in black and white." I tied a suitably somber black-bladed spoon on the line and flipped it out into the flat, gray waters of Stanwell-Fletcher Lake. The spoon had traveled to within five yards of the rocks at my feet when this pallid scene suddenly burst into color. Just as Dorothy's monochromatic Kansas whirled into the Technicolor of the Land of Oz, so now the leaden, lifeless waters of the lake blossomed into an extravaganza of silver and rose-pink.

"At last we meet, my beautiful Pink Lady!" crooned Nathaniel, our guide. The Pink Lady is a member of that sleek, mysterious, powerful race *Salvelinus alpinus*, commonly known as the Arctic char and found only in northern waters. Specifically, this lady was of the anadromous, or sea-run, manifestation of the species. And while she was a shimmering beauty, the char was shy enough — and strong enough — to have sped one hundred yards away in an instant on the six-pound-test, heading helter-skelter for the ice still out on the lake.

I found myself shaking with surprise. Not seconds ago, before the fish crashed my lure, those eight translucent feet of water that covered the dark boulders close to shore had seemed utterly empty. I estimated the char weighed around twelve pounds. That rosy flush on her sides, fading to orange on the belly, was the spawning color the fish had taken on when she entered the lake from the ocean. Yet she was no fragile beauty. As A. J. McClane, the doyen of American angling writers, says in *Game Fish of North America,* "This may be quite literally the strongest fish that swims."

It had looked for a while, though, as if I would have no chance to verify McClane's bold assessment. For nearly three days I had been socked in at Resolute Bay by freezing rain and fog. This bay is not capriciously named; it is an outpost of 130 indeed resolute individuals, 625 miles inside the Arctic Circle and about 262 miles short of the magnetic North Pole.

There at the Narwhal Hotel—a facility that had unmistakably started life as a couple of Quonset huts—others were also on hold. Among them: the crew of a Royal Canadian Air Force ice patrol; a group of tin miners waiting to fly into some unimaginable workings farther north; and one scholarly looking, silent man assumed by all to be attached to a Canadian-U.S. Star Wars project rumored to exist nearby.

Once there had been a bar at the Narwhal; an upstairs room still bore the legend THE RESOLUTE BAY YACHT CLUB. But "the privilege was abused," said a member of the hotel staff primly, "and it was closed down." Thus the wildest moment of excitement during my stay at the Narwhal came when a tomato blossom was discovered on a plant that grew in a hydroponic tank. "Unreal! Unreal!" gasped a corporal in the Mounties, the law in these parts.

Meanwhile I pondered the prospect, should I ever get out of Resolute, of meeting both an extraordinary family of Inuit—or Eskimos—and an extraordinary species of fish. The two groups happened to coexist at Creswell Bay Outpost Camp, on Somerset Island, a spot so remote that it made Resolute seem like a Club Med. At Creswell Bay would be found, I was told, one of the last families of the Inuit to still live year-round in the wilderness. It was also classic Arctic char country. Five miles of wild river linked the bay with Stanwell-Fletcher Lake, a thirty-mile-wide body of water. According to the map, extending from the far side of the lake was an unnamed stream where the char would mass for spawning.

It was noon, and outside the window of the Narwhal, the thermometer registered twenty-nine degrees. Ten feet beyond, the world was lost in cotton candy. Unless the fog cleared soon, this expedition would be over before it had started. Just as all conversation threatened to die, a tin miner suddenly yelled, "They're talking about a clearance around four o'clock!" Three hours later I was loading rod cases, tackle boxes and boil-in-the-bag Chicken Kiev into the chartered Twin Otter. In another hour the Otter was squealing to a high-tailed halt one hundred fifty empty miles away at Creswell Bay.

Historians tell us that the first serious misunderstanding between a European and the Inuit happened in 1576 when an irascible English explorer named Martin Frobisher sailed into what is now Frobisher Bay, under the impression that he had discovered the fabled Northwest Passage. He encountered problems with the locals that culminated when one of them "hurte the Generall in the Buttocke with an arrow."

As we jumped down from the Otter, I determined to be somewhat more diplomatic than Frobisher. I had been thoroughly lectured on the subject of the local people while in Resolute. "The Inuit are great guides, born guides," I was told by an Arctic veteran. "They'll stay out all day and night with you until you get your char or your caribou because it is regarded as shameful to come home without the quarry. But sport fishing they just do not comprehend at all. If you need to own some fish, they reason, they would be happy to net some for you. And don't let them see you release fish. It actually makes them angry, though that's hard to tell because they never shout. They always speak in a flat monotone, which evolved out of the necessity of living harmoniously as part of a big family cooped up in the dark for half of every year in a kitchen-sized igloo made out of tundra sod."

All this I recalled on the beach at Creswell Bay, where the Inuit patriarch, Timothy Idlout, and his wife, Nungat, their daughter Martha and son-in-law Nathaniel Kalluk awaited us, as did the characteristic detritus of an Arctic beach. There were the flayed carcasses of two beluga whales and enough empty fifty-gallon diesel oil drums to have fueled D-Day. The Arctic, it seems, is where fuel drums come to die.

Nathaniel, fluent in English, would be our guide, but first there had to be a ritual conversation with Timothy, translated by his daughter. "Of course the fish are here," Timothy said through Martha, surprised by our naiveté. "They come every year." He leaned forward and spoke again in Inuktitut. "He says," Martha translated, "you must cook the red ones, but try the gray fish raw." The gray fish are the yet-to-spawn char; the "red ones" are the males in scarlet spawning dress and the brilliant pink spawning females. Timothy continued: if we found it hard to catch char with the fishing rods we had brought, he said, he and his son-in-law could spear them in abundance in the river with the traditional *kakivak*, or gather them from the sea with the family net. Through Martha, we declined with thanks. Timothy giggled. "He thinks," said his daughter shyly, "that going after the fish with a rod is a little bit foolish."

Nathaniel rigged up living quarters on the beach for the six of us in the fishing party—three ancient, wood-framed tents. When we asked Nathaniel where we would be fishing, he pointed right in front of our camp. "High tide is the time," he said. "In a couple of hours from now. I'll be back." And off he roared on his three-wheel ATV to Creswell Bay Outpost Camp, about a quarter of a mile down the beach.

When Nathaniel returned, he had brought his boat, an aluminum craft with an outboard motor. "I thought we'd be fishing right here," I said.

"You are," said Nathaniel. "I need the boat to run my net out."

Remember Frobisher, I told myself. Carefully I explained that I thought perhaps a net would interfere with the rod fishing. Nathaniel looked at me. "You don't have to worry," he said. Then he leapt into his boat and began paying out the nylon net for fifty yards in a line from the beach, the white styrofoam floats bobbing on the gray surface. I began casting. Nothing hit my lures and it all seemed a little farcical, when, halfway along the net, the floats went into wild commotion. A patrol of char, working along the shoreline, had hit the entangling mesh in a silver explosion. We kept casting. Nothing. Then the net exploded again. And a third time.

At last I understood. "We're fishing on the wrong side of the net," I said, feeling stupid. "The fish are coming the other way." Nathaniel nodded in cheerful agreement.

Our group of five anglers moved a mere fifty yards to the east, and for the next two hours around the top of the tide, char hit our spoons. They ranged from four pounds to sixteen, and all fought like tigers, as advertised. They were all business, with none of the jumping or tailwalking of their trout and salmon relatives; instead they showed a steadfast refusal to give in to the pressure of the line—with sudden interruptions of powerful runs. The char were silver-gray, dappled with faintest pink and entirely beautiful. When we had landed them, we found they were stuffed, literally to the gills, with tiny, shrimplike creatures.

Nathaniel hauled in his net, so teeming with char that it took him an hour to clear it. I knew that gillnetting had already left some of the great char waters to the south barren and that the frontier of the species was being pushed relentlessly northward. But my immediate concerns were allayed when I was told this was not Nathaniel's regular practice. Today he was stocking up for the winter, and would cut a hole in the permafrost and freeze the fish. I think, too, that Nathaniel wanted to prove something. He had. We now knew that Creswell Bay was crammed with char.

Happily we kept proving that point over the next few days. But a further call beckoned: to set out for Stanwell-Fletcher Lake and that unnamed river on the map to try to find "the red ones" at the place where the char's spawning journey ended. Like the Pacific salmon's, the Arctic char's spawning livery is brilliant. But unlike Pacific salmon, the char does not die grotesquely misshapen and diseased at the end of the spawning run. The spawning char remain shapely, their color ranging from pink to vivid scarlet. These fish are a rare and spectacular trophy. Tomorrow, Nathaniel said, we would attempt to go upriver to seek them out.

That night a wind sprang up from the north with freezing rain and snow flurries that drove through the manifold fissures and rents in my ancient tent. To my personal research dossier I could add that for sheer, quintessential, miserable cold, nothing compares with being wrapped in a soaking wet musk-ox robe at three o'clock of an Arctic morning. After my tent roof collapsed, I spent the rest of the night in the commissary tent, cuddled up to a mound of freeze-dried Salisbury steak.

In the morning we started upriver with Nathaniel's smaller boat, forced to haul it by rope through the turbulent waters of high tide. We trudged along shore and had made less than a mile when the boat's stern swung toward midstream, caught a heavy current and dragged us toward the river. It was an equal contest as to which would get us first, the boiling current or hypothermia. It was luck that swept the boat into a slack eddy instead of downriver.

But the old craft had taken some knocks and now was taking on water. Nathaniel announced he would have to take it back to the outpost for repair. "I'll be back for you in a short time," he said. "Stay and fish. There's plenty here." He demonstrated with his *kaki vak*, spearing two char at once. I told Nathaniel I would accompany him while the others stayed to fish.

As we reached the outpost, two wild-eyed teenagers met us on the beach. They were Peter and David, Timothy's youngest sons, who lived alone on the far side of the river. Their shouted news—in Inuktitut—caused Nathaniel to run for his cabin. He emerged with an ancient brass spyglass and climbed to the roof, where he lay prone, focusing the glass out to sea. "Narwhal," he said. "The boys saw two narwhal in the bay."

Though I had never seen one, I knew that the male narwhal is that spectacular species of whale that, like a kind of marine unicorn, bears a single long twisted tusk projecting from its head. Before the Marine Mammal Protection Act of 1972 forbade their import into the U.S., just two of those ivory spears would have fetched enough to keep Creswell Bay Outpost in snowmobile fuel for a decade. Even now a spear brings around $500—more than enough to secure the undivided attention of Nathaniel. Moreover, eight or so properly butchered narwhals would provide enough red meat to feed his dog team through the entire winter. (The hunting of narwhals is not forbidden in Canada to the Inuit.)

Nathaniel stayed on the roof for more than two hours. Then he came down and said, "Let's go look for them at sea." I reminded him that we'd left the others, hours earlier, up on the river. Nathaniel stared at me as if at an idiot child. "Narwhal in the bay," he said.

We motored out to sea. Nathaniel watched intently for two more hours until he decided that the whales had left. We returned to the outpost, and I presumed the day was now shot. Tomorrow we had to leave; the beautiful pink fish of the lake would not be ours. But I had not taken into consideration the obverse side of Inuit psychology, the side that keeps them going indefatigably when there is a serious hunting or fishing objective. "Let's go to the lake," said Nathaniel. "The tide will be better now. It will help us." We rejoined the others. The trek upriver with the boat was indeed easier now, with the high tide holding up the water, but even so the five-mile push upstream was long and arduous. It was five o'clock before Stanwell-Fletcher gleamed in front of us, lying among bleak hills.

We all climbed into the boat and set a course for the unnamed river, still twenty-seven miles away on the far side of the lake. Soon we had the first intimation of further trouble—an odd tinkling music. The water became increasingly full of what looked like tiny crystal boats, broken ice fragments that, farther along, turned into an ice sheet. This year, we now saw with chagrin, there was no full melting of the ice on the lake. We would never reach the spawning grounds, and, it seemed, we would have no shot at a char in its brilliant wedding regalia.

But Nathaniel brought the boat alongside a rocky point. "We could try along the shoreline," he said. We scrambled out, looked around at those frozen monochrome barrens and began casting. "Canada's gulag," I said to myself. And then, in that flash of color, I met the Pink Lady.

I'll never know whether it was by pure luck or by Nathaniel's brilliant guidance that we had hit on the chief freeway used by the char to migrate to the far side of the lake. Mostly we hooked the gray char, recently arrived from the sea, but occasionally there came a male in vivid scarlet livery. Oddly, though, there was just one Pink Lady and no more.

But, perhaps, with such an elusive prize, one is enough.

DRUM SHOAL, OCRACOKE ISLAND, NORTH CAROLINA

CHAPTER THIRTEEN

The Once and Future Island

Time, perhaps, to head south again, and Ocra-
coke on the Outer Banks of North Carolina seems to make sense
as a stopover. There, though, the territorial imperative rears its
ugly head again as anglers move in by the truckload when the red
drum are running.

OCRACOKE,
NORTH CAROLINA

RUDY AUSTIN, bearded like General Grant and built like a scaled-down Hulk Hogan, eased back in his chair and gave the matter further thought. "Mostly," he said judiciously, "we call it Drum Shoal. But it has been called Vera Cruz Shoal, on account of a boat sunk there, the ol' *Vera Cruz*. But the original boat that went down there was the ol' *Albatross*."

Austin was talking on a mild, black-velvet midnight in a cottage on Ocracoke Island, on the Outer Banks of North Carolina, and the later it got, the more Rudy's voice took on the rich, creamy burr that is the inheritance of more than three centuries of Austins on the island. I dragged him back to the subject at hand—the youngest island in America, Vera Cruz Shoal, where I had just enjoyed the finest surf-fishing ever. "When did it first come out from under the water?" I asked him.

It wasn't Austin who answered me, but his friend Peter Nelson Stone. "It was always a shallow place," Stone said. "That's why all them boats wrecked on it. Just misread your chart a little and you was right up on it. Even in '75, when I first got here in the Coast Guard, there was a shoal abuilding and we was always getting calls from boats that had bottomed out on it.

"But it never come out of the water till '79," Stone went on. "And it'll disappear again just as fast. Last June it was as big as ever I seen it, half a mile long, like a big, long hook jutting out. But it's starting to go now. That Hurricane Gloria really did the damage, sliced it in two. Now we don't know if it'll build up again or wash away. If it does go, though, it won't be forever. . . ." Brigadoon Island, I thought.

"Hey, you really hit that little island hot, didn't you," said Austin. "You caught them real high tides coming off the new moon, big run of fish and you had it a few days all to yourself. What was it you got? More'n fifty drum? That was great."

It was not only great but something of a miracle. These days the two biggest runs in the American angling year consist not of fish but of fishermen. In April and then again in November you'll see them converge, from every part of the nation, upon the coast of North Carolina. All of them are in search of the handsome fish called the channel bass in the Northeast, the red drum in the Middle Atlantic states and the redfish from Georgia on south. The Southern usage is gaining in popularity, thanks to the growing taste across the country for Cajun cooking and one of its premier dishes, blackened redfish. In the spring and fall, long convoys of four-by-fours, surf rods mounted over the front fenders like strange weapons, roll down Route 158 from Kitty Hawk to Hatteras Island. It makes it seem as though this part of North Carolina is being invaded by guerrillas from the People's Army for the Liberation of the Outer Banks.

There are about seventy-five miles of beach on the Outer Banks, but only a fraction of them are fish-attracting spots, and these bear the brunt of the invasion. As you fight to find fishing room, you notice how the whole migration seems to have taken on the aspect of a paramilitary operation. It's impossible to fathom why, when they are seeking a fish that swims in turbulent, cloudy surf one hundred yards off the beach at night, many anglers feel the need to wear camouflage coveralls, and even harder to figure out why there is a growing fashion for camouflaged vehicles.

So, considering the population influx, I was not expecting great fishing on the Banks. I planned to spend several days fishing off Ocracoke before heading for the Georgia coast, where, I had heard, there would be less-crowded fishing. Because Ocracoke is accessible only by boat from Hatteras, I assumed I would find much smaller crowds there than elsewhere on the Banks. At least that had been the case in the past.

It was not so this time. The three o'clock ferry was boarded by a horde of camouflaged guerrillas who leaned their elbows on the hoods of their four-by-fours, chomped on gum or tobacco and stared across the water at the low profile of Ocracoke. Though it is about seventeen miles long, Ocracoke has only two real drum hotspots, and even twenty anglers would overwhelm them. That left me with just one possibility—a boat.

That evening, after settling into the cottage I had rented, I walked to Ocracoke's fountain of fishing knowledge, the Lakeside tackle shop, to find a boat and skipper. The shop is run by Sharon Miller along the lines of a rustic general store. All you have to do there is sit and listen, and you will find out as much as anybody on the island about where the fish are. On this evening, it wasn't very much. That is until the door opened and Sharon's husband came in.

Norman Miller is not your typical easygoing Ocracokian. He comes from a harder line, having grown up on Chesapeake Bay, and the silences into which he sometimes lapses are strange, introspective and uncomfortable. Not comfortable, either, is the way he fishes his thirty-six-foot charter boat, *Rascal*. The Atlantic off Ocracoke is a crazy pattern of white water, with steep seas breaking unpredictably over shallow banks, and it is in the midst of this that Miller likes to anchor. Still, he has earned an unassailable reputation as the best red drum skipper in the U.S. There is never any shortage of people waiting to sign up to go out with Miller. Indeed, you have to book months ahead, which was why I knew that my best shot on Ocracoke—to fish with Norman—was a feeble one.

Extraordinarily, I got lucky. Miller said he had a cancellation for the following Wednesday. That left me with two days to fill. I asked Miller if it was worthwhile to fish the surf off the island.

"Don't know nothin' about the surf," he said characteristically.

Sharon gave him a look. "What about the sandspit?" she said.

"Sandspit?" I asked.

"It's a tiny little island," she said, "that came out of the sea a while back."

"Don't know if anybody goes out there now," said Miller. "The last load of guys got into trouble, sank their boats."

"I could ask Rudy if he'll take you," said Sharon. She reached for the phone.

And so it was that the following perfect, opalescent morning I slid over the side of Rudy Austin's little boat and waded ashore on the sheltered side of Drum Shoal or Vera Cruz Shoal, an islet too young to know its own name. It briefly occurred to me that I could end up in some kind of Robinson Crusoe fix. To the east, the next landfall would be some three thousand miles away, roughly, at Casablanca, Morocco. To the west, a mere twenty-minute boat ride away, was the low silhouette of Ocracoke.

I looked around. It was low tide, but at high water on a rough day, I thought, the sea must break over the bank. Sweating, half-trudging, half-trotting as fast as my clumsy chest-waders would let me, I made my way across the spit to the seaward side, where the surf roared.

Surf? I wondered what surf was doing out here, with no wind to build it and the island beaches so calm. But then I realized that these waves were not the offspring of local wind but were engendered by ocean swells that hit the first shallow ground of the continent here. I moved into the turmoil cautiously, wading thirty, forty yards out as the water rose knee-, waist-, then chest-high. Then I waded cross-tide until I found myself knee-deep again. I was standing on a sand ridge that gave me casting command over a corridor of water that the smooth, green and unbroken swell indicated to be deep. It was what surf fishermen call a slough and pronounce "slew," a fish-holding trench. It was just what I needed.

I moved into the familiar pattern of surfcasting—legs straddled against the push of the tide, shoulders rocking to let the streamlined sinker swing behind me in a pendulum motion until enough power had built to compress the carbon fibers of the twelve-foot beach rod into a mighty spring. Then I released that spring, sending the sinker and cut-mullet bait far into the green water of the slough.

In orthodox drum fishing, this is the point at which the bait is allowed to settle, the rod is placed in a plastic sand spike and the cooler, probably camouflaged, is dragged out for lunch. Instead, I carefully reeled in my slack line, taking up the tension on the sinker. For some reason, from the very moment I had landed on the island I had convinced myself that I would hit a fish on my first cast. And after no more than three or four minutes of looking out over the heaving gray sea, brown pelicans flapping low over the water, there came, in glorious affirmation of my hunch, a brutal wrench on the line. My rod had taken on a battle curve, and one hundred yards away I could feel the beginning of the courageous, head-down, slugging resistance that a redfish of even eight pounds, which was what this one turned out to be, can offer. It was two battles, really; the second one started up the minute I thought I had won the fight, just as the fish rolled at my side, defeated. It was at that moment that it changed its mind and decided to head for Casablanca.

That fish was the first of many. Through flood and ebb tides over the next two days, the surf around the new island was full of eager war parties of school drum, some of the fish weighing as much as fifteen pounds.

By the second morning I had scaled my tackle down from the standard heavy artillery used for drum—the forty-pound-test line and eight-ounce sinkers—to fourteen-pound-test and three-ounce sinkers on a limber rod. This rig wouldn't hold a forty-pounder, but it was perfect for the fish I wanted. By the end of the second day, I had landed more than thirty. Only a couple ended up as broiled fillets; the rest I released, and they kicked away to liberty in an explosion of sand.

The third day was the one I thought I had been waiting for—the day I would go out aboard Miller's *Rascal*. Normally, that would have been a royal treat. But after the superb fishing out on the young island, it was merely an interlude I was eager to have done with. We took the same route to sea I had with Austin, for Miller had elected to anchor and fish on the seaward side of the surf that broke on what I now regarded as my island. I kept a lookout as the barely perceptible shadow of the island began to show.

What I saw reminded me of the scene from an old Western, the one where the wagon train moves into the gully and, one by one, Apache warbonnets break the smooth pattern of the horizon. As we swung by the island, I saw, gradually revealed, a line of surfcasters staked out across my beach.

Although my fishing diary for that day shows that all five of the fish I took from *Rascal* were bigger than anything I had landed from the island beach and were topped by a forty-pound-plus specimen, I can barely recall catching them. All I could think of was that my island had been invaded. Later, hanging his head a little, Austin would semiconfess, "I told a guy over to Buxton, and he must of passed the word around."

I knew the invaders would be back the next day, and I couldn't hold the whole island. But I could defend my slough, the best piece of beach, which was no more than twenty feet across, if I got to the island early. I set it up with Austin. And the next morning, for a couple of hours at least, it was like old times—just me and my island. Indeed I had landed my fifth drum before I saw the raiding party swarming ashore on the sheltered side.

It seemed to be highly organized. A beachhead was quickly established with a pile of multicolored coolers, sand spikes and rod cases. Then the faster-moving among them headed for the surf.

But they were moving to the wrong end of the islet. I knew that because I had earlier investigated that area. There was a sweep of tide there, and they wouldn't be able to hold ground with their sinkers, or not for long, anyway. As I watched them, I again felt the hit of a red drum and my rod doubled over. I doubled over, too, my back to the invaders. If I was lucky, I thought, they might believe I was hauling in a bunch of seaweed.

I wasn't lucky. I saw that immediately. Arms were raised and fingers were pointed. And now the entire line began slowly shuffling toward me. The nearest angler was still fifty yards away, but I could foresee how a small party might detach itself and move in on my far side to complete a pincer movement. So steaming hot was my paranoia that I didn't realize until much later that my actual fish score that morning was proving to be even better than that of the previous days.

Nor did I notice that the wind had begun to shift to the east and the sky to darken. What *did* register was that the fishing began to slow up, which proved that red drum were better at forecasting a sideswipe from Hurricane Kate than was the All Weather Radio from Hatteras.

In the meantime, Austin's Ocracokian weather antennae were at work, too. Our arrangement had been for him to pick me up at four o'clock, but three hours earlier than that I saw the white hull of his boat approaching. I also noticed that at least half of the guerrillas had quit fishing and were gathered around the two boats that had brought them across. I started to pack up. Rudy would not have come over early just for fun. I trudged across the island. On a dropping tide, it was a three-hundred-yard trip.

I would never have thought I could feel sympathy for the interlopers, but I did now. One of their boats was already high and dry, and its crew tried desperately and uselessly to haul it into the water through soft sand. I lent them a shoulder, and when I looked at their faces I discovered that they were not depraved storm troopers on the rampage but actually quite ordinary people. Some weren't even wearing camouflage.

Now, though, Austin shouted to me to wade out as far as I could in the increasing chop. I made it to the stern, threw my rod in the boat, and wriggled over after it. We pulled offshore a little ways, then both of us uttered the same thought: "What should we do about these guys?" One of their boats was now afloat and loaded. But the other guerrillas — no, fishermen — stood disconsolately around their stranded craft. "I can take just three of you with your gear," shouted Rudy over the wind. Holding their rods clear of the water, a hastily selected trio boarded our boat. The others faced a night on the island waiting for a new tide to lift off their boat. I savored no victory, as I might have a day earlier. I just hoped the marooned ones had bait.

By now, the normally calm waters inside Ocracoke Sound were a maelstrom and the rain had arrived; visibility was down to a few hundred yards as we started to cross. On the way home, we took two more small boats into our convoy. It was Rudy's moment of glory. "If you want Ocracoke, fall in behind me!" he roared majestically across the turbulent ocean. Less stirring remarks have become naval history.

That night in my cottage, as the winds of Kate beat up on the island, I savored the thought of my catch — close to fifty fish by the end — and talked with Austin and Miller about the miraculous little island, its birth and probable fate. For a while my paranoia had dissipated. When word got round of the stranded fishermen, I might even have the island to myself again next year. Unless, magically and mysteriously, on a full-moon midnight, Drum Shoal slips under the waves before I can return.

BONEFISHING, TURKS AND CAICOS ISLANDS, B.W.I.

CHAPTER FOURTEEN

The Provo Proviso

When the following was written, the tiny island of Providenciales—which was called Blue Hills until the property developers decided that a Spanish name might sound more chic—was still, very largely, pristine. Since then, though, things have changed. Club Med has moved in, and also an "international" airport; and there has been an ugly drug scandal involving the government of the Turks and Caicos. Nevertheless, I like to think that the ultimate bonefish flat is still there.

TURKS & CAICOS ISLANDS, BRITISH WEST INDIES

THIS starry winter's night the two of us were sitting in the bar of the Third Turtle Inn, Providenciales, Turks and Caicos Islands, one of the few remaining fragments of the British West Indies, a necklace of cays and islands and just over seven thousand people hung south of the Bahamas and one hundred miles north of Haiti. This was our fourth night there, the air soft, warm, tranquil, our mood quietly euphoric.

"Tomorrow, then," said Art, "we head out there again with the fly rods."

"The fly rods only," I concurred.

"They are going to climb all over those flies," said Art. He had made that remark several times that evening.

"But we take it steadily," I said, repeating another of the evening's themes. "One man casts, lands his fish. Then the other takes over in the bow."

"Better still," said Art, "you take the boat and maroon me. Leave me on a sandspit and I'll ambush 'em as they come by. Later we can switch."

We stood up, yawning. "No more tonight, Frank," I said virtuously to the advancing barman. "We have a big day ahead of us tomorrow."

You may recall that some years back there was a cult among surfers—a search for the Perfect Wave. I never heard the outcome of that. But here in the Turks and Caicos, after a mere four days of searching, Art and I had our hands on just as glittering a Grail. We believed we had located the Ultimate Bonefish Flat.

Plenty of people had had the chance of discovering it before us, from Ponce de Leon on. (He arrived in the islands in 1512, but some think Columbus got there ahead of him.) The Lucayan Indians might have fished there before the Spaniards shipped them out to work the mines of Hispaniola. The early colonists from Bermuda, followed by Loyalists from Georgia and the Carolinas who fled to the islands after the Revolutionary War, were more interested in salt production than bonefish. The present-day islanders, mainly descendants of slaves, go after bonefish all right, but our treasured flat was far from any of their settlements.

So the discovery had been left for Art and me, representatives of the latest wave of invaders the islands had seen—cosseted, airborne pleasure-seekers from the West, though we did not consider ourselves tourists but serious researchers. Months before, poring over marine charts, we had felt the kind of triumph that industrial geologists must feel when, from theoretical evidence alone, they pinpoint a vast oil deposit below the ocean bed.

Those charts had bellowed *bonefish*! The islands form a rough crescent embracing a vast area of shallows and flats, two thousand square miles altogether, and much more water than land, an enormous, bountiful area to fish, much of it, inevitably, virgin.

Probably the serious way to investigate such richness would be with a houseboat as a base, and a shallow-draft skiff to probe the creeks and channels. But that would have called for a prodigal investment of time of the kind that few anglers, since Zane Grey, anyway, are able to afford. A lightning strike would be all that we could manage. So we headed for Providenciales—as nobody actually calls it.

In the past, it had been Blue Hills, an island once notorious for its wreckers who hoisted lights to lure sailing vessels onto the rocks. Then, when modest development took place—some villas, a couple of hotels, a landing strip and a dock—it was rechristened Providenciales, maybe because that sounded more chic. Swiftly, though, it was anglicized to Provo. Now it is less than chic to call it anything else.

We arrived in Provo just before dark. A black squall was sweeping across the west of the island, and for a minute or two the eight-seater Beechcraft was driving through blinding rain. But then we were out of it and landing in the last of the sunshine. All the way down from Miami there had been thunderheads and patches of low, thick cloud over the Bahamas. Winter cold fronts heading south. "Don't worry," Art said. "All these fronts dwindle to nothing before they hit Provo."

After dinner on our first night, it seemed that he might be right. From horizon to horizon the sky blazed with stars. We stood on a wooden bridge spanning a cut of water in the little marina outside the Third Turtle. A dock light shone down, picking out a dozen mangrove snappers lying head-to-tide. Then a big fish was sidling into the clear patch. Slender, forked tail. . . . "Hey!" Art whispered, "*bonefish!*"

Dammit, they were right there in the hotel! Later, in the bar, a guest confided that, yes, he'd been out that afternoon and he'd got fifteen bones in an hour and a half. No calculator was needed to figure that this meant seeing, casting to, hooking and landing a fish every six minutes. Those bones could not have been very big. But who cared? Wasn't that the pattern in this area? Small fish but plenty of them. Deprived of bonefishing for many months, our appetites were as undiscriminating as a tiger shark's.

So in next morning's predawn blackness it was with a miserable sinking of the heart that we heard the small-arms rattle of rain on the windows and the wind howling in the bush. "Nobody informed that front that it was supposed to dwindle," I told Art.

There seemed no need to hurry. As we sat at breakfast, the sky was still a mess of tattered clouds, and surf boomed on the reef a mile offshore. Only the fact that this was our first morning made us consider going to sea at all. And it turned out to be the first time that either of us had been bused to a bonefish flat.

The rain was a result of a norther, coming right onto the shoreline where the hotel stood. Though the reef gave partial protection, there was still a lot of rough water to be crossed before we got into shelter, maybe twenty minutes of wet, bouncy ride. But delicate creatures like Art and me, the management had decided, should be spared this.

So the guide took the boat alone and we were loaded onto a pickup for twenty minutes of dry, bouncy ride all the way to Leeward Going Through, the sea passage off the northeast end of Provo. There, waiting for us with the boat, was Lemuel Stubbs.

A name with a fine eighteenth-century ring to it, and well in character. Not far from where we stood on the little quay there was a small island named Stubbs Cay and a gap in the reef called Stubbs Cut, named for some salty ancestor of Lemuel's who had hauled so many crawfish out of the rocks there that he had a kind of title to it. This latest Stubbs, square-cut, a little dour-looking perhaps, a man not inclined to speak unless he had something to say, seemed well in the tradition.

Some fishing guides are arrogant. Art and I would be spending several days in Lemuel's company and he in ours. It was natural for us to give some time to mutual summing up. Lemuel led with the first test question. "Bring your own tackle?" he inquired.

"Well, some people is beginners," he apologized when he saw our gear. "They aren't fishermen, but they want to catch a bonefish. So I takes 'em to the mud."

No mud fishers we, he was assured. For us, the classic stalk on the flats. To start with, we'd fool around with six-pound spinning outfits, just to get our eyes accustomed to sighting fish, just to get the feel of a bone on the end of a line again. Then we would switch to fly-fishing. "All right," said Lemuel briefly. We headed out along a dark, deep channel until the flats were plainly in view.

For a time, maybe for an hour, there is no necessity for bonefish to be present on a bonefish flat, especially on your first trip in a long time. The pleasure of poling along the flats is enough in itself. You see boxfish moving clumsily out of the way of the boat, barracudas hanging like poised spears, great rays churning clouds of white mud. Later, though, with no bones showing up, you start getting restless.

And on this first day out with Lemuel, he was restless long before we were. To start with, the visibility was poor—too much movement on the wind-stirred water, the sun breaking through only occasionally. "See, today, with the bad weather," Lemuel said, "this was the only place I could bring you. And this ain't the best of places."

On the horizon we saw a white boat, a twenty-footer it appeared to be, heading in. "Man," Lemuel said, "that boat going to be *filled* with bonefish. They been out on the *mud*." Fishing blind, that is, into the smoky-white patches of mud stirred up by shoals of small bones in the deeper water outside the flats. *Fifteen bonefish in an hour and a half!* Of course, that guest in the Third Turtle had stacked up his score in the mud. "If you want, I can take you to the mud," Lemuel said. It was another test question. We set his mind at rest. No mud fishers we.

The white boat came by us, the crowd aboard waving happily. "Tourists," Art snarled, failing to raise his arm. For a while we fished on, but it was hopeless. On the way home we cast MirrOlures into the deep channel in case one of the resident tarpon was in a questing mood. Only a big horse-eye jack showed interest but turned away when he saw the boat.

"What I'm going to do," Lemuel said, "is, when we get ashore, I'm going to drag the boat out, hook up on the Jeep and take her right over the south side. That will take me the afternoon. Tomorrow we'll fish in the lee of the wind on the other side of the island."

That evening in the hotel, Art and I could have done with T shirts with something like WE DON'T FISH THE MUD emblazoned on them. The innocents who had been out in the big boat didn't understand concepts like wind and visibility. "I caught *four*," caroled a plump lady as we dourly sipped our drinks at the bar. She got about half a thin smile. At dinner Art dealt with his grouper fillet with silent, savage intensity. We went to bed early.

The sky looked better next morning. The wind was down, too, and over on the south side of the island the water shimmered. For half an hour we ran along small, perfect beaches, the sand white as bleached bone, and low cliffs tunneled with caves. Ospreys soared over us. Only puffs of white, fair-weather cumulus hung in the sky. The cliffs gave way to low ground and then we were into bonefish country again.

That second day we did a little better. One place, especially, an indented bay of white sand, held a school of a dozen good fish, and it was possible to slip out of the boat and stalk them. For the moment it was enough to see the fish turn in unison at the one-eighth-ounce pink shrimp that I flipped just ahead of them, follow it toward me and the leader of the shoal take it firmly. After that the well-remembered, endless wail of the drag, the rod held high to keep the line from rough patches of bottom.

That first bone was a six-pounder. In the next hour, three more fish hit and were landed. All of good size: these were clearly not the small fish in big schools that one finds in many places in the Bahamas. It all looked promising, but from then on we ran out of sightings. Maybe it was the turn of the tide that did it.

"You ever talk with Tommy Coleman?" Lemuel said on the way home. "He used to have a bonefish camp, private little bonefish camp, on the south side here. Lives on Parrot Cay now. Used to fish all the time."

"Maybe it wouldn't hurt to talk to Tommy," Art said.

"You still have plenty of time left to fish," said Lemuel. "Tommy knows a lot. I could take you over tomorrow."

Coleman, in his fifties, baked brown, was, he proudly told us next day, an ol' Florida cracker from Saint Cloud, twenty years out from home via Nassau and the Exumas. "I'm the only man I know," he said, "that called it quits at the age of thirty. With no money. But I made it so far. I was thirty-one when I hit Nassau, and I'm still fishing for my frying pan."

He sat in his rocking chair as if it were a throne, and indeed he was king of his small island domain. United Parrot Republic, said a coat of arms on the wall. Fittingly, also, at first he talked about treasure, not fish.

"Most of the treasure 'round hereabouts," he said, "come after that slaves' uprising in Haiti. 'Bout 1800, was it? All them French plantation owners came here. Real rich. All this fancy silver and gold. Buried it when they come ashore. But *my* treasure, it came from ol' King Christophe. He built himself a retreat here, and he reckoned, if the French ever kicked him out of Haiti, he was going to come pick up his treasure and head to New Orleans. Now for sixteen years I was looking for it. I used to bum a ride from the Exumas and walk the shore. Then about six years ago, well, hell, here was the treasure. Matter of fact, it was a fellow over from Provo that found the first gold coin. So, man, I got my buddies together, we got one of them metal finders and we went over and we dug a place. It was all scattered, the box was all broke up. But it was there."

Naturally, Tommy told us, he had put it back exactly where he found it. "Do I want the government to come to me? Taxes? Claims? Man, forget it. It's still buried where it was." He looked at us unflinchingly.

Provo and the cays around it might well be hip-deep in treasure. It is no legend that Teach and Morgan quartered there and so did those two demonic women pirates, Ann Bonny and Mary Read. The Spanish treasure ships used to come out of Port of Spain, Trinidad and use the deep Caicos passage to clear the Indies. Provo was a perfect ambush point. Parrot, as in Parrot Cay, is a corruption of pirate.

Art and I were concerned with a different kind of treasure, though. We steered Tommy onto fish.

"Bonefish?" he said dreamily, his mind perhaps still on the treasure. "Listen, I *eat* a thirty-pound bonefish one time. Well, I *helped* t'eat him. That was in Mayaguana, fifty miles from here. Listen, they've had them here, twenty pounds, in the seine nets. Never on a line. Biggest one I ever caught here, listen, I didn't weigh him because I had to *eat* him. 'Bout ten years ago I built a camp, real, real pretty, over the western end of Provo. And when I was building it I had this boat anchored there, and me and the troops were sleeping on this boat, working, building things, and I thought I'd go catch a bit of fish for supper. I walked back and I saw a creek there, a hole. So I took my rod and threw my feather across it. And man, he had it! And I caught him! I said to this man on the boat, 'What he weigh?' And he says, 'Listen, man, that thing is fifteen pounds!' But there weren't no road going over the island then, so I can't get him to a freezer, ship him to the States. So I was just stuck, eating the biggest damn bonefish I ever caught!"

We listened reverently to all this. "Fifteen pounds," Art said. "That's close to the record."

"World's record from someplace in Africa, ain't it?" Tommy said. "The record up around here is about sixteen pounds, ain't it? Caught up in Bimini. But the world's record, nineteen pounds, come out of Africa. Listen, we had a fellow here, Reindeer Sturges, he's one of the best bonefishermen in the world. But he don't write about it. He just goes bonefishing. Where there's bonefishing, he goes. He swears that the world's record will come from that place down there." Tommy's brown thumb jerked to the south.

Lemuel had been listening attentively to all this. He looked where the thumb was pointing. "Ocean Hole?"

"Right," said Tommy. "Ocean Hole, south of Grand Caicos. Supposed to be bottomless but it's three hundred feet. Big black hole in the bank. North of there is the bonefish flats. Some of them flats ain't never seen a feather."

From then on, there was no possibility that Art and I would head anywhere other than the Ocean Hole, even though, Lemuel explained, it was a two-hour run from the Third Turtle Inn. We left Tommy Coleman to his treasure and his kingdom. We had preparations to make.

Next morning, at five o'clock, I was listening anxiously for the patter of rain, for the wind to spring up. But the weather held. The sun was strong when we slipped out of the marina for the long haul south and east. The trip was strangely like climbing one of those hills when, every time you reach what you think is the crest, another is rising ahead of you. In the distance there would be the faint smudge of a cay. We would come up to it, then see that beyond it was another cay. Then another. It was the full two hours and more before we moved inshore again to the Promised Land.

It was good, almost from the beginning. At the first flat, Lemuel switched off the motor, picked up the pole and scattered a shoal of bonefish that must have just moved out of the deep. The only thing to complain of was the bottom. Mostly it was dark, making it a little difficult to spot fish. Nevertheless, there were abundant bonefish there and of a high average size, four pounds and upward. Upward to what? Eight or nine pounds, possibly. Tommy Coleman had probably eaten the bigger ones.

"Three years since I been here," Lemuel said suddenly as we poled along. "You ever hear of a man, Ted Williams? A sport player? I didn't know who he was till they told me. Good fisherman. He didn't want no mud holes, either." He gave one of his short, rare laughs. "He did some fly-fishing but not out here at the Hole."

Art and I had our fly rods in the boat, but so far we had not picked them up. It was a long time since we had met bonefish. Humanly enough, perhaps, we were settling for quicker action with the spinning rods and the lures. "Maybe after lunch we'll do a little fly casting," Art said.

How were we to know that after lunch we would come upon the Ultimate Bonefish Flat?

In the morning, over the dark flat, the sport had been modest but interesting. Now, with the sun high overhead, we followed the coast of Grand Caicos to the east. We all felt some kind of sharp anticipation, and the instinct was not false. We rounded a low headland, and there it was in front of us.

It was pure sand, a clear white. A band of it, perhaps two hundred feet wide, stood out between the mangroves and the greenish, deeper water. It ran, I guessed, for close to five miles. Lemuel started the motor and we took a wide swing out to sea. The gentle breeze was from the north: we would head up to the top of the flat and pole down with it.

In fact, we could have gone higher up than we did: there seemed almost an infinity of water to fish. But there was no need. Lemuel cut the motor, got the skiff into its fishing position and said, immediately, "Bonefish." Quietly, like that. Not the least of his virtues as a guide was that he never shouted, let alone shrieked as some do, putting the caster off.

Now I could see the bones, a pair of them, fish maybe five or six pounds, inshore of our boat. I flicked my little lure to them. One lunged and took it. Over that white sand, the visibility was perfect. One extraordinary thing we saw was that the other bonefish did not immediately vanish. For several seconds it held position, as if puzzled.

It would be repetitious to detail the events of the next two hours. Like waves of hapless infantry committed to a frontal attack by a mindless high command, schools of bonefish moved toward the boat as we poled slowly down the sand corridor. Some of the schools numbered thirty or forty fish. None of them were small. The biggest we hooked was around eight pounds but others might have been bigger. We hooked more than we landed: inevitably, on the six-pound-test, some fish crashed the mangroves and cut the line. Fishing etiquette went lamentably by the boards in the excitement after we discovered that one angler could hook a fish and not spook the school, giving the second man a shot. There were more double hookups than anybody needed. The only calm man in the boat was Lemuel. And the fly rods, forgotten, lay where they were.

We kept no account of the fish, releasing them as they came to the boat, and by three in the afternoon we found ourselves in a state that must be very rare in angling history. We were satiated with catching bones, and the only one not willing to call it a day was Lemuel. It distressed him, clearly, to quit. We had to sit down, like men on strike, before he reluctantly started the motor.

The Ultimate Bonefish Flat. Big, unsophisticated fish. Perfect visibility. Firm sand, so that, had we thought of it, we could have waded with ease. And used the fly rods. Before we had arrived back at the Third Turtle, the thought was already tarnishing the pure pleasure of the afternoon.

But we could return next day, in a more suitable frame of mind, with the fly rods. It was with controlled glee, that night in the bar, that Art forecast with what abandon those bonefish would climb all over our flies the next day. It could not have been ten minutes later that the wind sprang up. A big wind. From the south, right into the Ocean Hole.

That would seem to have been that. The Ultimate Bonefish Flat had one drawback only, as we saw it. It could not be fished in a southerly wind. We went to bed accepting that there would be no last, fly-fishing day. It would have been less messy, certainly, if it had been left at that.

But at breakfast the next morning the wind had gone down, though heavy swells — rising, no doubt, ahead of a big front — were breaking over the reef and running into the sheltered bay. The first half hour of our run to the Ocean Hole was rough and wet, and the waves were breaking white over the sandbars we had to cross. We weathered all that, though, slid into the Leeward Going Through passage and punched east for the bonefish.

It looked pretty good when we got there: the water was calm. Art demanded to be put ashore with his fly rod, and so he was. Lemuel and I headed a couple of miles up the flat, promising to pick him up later.

This time there was no instant action, but that, we felt, was easily explained. The water was still very shallow: the tide had not yet begun to rise on the flats. Art must have realized the same thing. It seemed a kindness to pick him up again, we felt, to wait for the flood to start.

So there, in the end, were the three of us, watching and waiting. And, of course, as it always does, eventually the tide started to run. If there were any bonefish in it, though, they were well concealed from us. For instead of its pristine transparency of the day before, the water was the color and opacity of milk. The overnight storm had compounded a thick emulsion of water and mud. The fly rods, after all, would not be used on the Ultimate Bonefish Flat.

But at least we were in a stronger position than that organist who mislaid the Lost Chord. We know precisely where what might well be the finest bonefishing flat in the world is located. We saw it again the next day when our Miami-bound Beechcraft flew low over the Ocean Hole, and for a moment Art looked ready to hijack the plane and order it down on the nearest sandspit. Understandable. Hell, his fly rod was right there at his side.

CHAPTER FIFTEEN

Invasion of the Red Horde

Club Pacifico on Coiba Island was the scene of perhaps the most ludicrous misadventure that ever befell me fishing. It was also one of the most fish-filled trips I have ever been on. Perhaps that was a reasonable trade-off.

PANAMA

Tom WAS grunting like a baboon, his red neckerchief dark with sweat, his rod butt creaking and his reel drag making terminal noises. "Take it easy," I advised him from the shade of the canvas awning. "You have merely encountered one of their outlying pickets. The Horde itself will be in the lee of the reef. I want you to save yourself for the real test."

Like a boozy old duchess curtsying to the Queen, our twenty-four-footer teetered on top of a swell, swooped into a trough, then staggered up onto an even keel again. Tom hung on to his fish. The line snapped like a firecracker and he let go a King Kong roar of frustration, slumping onto the cushions. "But I saw them coming for me," he panted. "The Red Horde . . . I saw the Red Horde!"

"Take a grip on yourself, Tom," I told him sternly. "We can hold this boat for hours yet. I'm putting you to defend the bow. I will take the stern. Meanwhile Rafael will remain amidships arming plugs and making up fresh leaders." We fell to laughing as Rafael, the skipper, turned the boat around to make another pass at the reef. At this stage of the trip, you see, the Red Horde was still a joke.

A joke, in fact, that had started in a restaurant in midtown Manhattan, where Tom, myself and our guest were having a serious, working lunch. The lunch was intended to acquaint Tom and me with what to expect when, a few weeks later, we would head down to Panama to fish Coiba Island on the Pacific coast. Fortified by several martinis, our guest, an old hand in those waters, confirmed

COIBA ISLAND, PANAMA

what we had heard: that the fishing was remarkable for its variety, that we could expect acres of wahoo, sailfish, roosterfish, amberjack, miles of rainbow runners, truckloads of blue-water game fish. Was it correct, we asked him, that at Club Pacifico, the fishing camp we were booked into, the emphasis was on light-tackle fishing from small, fast boats?

"Light tackle, yes," he said. Then his expression seemed to change. "Except for the cuberas, of course," he added, absently rotating his empty glass. We hastened to have it replenished. Cubera snapper I had heard of but once, from a fisherman at Key Biscayne who told me that they always got a few there in summer and that you fished them with a live lobster. ("Isn't that expensive?" I asked him. "Nah," he said, "first you go out and rob a lobster pot.")

"You mean that you have to use heavy bottom gear?" I asked our guest.

"No, no," he said, sipping moodily, the look in his eye that of a man who has experienced heaven and hell and found both places lacking in color after the reefs of Coiba. "You use plugs. Huge plugs." He leaned forward confidentially. "The best place is down south from Coiba. Small island called Jicarón. There's a reef down there. . . . Listen," he said, "you want to take plenty of big, heavy poppers. You want to cast seventy, eighty yards, you want a big conventional reel and a heavy two-handed rod." Carried away, he slammed an invisible plug at an invisible cubera snapper lurking near the checkroom, just failing to send a steaming plate of veal parmigiana, which was being proffered him, skimming into the other diners, some of whom were beginning to look around, the nearest of them pricking up their ears at our guest's dramatic recital.

"Only remember this," he went on. "As soon as that plug hits, bring it back fast. Fast! And don't be scared of what's behind it, because what you're going to see is . . . what the ocean is going to look like is . . . *all red!*"

"All red," nodded Tom.

"The sea turns red," intoned our guest, fixing us with an Ancient Mariner look, "with *huge cubera snappers.* Hundreds of them, all red, coming up at you from the reef. Sixty pounds, eighty pounds, some of them."

"A Red Horde," Tom confirmed.

Our guest looked at him suspiciously, but continued. "Those cuberas are slow to take the plug, though. They'll roll two or three times at it before they hit. So if you are fast, you can draw them away from the reef and then you can fight them in the deep water, which gives you about one chance in five if you remember to tighten the drag and get them into the boat before the sharks come."

"Sharks?" I asked.

"More sharks around Panama than anywhere in the world. Chop even a big cubera right behind the ears so all you bring up is a big toothy head and a few fronds of insides."

A man at the next table pushed his plate away abruptly and rose. "I wish I was going with you," our guest went on. "Built myself a new rod for those big ones. There are one hundred-pound cuberas on that reef, like huge red bulldogs." By then he was twenty-five hundred miles south-southeast of Seventh Avenue. "Watch for that blood-colored surge," he urged us, looking from one face to the other. Gravely we assured him that we would. "Good luck," he told us as he left the table, moving out into the sunlight and the swirling eddies around the Manhattan reefs.

"Red Horde, eh?" Tom sniggered when we were alone.

"We'll attend to the Red Horde when we've dealt with the big wahoo," I said. "And the sails on fly tackle. And the roosterfish." Lazily, over dessert, we leaned back to savor the delights of our forthcoming trip.

Three weeks later, in a light aircraft wobbling through the rain clouds toward Coiba, our mood was still buoyant. The previous evening, from the balcony of our hotel room high over Panama City, we had practiced roll-casting the No. 12 fly line we planned to use on the sailfish. Not even the rain could damp us, not even (we should be forgiven) the sight of long-term prisoners near the Coiba airstrip listlessly chipping rust from the hull of the beached World War II landing craft used to ferry them from, and maybe one day to, the mainland. Coiba has only two settlements: the penal colony on one side of the island and Club Pacifico on the other. We piled our gear into the twenty-four-foot Aquasport that was going to take us to the far, non-penal side of the island, and as we cleared the point and put the prison out of sight, a sailfish jumped nearby. A fine omen.

At Club Pacifico Bob Griffin, the camp's founder, was in the middle of a warming story. "So there was this man from Illinois," he was recounting, "who came back for his second trip with a full set of artillery: marlin rod, 130-pound-test line, 14/0 reel, full harness and his own fighting chair to screw down into the boat." The tale was about Hannibal Bank and the mysterious monsters that lurk there; no one, it is said, has ever lowered a jig into those waters and managed to fight to the surface the fish that hit it. But the man from Illinois had returned to Coiba determined to solve the mystery. Once more, though, he had had to admit defeat.

"He came back that night destroyed," Griffin went on, "and I asked him what had happened. 'It was going fine,' he said. 'I got out there, started to jig and got a hit right away. I was all strapped up, I had powerful tackle and after a while I had that fish, whatever it was, coming up nicely—one hundred fifty pounds, maybe two hundred pounds it felt. Then one of the big ones grabbed it.' "

There could have been no better captive audience for a fishing story than Tom and I, together with the four other anglers who had arrived that day—the brothers Gore and the brothers McGinn. But Hannibal Bank would not be on our program, Griffin told us. It was a four-hour run, too long and risky a haul for small boats in the rainy season. Instead we would head over toward the mainland, where the big wahoo run should be on. Should be on? Didn't anybody know? No, because the camp had been closed for two months. Not only were we going to fish teeming waters, but also waters that had been *rested* all that time.

They were calm waters, too, we found next morning, the currents sliding easily through a pattern of islands humped high and green with dense rain forest. Five minutes out from the jetty we saw the ocean's mirror fretted with a hailstorm of frantic needlefish, obviously beset by some predator below. Frantically, we began grabbing for our rods. Rafael held up a sophisticated hand. "Is jus' rainbow runners," he told us kindly. He slowed the boat until we could see the runners flashing cobalt and yellow in the water, then picked up speed again, heading for where the wahoo were said to be working through a channel that ran between a small island and the mainland.

Long before we reached it we tossed out deep-running plugs. Spanish mackerel hit them at once. Next came a boisterous half hour with jack crevalle. Afterward, nothing for a spell that must have gone on for close to twenty minutes. Then Rafael picked up the radio transmitter and smiled slowly as he interpreted the crackle at the far end. "My cousin finds plenty wahoo," he told us, grinning happily. "They smash up all the tackle, them and the sharks. My cousin's tourists got no plugs left!" Tom and I regarded one another smugly.

We had with us enough plugs to account for all the wahoo between there and Acapulco. Despite a slight unease at hearing our fellow anglers described as tourists (Was that what Rafael called us when the guides got together in the evenings?), we looked forward confidently to some gentlemanly sport. Red Horde, eh? Nothing so crude. This was going to be elegant fishing: thoroughbred, black-and-silver wahoo on light tackle. Well, not too light. Maybe fifteen-pound tackle. The Coiba wahoo ran big, we'd heard.

To begin with, all went according to the brochure. As we started to troll tight in to the rocks, so close that we were in the shade of the jungle overhanging them, Tom's rod began a wild attempt to free itself from the holder and his reel made a noise that no mackerel could produce. "Is fifty-pound wahoo," Rafael told us fifteen minutes later as, too big for the fish locker, it drummed its life out amidships (fifty-five pounds twelve ounces on the camp scales that night). "Not bad for a tourist, hey?" Tom asked Rafael.

"Is *big* wahoo here," he replied cryptically, coming on course again. Did he mean that this one was a tiddler? Or was he endorsing Tom's pride of achievement? There was no chance to question him because my reel was into its battle song now and I was bracing myself in the stern. "Is wahoo," Rafael observed superfluously. "Is fifty pounds." For maybe ten seconds my wahoo went on being an orthodox fifty-pound wahoo, then changed very briefly to a three-hundred-fifty-pound wahoo, and finally metamorphosed into a U-boat making ponderously for the ocean floor. "Shark come eat him," Rafael said, unwrapping his sandwiches. In his experience, it emerged later, a tourist always tried to land his first shark, which always ended up immovable, hanging deep under the boat, providing Rafael with a useful lunch break as the Aquasport drifted quietly and the tourist heaved and grunted fruitlessly.

And undoubtedly I reacted like many anglers had before me. "This is no shark, I tell you," I roared passionately.

Rafael sank his teeth deep into an apricot jam and peanut butter sandwich. "Is shark," he repeated, bored. "Is shark," Tom said unsympathetically. The rod was doubled over. I might have been into a coral reef except that occasionally there came a dull thump. Only a shark could act like that. "Is shark," I had to admit in the end. His sandwich jammed in his mouth, Rafael throttled forward and I hung on for the brief moment it took to snap the line. "Is many sharks in this place," he said in a moment of garrulity. And he was entirely right about that, too.

From then on, sharks hit all the time. I landed one lightweight, a ninety-pound mako, but most of them were heavier and impossible to haul on our light tackle. We went around to the seaward side of the island, took two roosterfish and then the sharks moved in again. Mostly there would be just a vastly increased weight on the end of the line, but sometimes, when a small fish was on close to the top, we could see a shark attack, bulging huge and brown under the surface like a gargantuan trout sipping nymphs. "Is ridiculous," Tom said around midafternoon. Even our formidable armory of plugs was beginning to dwindle. The channel was full of wahoo but there was no point in hooking them when every time they would be fielded by sharks. Rafael sensed our desperation. "Orright," he said. "We find the other boats."

They were tucked in a little cove, refugees like us. But they had sold their plugs dearly. One of the Gores had a 58½-pound wahoo, and Frank McGinn had taken a good one on six-pound-test — significantly, at the start of the day's fishing before the tiny brains of the sharks had awakened to the fact that there were easy pickings about. "You know," McGinn said, grieving over his lost plugs, "there are actually men who go out deliberately to catch sharks." We shook our heads wonderingly. Maybe the Club Pacifico should employ a task force of such coarse-grained anglers to sweep the seas clean before the serious sports fishermen arrived. Short of that, there didn't seem to be a lot of future in Wahoo Alley. Reluctantly, we had to admit seeming defeat, not knowing at the time that one very significant trophy had been wrested from the sharks; McGinn's wahoo turned out to be forty-eight pounds three ounces, later to be ratified as an IGFA world record on six-pound line.

In the camp bar that evening, we drew up new plans. Maybe there are shark-repellent qualities in vodka martinis; the McGinns decided they would hit Wahoo Alley again next day. The Gores were going to potter around close to camp. Tom and I were going to break new ground.

"If you don't mind the half-hour haul down there," Bob Griffin said, "you could head for Jicarón, try for a sailfish on the way down, then plug the reef."

The name closed a memory circuit. "You want us to tangle with the Red Horde, eh?" Tom asked him dramatically. We were well into the third round of the cocktail hour. "We'll make a movie," I sniggered. "We'll call it *The Sea Turns Scarlet*."

"No," Tom guffawed, "it's going to be *The Plugs of Jicarón*."

Only Griffin's pet howler monkey, tethered outside where he could ambush small iguanas and eat them like Popsicles, reacted appreciatively, with cartwheels and a manic laugh. The others, Griffin in particular, looked at us curiously.

"Down there," he said, "are more cubera snappers, probably, than anywhere else in the world. And when they are really feeding, patches of the sea do change color. You'll see tomorrow."

We were momentarily chastened but after dinner, as we made our way through the warm darkness to our cottage, the somewhat ludicrous notion of the snapper army took over again. Even so, we both had brought heavy casting rods and reels with us. For all the fantasies, for all the jokes, something had got through to us that lunchtime in Manhattan. Clearly there could be no such thing as hundreds of fish of fifty pounds and more making a massed rush for a plug. But there was a certain depth of feeling in the way our guest had talked that afternoon. Probably the cubera fishing would make a pleasant interlude of relief after the serious business of the wahoo and the sails. If there was time, we concluded, we might just try it for an hour.

So we headed south that morning, leaving the penal colony to starboard, roaring by islands humped like camels, low and twisted like sea serpents, all of them lush and green, some alive with frigate birds. We weathered point after point as the ocean swell became more apparent, and then just off a tide rip Rafael slowed down. Time to look for a sail, he said.

Now the idea was, you see, that we would try to take at least one sailfish on fly. But, naturally, we didn't want to rush things. The right course, we reasoned, would be to have at least a couple of sails under our belts before we would be psychologically ready to use up what might be a long spell of fishing time on a problematic venture. So although the large saltwater fly rods were readied and laid out in the bow, we suggested to Rafael that first we would just act like ordinary fishermen and troll. At Club Pacifico, we'd been told, flyfishing for sails was a kind of specialty of the house and the guides were well versed in the techniques of teasing the fish up. Rafael, though, didn't seem very much put out when we made our suggestion. Indeed, with hindsight, one might well have identified a look of relief in his expression.

So we trolled, and for a long time the trolling turned out to be what trolling is often like, that is to say, the most boring form of fishing yet devised by man. Indeed we were restlessly talking about hauling in the lines in another ten minutes when two beauties came right up behind the plastic squids and grabbed one apiece in a classic double strike. We got them both, 102 and 109 pounds, and naturally then would have been the moment to take the hooks out of the lures and go ahunting for another sail on the fly rod. But by the time we had landed our brace we had cleared the last, southerly headland before the island that had already passed into our private mythology: Jicarón.

It was really very similar to the other small islands around Coiba, lush and verdant, a neon-green sea sluicing its rocks and falling white on its beaches. In addition, Jicarón wore, like an ornament, a rusting tramp steamer that had run aground on its northernmost point. "Trying to get away from the Red Horde," Tom said—predictably, I thought. "He don't see the light," Rafael corrected him.

We headed a point or two out to sea, and it was possible to see the reef, even though it was covered at high tide. The swells moved across it, frothing white, and as we came nearer and it became more defined, we could see its extent—a long reef, parallel with the shore, with three pinnacles almost breaking the surface.

We stood off to rig the heavy casting gear and Rafael put us in position two hundred feet from the nearest break. Tom's popper went out first, splashing into a smooth hump of water that was building over the rock; then he was working it back, jerking his rod tip violently and reeling fast. "Hey! Hey!" Rafael yelled. A big, sullen swirl broke astern of the popper. Tom reeled faster. Two more swirls and then his rod was hard over and he was frantically trying to tighten the drag. Under no circumstances, our luncheon guest had told us, was any line to be given. If it was, the cubera would be straight into the reef, cutting us off. So to encourage Tom as he sweated and panted to hold his fish, I told him that he had one of the lesser cuberas there. "You have merely encountered one of their outlying pickets," I told him.

Tom lost his fish and we turned to our comedy routine again. Rafael listened silently to our plans for defending the Aquasport against the Horde, then said crushingly, "Is not cubera you have. Is little surface snapper. About fifteen, twenty pounds. Small cuberas is twice as big. I take you to them now, and maybe to some big cubera." He swung the boat around and headed uptide again. "You cast that way," he said, pointing. Two poppers flew out, started to jerk back on the surface and then, quite suddenly, the sea turned red.

Not an acre of red, but a patch as big as a medium-sized hotel lobby. And not primary red either, more a dull brick color. There were crashing explosions all around the plugs, then both our rods were wrenched down savagely. "Cuberas come," Rafael said nonchalantly.

Silently, Tom and I fought our fish. This time we were in better shape than during Tom's first snapper encounter because now there was a lot more water beneath us and we had some room to maneuver and to contain the repeated crash dives. Even so, and even on heavy gear, it was fifteen minutes before both the fish were subdued, coming up dull red, the dog-fanged jaws moving slowly. "Is small cuberas," Rafael announced, lifting them out on the gaff. "Go maybe thirty-five pounds. Now you cast again."

Tom and I looked at each other. If those were small fish, we were not entirely certain that we *wanted* to cast again. The Red Horde that was a joke had now turned out to be real. Maybe another of our fantasies was real, too: the Cubera King, deep in his rocky, weed-fronded fastness, might come out and accept our challenge, all one hundred pounds of him. Or something similarly nasty. Such a thought, comical thousands of miles north, was easy to entertain when you were riding an ocean swell surrounded by lumps of Central American jungle.

Even so, we cast again, and once again the Red Horde sallied out from its fortress. We dragged the plugs away from it frenetically, in the hope that they wouldn't be hit until they were over deep water, but they were engulfed before they had traveled fifty feet. There was a difference this time, though. Even before the first power dive could materialize, brown shadows appeared in the subsurface and we felt the familiar, sickening deadweight of sharks on the line.

There was no fighting them; they were simply too big. We broke off and cast three or four more times. The same. "When sharks come, they stay," Rafael said. "We shift away from here now."

So we did. We trolled a wahoo channel on the far side of the island and by the time the second fish was aboard the sharks had arrived. Landing wahoo heads is not really fun. We set out for home. "Tomorrow I want to stay away from Blood Island," I told Rafael. "Let's try to take one of those sails on the fly."

The technique of catching sailfish on flies is now well established, since Dr. Webster Robinson's first successful experiments in 1962. You troll hookless teasers until you raise a sail. Then you enrage the fish by snatching the teaser from it until it turns blue and green with fury. Then you haul in the teaser and substitute your fly. More sails have been caught this way out of Club Pacifico than from any other fishing camp in the world—or so it's said. And the guides are naturally very experienced.

Next morning, though, when we hit the sailfish grounds, we had a hard time convincing Rafael that the hooks should be removed from the plastic squids we planned to use as teasers, but finally, looking at us as if we were crazy, he consented to do this. And we hadn't been bouncing the teasers along for more than fifteen minutes when everything started to happen according to the rule book.

Up came the sailfish, yawing about behind the starboard teaser, and Tom then commenced the teasing operation. Just as the book said it would, the sail became very upset. It changed color violently and tried to rush our transom. It was time to cast the fly, a big arrangement of white feathers and silver Mylar strips with a polystyrene popping head. As the rule book instructed, Rafael took the engine out of gear. Then he hit the deck as the fly whistled past him on the back cast and I launched it at the sail.

Perfect. It landed to the sail's port side, I twitched it a couple of times and it was comprehensively grabbed. The slack line slid through my fingers and I set the hook hard four or five times. The sail went into its hopping-about routine, did all its dangerous antics, and the hook held firm. By all the rules, given a little patience, it was mine. Then, as the fish surged off steadily, I realized that something unusual was happening. The backing was melting off the fly reel but the boat was still revving in neutral. "Come on, Rafael," I yelled, "let's go after him!"

Rafael said, "Señor," and paused. It was the first time that he had called me that. "Señor," he repeated, "I am sorry. But the propeller have fall off the boat." A moment later, with the line in a great arc, the fly fell out of the sail also.

That took care of most of our fishing day. It turned out to be a three-hour tow back to camp and another hour while Rafael fitted a new prop, one of the shortest-lived in marine history, because when we headed out to sea again Rafael struck a submerged log.

But at least it all made way for a longer planning conference at cocktail time. With the time we had lost, the next day would have to tell. Wahoo Alley was out for a start. The McGinns and the Gores had been fishing in the area since the first day and it looked as if the big wahoo had gone, though they had had a great variety of lesser fish, and Frank McGinn had spent the best part of one day fighting something that he never saw on his six-pound line, a big amberjack possibly.

"If it weren't for the sharks," I said to Tom, "I feel strong enough for the Red Horde again." Between us it had been agreed that my lost sail was to be regarded as a release, a piece of mild sophistry that enabled us to tick "sailfish-on-fly" off our list. And secretly we didn't want to use up another whole day looking for billfish that might never show up. A consultation with Rafael seemed in order.

"Is there any place," I asked him, "where we could throw a plug at the cuberas without the sharks arriving?"

"No, señor," he said. He was a much chastened Rafael since the two props had gone, and he waited a few seconds before telling me that nevertheless there might be a way of coping. He and his father had once worked together as professional snapper fishermen, he said. They had the shark problem, too, and they solved it, simply enough, by catching some sharks to start with.

"Then, señor," he said, "we kill them and put them back in the water. Soon there are no more sharks. Maybe the others don't like the taste in the sea."

So we had to cut our way through the sharks if we wanted the cuberas. Our problem was that the heaviest tackle we had brought was 25-pound-test and that was totally inadequate for the sharks around Blood Island. Heavy handlines perhaps? We went to Bob Griffin to see what he had in his tackle store. "There's just this," he said.

It turned out to be a heavy marlin outfit. There was no fighting chair and no harness in the Aquasport but it might be possible to manage. Rafael approved the gear and bore it away to the boat. "Light tackle, eh?" scoffed the Gores and McGinns as it was carried past them on the patio.

"In war all tactics are fair," Tom told them intensely. "The artillery will clear the ground for the infantry to move in."

A small tuna feather attached to a heavy wire leader on a mighty marlin rod looks faintly ludicrous, admittedly, but next morning, off Jicarón, that seemed to be the logical approach. We would troll close to the reef of the Red Horde, not with cuberas in mind but in the hope of contacting a school of bonito or small yellowfin tuna. Shark bait.

That morning the sharks were lazy. We actually boated three yellowfin before the first shark struck, swallowed and sounded. I bent into it with the big rod and started to pump. There was no possible chance of it breaking the 130-pound line, but on the other hand, standing up in a twenty-four-foot Aquasport with a cumbersome 14/0 reel to hold and a great deal of shark at the other end is a somewhat demanding occupation. After ten minutes I had gained a bit of line, but my knees were beginning to feel as if they were melting in the sun. I passed the rod to Tom. "Work him a little," I said.

So Tom worked him, then I worked him, and Tom again, until finally we were handing the rod back and forth like a pair of jugglers. It was half an hour before Rafael could get hold of the leader and a brute of a white-tip, three-hundred-fifty to four-hundred pounds by the look of it, was in range of the bang-stick. The shark was dispatched and sent to float downtide with its belly open, but at this rate both Tom and I were going to be too exhausted for the cuberas when the time came.

But help was at hand. As we labored over that shark, Rafael was hard put to conceal his amusement, so much so, indeed, that after it was beaten I told him courteously that the privilege of landing the next shark would be his. "Orright, señor," he said, "but I do it different."

That was an accurate remark. When the next shark hung on, Rafael screwed the drag all the way down, planted the rod in the holder and opened the throttle. "Orright, *tiburón*," he yelled happily. "Come up and see the butcherman!" A three-hundred-pound white-tip being pulled haplessly to the surface and then aquaplaning behind an Aquasport is a formidable sight. From the moment of hooking, Rafael had him bang-sticked, butchered and drifting away from the boat in, overall, not more than ten minutes. Then he performed the feat over again. Would three sharks be enough? we asked him.

"Take about one hour to work," Rafael said. "Three is enough."

If the Cubera King were really down there, he should have awarded us the Order of the Red Horde, because, it proved, we had done his people a real favor. Unmolested by sharks, they surged out of the reef that afternoon and grabbed plugs. Oddly enough, though, when it was time to head back to Club Pacifico there seemed to be only four cuberas in the boat. At least we could not blame the sharks for that. The big snappers were just too strong and the rocks were just too close. We could only get midgets, up to forty pounds or so, to the side of the boat.

It was strange to think how we scoffed at the honest fellow we had taken out to lunch so recently. At the bar of the Club Pacifico that night I listened to Tom, with that haunted, Ancient Mariner look in his eyes, lean forward to give the message to the McGinns and the Gores. "The ocean turns all red," he was saying. "They come at you from out of the reef. . . ."

"Look for the blood-colored surge," I found myself telling them. One of the McGinns rose uneasily to pour more drinks. I could see they didn't believe us. But it didn't seem to matter. When we left they would be sniggering, "Red Horde, eh," at each other, but the spell would start to work on them. Gravely we bade them good night. They would thank us one day. As we walked off into the night, I'm fairly sure I heard Frank McGinn say to his brother John, "Do we have any of those, uh, big popping plugs with us?"

The Red Horde, I reckoned, was about to claim another victim.

Noble Fish and Royal Ruins

*As has happened to me in many another place,
when I got to Guatemala to fish tarpon in a lake a couple of
hundred miles from the sea, the fish didn't particularly matter. It
was a homesick old man that did.*

GUATEMALA

JUST BEFORE dinner, flocks of egrets came in
low over Lake Petexbatún and roosted on a single tree among the
thousands around the shore. "That is a 'salam' tree," Albert Gillet,
my mentor, told me the first evening we were out on the water.
"Its leaves and wood smell very sweet, mon. Very fine and sheltery
for the birds. Only one salam tree on the lake now. Upon a time
used to be a bigger one than that, but it fell down. From the burden
of the birds, mon." You could assume that would be the fate of this
one as well. By dusk, uncountable egrets had settled on the tree,
turning it as white as if this were Christmas in Vermont, not the dry
season in Guatemala.

The bird-watching on Petexbatún was incidental: egret time, Albert reckoned, might also be tarpon time—when, we hoped, the
indolent, seemingly purposeless rolling of the fish would change to
water-slashing action. But from the evidence we would come upon,
it seemed more likely that somewhere below the surface there was
a fishy equivalent of a salam tree, to which the tarpon quit for the
day when the breeze dropped and the skin of the lake became calm.

Albert himself was always calm. Seventy years old, black, with a
wisp of white beard, a shock of white hair and the manner and the
vocabulary of an Old Testament prophet. He is a carpenter by trade,
and he had first come to Guatemala thirty years ago, from what is
now Belize and was then British Honduras—to Albert, and forever,

ALBERT GILLET AT LAKE PETEXBATUN, GUATEMALA

"B.H." "We bulled a road in from B.H., mon," he said. "Then I stayed here in this republic, loggin'."

Albert knew that you couldn't hurry fish and that I'd been a trifle perverse in coming to Petexbatún in the dry season. "The heavy fishes, mon, they come up on the big floods in July, August," he had said, confirming what I'd been told previously. "That's when the two-hundred-pounders come, when the waters is up. Look in the *Farmer's Almanac*, how the moon is in July, and you'll know."

The run of giant tarpon to Lake Petexbatún is one of the most extraordinary phenomena in the world of fishing. The lake lies in northeast Guatemala, in the Petén, a low-lying subtropical rain forest that adjoins the Yucatan Peninsula of Mexico. For much of the year the lake spills out into the Petexbatún River, a tributary of the Río de la Pasión, which in turn feeds the mighty Usumacinta, which empties into the Gulf of Mexico four hundred miles from the lake.

A four-hundred-mile freshwater migration of huge fish that ends in a smallish lake. Why? To feed? It would seem that in the ocean itself or in the Usumacinta there would be infinitely more forage. To spawn? No evidence of this. An epic journey, longer than most salmon make, and an apparently motiveless one.

It is as mysterious, indeed, as the fall of the Mayan civilization, whose great plazas, temples and overgrown pyramids are so numerous in the forest around Lake Petexbatún that many of the ruins are still waiting in line, so to speak, for the attention of archaeologists. And, oddly, if it hadn't been for archaeologists, the great tarpon of Lake Petexbatún would still be known only to the villagers along its shores.

Long before sport fishermen became aware of the odyssey of the Petexbatún tarpon, archaeologists had arrived, and upon finding the area so richly endowed in ancient wonders, they built a permanent camp on the lakeshore in the early sixties. Much of the camp's carpentry had been done by Albert, who was also its guardian. To it came such notables as Ian Graham of Harvard's Peabody Museum.

Later, there was a secondary wave of guests, archaeology buffs traveling to the lake not to excavate but merely to view the ruins. A Guatemala City travel firm refurbished the camp to accommodate the newcomers. For more than twenty years, Albert had had the fishing almost all to himself, but with more people coming in and the fact that by the law of averages some archaeologists have to be fishermen, the secret got out. Last year sport fishermen started to arrive, and Albert, pressed into service as a guide, would have little time for the lonely epic fights with huge fish hooked on his handline. "It is beautiful to mess with them, mon," he says. "They are huge beasts that lurks in the pool. I has the good judgment with my handline, but there was oftentimes when I was afraid I would be carried out of my dory."

Because we had only a few days, Albert delicately rebuked me for having come at the wrong time of year. The very big fish come when the heavy flooding of the rainy season backs the river water into the lake, so that the flow is reversed. "The drifting in of the first flood, mon, when you sees the sticks and bushes coming into the lake, that is when the heavy beasts, the noble tarpons and snooks, are here," he'd say, as though repeating a lesson to a backward child.

But I didn't think that coming in the dry season had been entirely perverse. During the wet season the banks are flooded as high as the lower boughs of the trees, so that there's no fishing *except* for big tarpon: the smaller species are deep in the swamps the floods create or inaccessible in the submerged bushes.

In the dry, though, diversity made up for size. So I had been told by Andy Sherman, a New Yorker living in Guatemala City, who had fished the lake half a dozen times — except for Albert's, the most experience that anyone had there. In the dry season, he had written me before the trip, though the big tarpon were absent, there were plenty of smaller ones, up to forty pounds or so. And the other lake species — snook, peacock bass, local fish they called *mojarra* and *muchacha* — became available. And, besides, what was so Lilliputian about a twenty-five-pound tarpon on the right light gear?

So in April I met up with Sherman in Guatemala City and headed north with him, first in a rackety DC-3 to Flores in the Petén and then by Jeep over a dirt road to Sayaxché on the Río de la Pasión, where we dumped our gear into a dugout canoe in the gathering darkness and started on the last leg of our journey, a two-hour trip upstream, switching from the Pasión to the Petexbatún River. As the rain forest slipped by, alien night sounds, the explosions of birds awakened by our passing, were all about us. Only a faint sense of space, of there no longer being banks close to the canoe, told us we had reached the lake.

That night there were two separate disturbances: a scrabbling, scratchy noise on the balsa leaves that make up the roof of the two-story wooden camp building and, later, furious barking from the guard dogs. "What you heard, mon," said Albert the next morning as we edged his dugout to the lake, "was a kinkajou dancing. He's a little furry bear, but more of the cat tribe. This is a peaceful piece of the forest, mon."

As soon as we rounded the first rocky headland, we could see a spot where the water had been lashed into foam. "Snooks been eatin'," Albert said. Something had been working there, no doubt of it, but there was no response to the lures we threw all around the area. "Let us try the pool," Albert said.

When we reached what Albert called the pool, it looked no different from any part of the lake. He knew what he was talking about, though. This was a deep hole—soundings showed it to be one hundred feet deep—and it was here that the tarpon seemed to concentrate.

They were rolling idly in almost exactly the same way that Atlantic salmon do when they aren't inclined to hit a lure. Spoons, Andy said, had been the most effective lures when he last fished Petexbatún, but hundreds of tarpon must have seen ours pass them and showed no interest. Those tarpon didn't care if we stayed or went, and they outlasted us. After two hours of frustration we were reduced to trolling the margins of the lake for whatever might come along. Which were a few small peacock bass that Albert called "blancos."

At a kind of jungle brunch, Albert chewed on one of the small bass, spitting the bones out expertly, while on his shoulder sat his green parrot, Lorenzo, a malevolent creature. "I'm the onliest person in the world who can handle this *bravo* bird," was Albert's boast, one entirely justified, Andy and I would discover later at some small cost in blood.

"That fishing this morning was very bad," Albert pronounced between fusillades of fish bones. "You hear the dogs in the night? Chepita and Lassie and Jet? They hear the people from Sayaxché comin' to fish at night. All last week the Sayaxché people were on the lake with their nets. They clean the fish, and they dump the remains in the water. And the other fishes scent the blood, and so they seek to find a sheltered place where they become more peaceful. That is why there is no snooks, no noble blancos. But I still have hopes."

On the cut grass around the camp, blue buntings were foraging. "We has lots of them," Albert said, "and hummingbirds. But the little hummingbirds are all hatched and gone now. I love them small little birds, mon."

In the heat of the day, a timelessness settled over our party. The dogs lolled at Albert's feet. "They hunt armadillos," he said, "all of them rodent tribes. But not as a job to *go* to. Mostly they sits around. Like me."

It must be a lonely job, I offered, when no anglers, no archaeologists are in camp, which is most of the time.

"I like it in the woods," he said. "I have a brother in the States. To be truthful, I can't recall exactly where he lives. But that would be too big a city for me. I went to Guatemala City once for eight days, but it was too cold."

And he'd never married? No, he said, with a patently false look of melancholy on his face. "That happiness I do not know. I never reached that distance, mon. But I have known many good ladies, and bad ladies, and I love to dance. When I was young, I *got* to learn to dance, because at home in B.H. they put you to dance when you are small, and if you do not dance good, you do not get chocolate, you do not get peanuts, you do not get nothin'. But once you can dance a bit, you gain *pride*, mon."

Late that afternoon we went out again, trolling the shores. Again, only insignificant fish hit. We worked on until we were in sight of Albert's deep pool, but even the tarpon had stopped their rolling. "When the birds come home to the salam tree, mon," Albert said, "maybe those fish start working. Sometime it happen like that." And then, incongruously, he broke into verse, maybe to pass the time for us. " 'It was the schooner *Hesperus*,' " he declaimed, " 'that sailed the wintry sea.' " He went through all the stanzas without error.

"Learned that in St. Mary's, in B.H., mon, from my *Crown Royal Reader*," he said. "At home we has the Carib tribe to the south, the Mayan to the north, and in Belize we has the mixed people, the African men that speak the broken language, the Chinese and the Japanese. But in St. Mary's you learn the proper way. They force you, mon, with the *Crown Royal Reader*. We were forced to read the great *Macbeth*. 'Toll for the brave.' 'Under the village chestnut tree.' 'Into the jaws of hell rode the six hundred.' But I lost my book, mon. I lost it in Flores to a nurse. She used to permit me to read English to her, and it remained with her." Now all he had to read was the current *Farmer's Almanac*.

The rundown on the St. Mary's curriculum might have continued, but now, just as the salam tree looked as if it should have been equipped with a neon sign reading NO VACANCY, Albert stopped reciting, sat upright and pointed across the lake. "Mon," he said, still calm, "the noble tarpon is *feeding*."

Half a mile away, the water was being sliced white, the spray being sent flying. Hundreds of tarpon were crashing into shoals of baitfish. Albert pulled on the little outboard, and we started to move in a big half-circle so we could cut the power when we were ahead of the fish and let them catch up to us. But at that moment, a wind sprang up, first a breeze, then gusting, finally blowing at half-gale strength. It held our little craft as if it had us on a rope. Baffled, we saw the great shoal of feeding tarpon move away, growing faint and eventually disappearing from the surface altogether. And then the wind dropped as suddenly as it came.

"That wind was perplexing," Albert said that night in camp. "Let that wind come from the south and they cease feeding immediately. If we was in the *sea* now, yes, mon, the south wind fishing is *good*." Huge beetles made science-fiction noises and fireflies were out in strength, but mention of the sea immediately carried Albert miles away. "I used to fish my little dory in B.H.," he said, with true melancholy this time. "All the way up to the north, stoppin' to lodge on a different little cay every night. I miss the sea to a great extent, mon. I'm goin' to get out to B.H., out to the cays again. I could save up $500, build a little skiff. No fisherman *starves*, mon."

Our first day's experience showed that we were lucky we weren't relying on that bold statement: the few little peacock bass we had taken hardly fell into Albert's "noble" category. Still and all, I'd wanted to fish in Lilliput, had I not?

There were compensations, though. By its nature, Lilliputian fishing is a relaxed sport. Wouldn't we be crazy, Andy speculated at supper, to have traveled all this way and missed seeing something that most archaeology buffs would have signed away half a year's salary to visit? I could see his point. In my skewed mind it would equate to some astigmatic scholar bending over a Maori artifact while, unheeded at his back, leapt the great rainbow trout of the Tongariro River in New Zealand. I allowed as how it would be fine if next morning we headed across the lake and up the feeder stream that would bring us, after an hour or so, to the Mayan ruins at Aguateca. But I stipulated that we'd take a couple of light spinning rods in the canoe.

We left at dawn, and as we crossed the lake we made a few passes at the shoal of feeding tarpon that had reappeared. Our plugs and spoons passed among them unmolested. Clearly it was time for the ruins, and we made for the stream mouth at the far end of the lake.

Soon we were in a green tunnel in the rain forest. In the shallow, extraordinarily clear water, the little gray bass that Albert called *muchacha* skittered away—too small even for us to bother with. Once, as the stream opened out into a reedy lagoon, we found the biggest stork I'd ever seen standing sentinel—white, with a chestnut-red head and a black beak. "*Javaru*," Albert said. "I love all the things of nature, mon!"

As Albert spoke, a little sun-grebe, brilliant blue, incautiously surfaced close to the canoe. *Whack!* went Albert's paddle. There are some instincts that lie deeper than the precepts taught at St. Mary's. Fortunately, the bird bobbed away unharmed.

After the river journey came the long, sweaty climb to Aguateca and, for a moment, a sense of anticlimax. The great temple pyramid was there, certainly, and the outlines of the plaza and of the elevated walks. But the rain forest covered them; this was no tailored site, like Chichén Itzá. But then we saw the stelae in the clearing, three great slabs of green stone that had fallen from the pyramid, carved with the elaborately headdressed, brutal-featured figures of a race that gave birth to the mathematical concept of zero some one thousand years before it occurred to any Europeans.

Possibly they had hit on it after tarpon fishing in Lake Petexbatún, was the unworthy thought that came to me as we headed back downstream. We came again to the lagoon, from which the *Javaru* had long since flown. "Try your baits," Albert said, and we flipped out spoons in the hope a noble peacock bass might be hiding under the stumps. Nothing. "Let me try," Albert said.

I handed him my rod, but he didn't want it. Instead he was fumbling in his bag, coming up with a bottle. "Just a vermouth bottle," he said. "Not so good as a burgundy, not so much room." I looked at it mystified for a moment, and then I traveled back a good many years, to catching minnows as a kid in Wales. Take an empty wine bottle with the cork in, knock the glass disc out of the blunted cone at its bottom, tip in some bread crumbs. Lo, a minnow trap.

It worked in Guatemala, too. Inside two minutes we had fresh bait, one hundred silvery slips of minnow. Albert presented us with a hook apiece. "Fish!" he said.

Now we were doing it his way. Freelined, the minnows worked their way to the shoreline. Then, each time, *thump!* "Did I not tell you we have noble blancos?" Albert crowed. They were two- and three-pounders, and for Lilliput fishing they were noble indeed. Who cared about such a vulgar concept as size, anyway? We caught them until the sun was high and the water went to sleep. Next day, our last, would be time enough to deal with the recalcitrant tarpon, because Albert promised us more bass fishing, right at the camp's landing.

And so, in the evening, we caught yet more noble blancos, and when it grew too dark to fish we walked up the bank and broiled them, having turned down Albert's seductive urgings to get in the canoe again. "We has some noble catfish in this lake," he told us temptingly. "Fish for them in the pool at night. Huge alligator gars as well, mon. And we has about three classes of fish that hauls its way up here from the sea. We has the drummer. We has the goathead, plenty of good flesh it has. And we has another fish here that has a small mouth but it is huge; we calls it the mountain mullet."

Good talk to go to sleep on after a nightcap. Had there been time, it would have been fascinating to hunt down the drummer, the goathead, the mountain mullet. But we had just the morning left and a last shot at the tarpon.

Maybe the fact that it was my last shot on Petexbatún sharpened my wits the next day. There were the tarpon again, predictably rolling, predictably scorning everything thrown at them, until I recalled an autumn morning in Costa Rica when much bigger tarpon than these had behaved the same way. What was it the guide had said? Yes, *the tip of the iceberg.* The fish we could see on the surface were the tired ones, the satiated ones. The hungry tarpon would be deep.

I put on a silver-and-black deep-swimming plug, counted thirty while it sank, retrieved slowly, a quick twitch at long intervals. *Whack!* The first Lilliputian tarpon, twenty pounds maybe, had slammed the bait and headed high out of the water. That first one threw the hook. But there were others. And others. Once you had it figured, it was absurdly simple.

Albert wanted two to take back to camp. He liked to smoke them, he said. He also smoked alligators when he got the chance — though not the dead one he discovered as we returned to camp and which he displayed with the bravado of a 1930s-style great white hunter.

"Maybe the next time you come here there'll be a bar, showers, ice . . . ," Andy said. And indeed, as he spoke, there were carpenters at work building cabins for future fishermen. "The Mexican and the Guatemalan governments are talking about a joint hydroelectric project on the Usumacinta River," he added. "That's five years off, but it could be the end of the tarpon run."

"I'll be gone before that," Albert said. "Five hundred dollars, buy me a skiff. Get out to the cays. In B.H. we has freedom, and the newspapers, and the legal courts. In this republic, mon, they can beat you and grab you and carry you off, but in B.H. they have to prove you done wrong in the courts. But society all changes, I suppose, everything moves on. Maybe I don't know anybody up there anymore, except my sister. She lives amongst the nuns. I'm seventy years old. I just want to make my tables and chairs and fish my little skiff in B.H." He brightened. "Mon, there is huge beasts up there on the coast, the noble marlins. They take the shad bait and you use a hook and a chain. . . ."

It was time to leave him to it, cleaning the tarpon, throwing the offal to Lassie and Jet and Chepita, handing a tidbit up to Lorenzo the parrot. In a few weeks, the big water would be pushing up again into Lake Petexbatún, and with it the big tarpon, the two-hundred-pounders. Maybe Albert will be waiting for them and maybe not. We pushed out our dugout with our gear loaded in it, yelled our farewells, but Albert had his nose in the *Farmer's Almanac*. I hope it forecast a long voyage for him, in a small skiff.

CHAPTER SEVENTEEN

Deep in the Green

*Until very recently, Kay Brodney was a li-
brarian at the Library of Congress, concerned with the Life Sciences. During her time there, she'd take her vacations in the more
impossible parts of the South American rain forest, flyfishing for
creatures with names like arapaima and arawana. Now that she's
retired she probably does nothing else. This is an account of how
I first met her.*

AMAZONIA

W̄HEN THE tall lady in the sun hat came wad-
ing ashore from the dugout canoe, in the battering heat, deep in the
Amazonian rain forest, it was an ideal moment for a memorable
greeting, H.M. Stanley style. In the event, though, my words came
lamely: "Oh, uh, there you are, Kay!"

Her response was altogether more relevant, sharper. "Splash!" she
called. "Kick your feet up!"

I stopped as I waded out from the sandbar to meet her. "Why?"
I wanted to know.

"Stingrays," she said brusquely. And that was the first piece of
jungle-river lore that Kay Brodney, sixty-one, head of the Life Sciences Subject Catalog Section of the Library of Congress, had to
impart. And she elaborated: that in the Amazon system, stingrays
will lie in the shallowest, warmest water; that if you step on one you
can expect twelve hours of pain so intense that victims have broken
their own limbs in their agonized thrashing; but that if you splash
as you wade, the rays will scuttle out of your way.

However, when both of us were on dry land, shaking hands,
Brodney was careful to avoid drama. "People think that I'm a mad,
brave old woman to come out fishing in a place like this, living like

VICTORIA REGINA WATER LILIES, AMAZONIAN BACKWATER

an Amerindian," she said. "But, hell, I've been robbed twice on the streets of D.C., and each time it was more frightening than anything I've met in a rain forest."

The baking sandbar on which she now stood was about thirty-five-hundred miles from D.C. as the vulture flies. It was one of the bleached, dry-season bones of the Rio Branco, which flows south out of the highlands of Guyana into Brazil to join the Rio Negro, which, in turn, meets the Amazon at the city of Manaus. On the map that she had sent me months earlier, Brodney had circled Manaus in red ink. Alongside she had written laconically, "Beds. Ice." On our Rio Branco sandbar, those beds, that ice, were more than three hundred tortuous river miles distant, a two-week journey, give or take a day or two, by a chugging old river launch.

It was from Manaus that photographer Mick Brennan and I had set out to rendezvous with Brodney and her companions in the Amazonian wilderness. They had set out ten days earlier, from the northern Brazilian town of Boa Vista, way upstream on the Branco. From there they planned to truck down to the village of Caracarai, below the last rapids on the Branco, pick up boats and meet us at the tiny settlement of Santa Maria, halfway to Manaus and forty miles south of the Equator.

"We'll have done all the scouting by then," Brodney had written me. "We'll have the fishing pinned down. [In the dry season in Amazonia, the fish tend to mass in tributaries and lake systems.] We can fish the Itapera, a veritable brood-pond of large *tucunaré, arawana, trahira, pirapacu*. There may be some *arapaima*."

Those are the Indian names, half-rendered into Portuguese, of fish that only the head of the Life Sciences Subject Catalog Section was likely to be acquainted with. Fish, one was tempted to imagine, that were caught using alligator tails for lures. Or maybe live snakes.

But one would be wrong. Brodney had made it clear that she would be taking only fly-fishing gear into the jungle, and she would be making no compromises. Into the simmering Amazonian hot-house she would bring the ethical standards of the purist fly-fisher. And those crazy-sounding species, she promised, would be worthy of them.

Brodney has devoted most of her life to fishing. She started out on pike and bass near her hometown of Fond du Lac, Wisconsin, and in her twenties hitchhiked to California. "A classic dropout," she calls herself. One day in 1948 she happened to be in San Francisco's Golden Gate Park while a casting tournament was taking place. "I saw those lines swishing about and it changed my whole life," she says. "Women weren't recognized for doing much distance casting then, just accuracy events. Once I took third place in the Western Championship down at Long Beach. I went to get my prize but I found I hadn't qualified because I wasn't a man."

By the time she was in her mid-thirties, Brodney reckons, she had become a card-carrying fishing bum. She never had much money and she went through about fifty jobs, the steadiest one clerking at a railroad office. But she did manage to acquire a Volkswagen Camper. It took her all over northern California fishing for steelhead and shad.

That didn't satisfy her for long. She moved up to Eureka, California, and continued to try to make do with odd jobs, mostly as a waitress. But the work was seasonal. Sometimes Brodney couldn't raise gas money. So she moved to Seattle, on the grounds that it was eight hundred miles nearer to the Kispiox River in British Columbia. And it finally came upon her that she had better qualify herself for some occupation. She took a job as a clerk-typist at the State Fishery. At night she worked in the University of Washington Fishery and Oceanography library cataloguing reprints, the bottom end, she says, of the library business.

When the Washington Department of Fishery moved to Olympia in 1960, Brodney dropped her state job for one with the Feds. And she kept on with her cataloguing job. For five years she went to school and worked a sixty-hour week, in her two jobs. At the end of that time she had a B.A. in zoology and $1,000 in hand. All of which she blew on a marlin-fishing trip to Baja California that turned out to be a bust.

In the ensuing years, she saved enough from her dual employment to take an annual fishing trip: Nova Scotia for salmon, Florida for tarpon, but nothing truly off the beaten path, nothing that could be called exotic angling. Apart from those trips, Brodney's life was a little boring. Mostly she was "reading" fish scales. "After a while I could see that it was going to be either fisheries work or the library," she says. "And the more I saw of those damn doctorate guys, the more it looked to me like books. Big-shot doctors reading scales all day, racial analysis of the red salmon. All that chemistry of the blood stuff! And then something happened that really turned me off. A field trip to the Kispiox came up and they wouldn't let me go. This would be around 1963, before Women's Lib really started up. They sent some pip-squeak male instead, junior to me. That was the end of my scale reading.

"I checked and found that a master's program in library science at Rutgers was the fastest and cheapest way for me to get an advanced degree. It took a year. Then I got a job in the Library of Congress. I've been there sixteen years, and I can blow five or six grand a year on fishing!"

On the Saturday night before Brennan and I were to leave for Brazil, Brodney got a call through to me in New York City from Boa Vista. There was a little delay in obtaining the boats, she said, but the governor of Roraima Territory, in which we would be fishing, was taking a keen interest in the expedition. Meanwhile, by the time Brennan and I arrived in Manaus, officials would have made arrangements to fly us into the strip at Santa Maria by light aircraft. A message confirming the arrangements would await us at the Tropical Hotel.

It's five o'clock when you get to the Tropical after clearing Manaus customs following the weekly airline flight from Miami, and at that point your main interest lies in getting to bed, which seemed all the more reasonable when we found no message awaiting us. But it was sure to be there soon. The morning would be time enough to study the governor's instructions, we felt.

I arose at the respectable (considering the circumstances) hour of 10:30 the next morning, and after breakfast sauntered over to the main desk. No message. No message? How strange. A message for a Mr. Brennan, then? No, sir. No need to worry, I told myself, suppressing a qualm or two. The officials were being considerate. Knowing at what hour we had arrived, they were holding off until lunchtime. It occurred to me that I was doing all the donkey work, so I woke Brennan up. "We ready to leave?" he grunted sleepily. I told him that I didn't know.

At lunchtime I still didn't know. "Better call the airport," Brennan said. "The air taxi company. They're probably waiting out there for us."

The interesting news from the airport, politely conveyed to us by the young man at the hotel desk who had made the call for us in Portuguese, was that no one had heard of us. Also, that the last aircraft to head to Santa Maria, three years previously, had disappeared into the jungle with all hands.

Brennan, an Irishman raised in London and transplanted to Manhattan, sat down on his suitcase and put his head in his hands. "I could call the priest," the desk clerk said.

Brennan looked at him alarmed. "It's not as bad as that," he said.

"I mean the priest with the airplane," said the clerk. "The one who goes to see the Indians." He looked at our tackle. "The priest who catches the *tucunaré*."

The Reverend Bennie de Merchant of the United Pentecostal Church of Brazil, a native of New Brunswick, Canada, and sixteen years a jungle missionary, might have been a little disturbed to be described as a priest, but he responded to our call. The trip up to Santa Maria would be a long one, he said in his mild-mannered way. With some embarrassment he told us how expensive it would be—about $1,350—with the huge cost principally accounted for by the $3.20 a gallon that aviation fuel went for in Brazil. But we realized, did we not, that the money would be helping a good cause? It would go to the church.

That was understood, we said, but what of the sad reputation of the Santa Maria airstrip? Well, that was all right, the reverend said, because he had a Cessna floatplane. Could we be ready in half an hour? The trip would take maybe three hours and we'd have to get in before dark.

Almost certainly the reverend would have helped us anyway. But it turned out that the clerk had told him we were going fishing. And perhaps for the first time since he had arrived in Amazonia as a twenty-three-year-old missionary, he had found somebody to talk to about fishing. *Fly*-fishing, that is. Diffidently, after he had stowed our rod tubes in the Cessna, he dug into his hip pocket and dragged out a glassine envelope that held a couple of salmon-size Mickey Finn streamers. "Tied these up myself," he said. "Best flies going for the big *tucunaré*. Take 'em with you."

It seemed a good moment to ask what a *tucunaré* was. "In Spanish, it's *pavón*," de Merchant said. "You probably know it as peacock bass." I did, but by reputation only as one of the finest freshwater game fish of South and Central America.

"See my fly rod in the holder, back of the cabin?" the reverend said. "That's my spare tire, that's my survival kit. Reckon if I ever crash in the jungle—manage to miss smashing into a tree trunk and just rip the wings off—I could grab that fly rod and maybe make it for a week or two."

Brennan said he didn't want to hear about that, but de Merchant was carried away by now. "What I do," he said, "as long as I'm not pressed for time, is stop en route to church—I plant churches out here, using that floatplane as a tool—and if I see one of those black holes in the jungle, I drop in and roll out a Mickey Finn or something else I've dreamed up on the vise. Best fish I ever got was twenty-four pounds, but I've had bass on that have towed the Cessna along. *Slowly* towed it along," he added with pastorly accuracy.

"Black holes?" Brennan asked. It did sound a little science-fictitious. "I'll show you," the reverend promised.

By then we had lifted out of Manaus. Against all the odds it looked as if we were going to meet Brodney and her party. It would also add a little spice to the encounter when she discovered that the Reverend de Merchant had been laying out fly lines in Amazonia for sixteen years now. Below us was the vast expanse of the Rio Negro, incredibly, a mere tributary of the Amazon. "Here's a black hole," de Merchant said.

He banked the Cessna away from the river. Below us in thick jungle, looking as black as ink, was a little lake. "Just part of the Negro in the rainy season," he said, "but when the water drops the fish stay in it because it's deep and cool. And nobody can get at 'em. Except me! Wish I had time to take you boys in there, but we have to make Santa Maria before sundown."

We had left behind the last of the riverside shacks long before we hit the confluence of the Branco and the Negro. Soon we were flying over a tributary of the Branco, the Jauaperi. "Bad river," the reverend said. "Nobody takes a boat up there. That's where the Waimari Indians are. The ones who did the killings in '75. Wait a bit." He went down to little more than treetop height and flew away from the river for ten minutes. "Look over to the left," he said.

A patch of jungle had been cleared and in the center was a great Indian roundhouse. "Nobody home," de Merchant said. "Whole tribe away somewhere." It was hard, in the cooled cabin of the Cessna, to appreciate that down there were some of the last people in the world holding out against the tide of petro-civilization, who had killed when they saw their hunting grounds threatened by construction projects such as the Trans-Amazonia Highway, who themselves would probably not survive this decade.

Now, though, the Branco itself gleamed silver ahead of us. We had been a long time in the air. "Twenty minutes to go," the reverend said, and finally, there in the fading light, was a group of shacks. It was Santa Maria, and as we landed all of its couple of hundred residents came out and stood in ankle-deep mud on the shore to greet us. There was no sign, though, of the Brodney group. "We'll have to stay here tonight," said the reverend as he secured the Cessna, "if we can."

There had been one small miracle that day already, when de Merchant and his floatplane had materialized. Now there was another. A man emerged from the crowd speaking the slightly pedantic, modulated English of an Indian, an *Asian* Indian. A political refugee, we learned later, from upriver, from Guyana, which has a substantial Asian Indian population. "Wait here, please," he said, "and I will see what I can do." He was back in five minutes, triumphant. "I have three hammocks for you," he said.

It occurred to both Brennan and me that we were going to have to gamble. We could call the trip off, head back to Manaus next morning with the reverend, or we could take the chance and wait in the settlement for Brodney. If she didn't show, we were in for a long vacation in Santa Maria and a long boat trip back—when the rains came.

That thought kept sleep away after we'd slung our hammocks in a bare wooden hut on stilts at the river's edge, but the animal kingdom would have ensured a broken night, anyway. It was our first taste of the jungle: the insane chatter of roosting parrots, the howler monkeys giving their celebrated imitation of a Cape Cod nor'easter, the frogs in divisional strength. Brennan claimed he heard a jaguar roar that night, but that was County Kilkenny imagination, I told him. With pelts fetching $60 on the illegal market, there would be few wildcats this close to Santa Maria.

Dawn was decision time. Back with the reverend, or stay put? Unsolicited, de Merchant made us an offer. There would be no extra charge for a twenty-minute scout further up the Branco—a little better than thirty miles. For the moment we could postpone making our choice.

Santa Maria turned out again to see us off and we headed upstream. For ten minutes, slightly more, there was no sign of a craft on the river. And then, way ahead, barely in sight, was a whitish patch. A cliff? A rock? A boat! Not them, couldn't be them, Brennan and I told one another, not daring to look too closely as the Cessna came in low to check what we had glimpsed. And then, no mistake, there were Brodney and someone else setting off in a dugout from a big white river boat. The reverend put the Cessna down, gently running it ashore on the sandbar. "Oh, uh, there you are, Kay," I said. Or something like that.

Not only was Brodney there, but so were Pete Gorinsky, his mother, Nelly, skipper Lauro Bamberg, his son Glenn and a stout crew of Brazilians recruited in Boa Vista. But things hadn't gone well for them, either. Instead of the three big dugout canoes they wanted to hire, the officials at Boa Vista had insisted they take an old Manaus-built *barque pescero*, a cumbersome Amazon commercial fishing boat with most of the deck space taken up by an enormous fish box that normally held an iced-down catch and left little room for people. As auxiliary craft there were one big dugout, a tiny canoe and an old aluminum skiff with two outboards. The outfitters in Boa Vista seemed to be more concerned with cornflakes than boats. Americans, the governor's men were convinced, could not function without cornflakes, and they had vainly scoured Boa Vista for breakfast cereal. It had taken Brodney and the Gorinskys a long time to convince the solicitous bureaucrats that this wasn't necessary. What with the great cornflakes chase and other delays, Brodney and company had been three days late leaving for the rendezvous at Santa Maria.

This meant that they had had to head straight down the Branco, with no time for scouting fish on the way. The lumbering old forty-five-footer had gone aground on most of the available sandbanks downstream of Caracarai and had finally got firmly stuck at the dry mouth of Lago dos Boto a couple of hours' traveling time from Santa Maria. When we spotted them from the Cessna, they had just managed to get it afloat again.

But another difficulty arose. Brennan and I had planned to spend a couple of weeks with Kay's expedition. Now we found out that in three days the reverend was scheduled to leave Manaus for a month-long circuit of his outlying churches. As a fisherman, he responded to the disappointment on our faces. All right, he said, he'd postpone his trip and pick us up in seven days. It was the best he could do.

We said goodby. De Merchant walked off across the sandbar as reluctantly as a kid being dragged away early from a birthday party. "I'd love to go fishing with you," he said, reeling in the line he'd been using to get in a few moments of angling as his passengers had talked with Brodney. The Cessna took off, wagging its wings, and' there was a sudden feeling of desolation, a realization of the utter remoteness of the place we now found ourselves in.

Nelly broke the spell. A brisk, tough old lady, whose father had been one of the pioneers in Guyana, which was then British Guiana, she's now virtually dispossessed in her native land. Until recently she had lived alone on what was left of the family ranch; her children were scattered—two living in Canada, one in London, one in St. Maarten, one still in Georgetown, Guyana, and Pete, now of our party, in Costa Rica. "Time we made camp," she told us, in a sharp, pioneering sort of way.

So we headed downstream until we hit the mouth of the Tapera Grande, another tributary of the Branco. Nelly led a machete-brandishing party ashore to clear away a patch of jungle at the water's edge, an operation that moved slowly and circumspectly. First, with sticks, members of the party had to check the undergrowth and the holes in tree trunks for snakes. Then they hacked out a clearing, leaving strategically placed saplings for slinging hammocks and mosquito nets. Next came the burning of the undergrowth and the dead leaves: snakes, apparently, hate to cross ashy ground. The fire also killed the ticks. A timber fire had to be set to smolder damply, in spite of the oppressive heat, to keep away the *cabouri*, the tiny, viciously biting black flies that are universal along the river. It all took a long time.

"Why don't we just sleep on the boat?" Brennan wanted to know. The *crewmen*, he was gravely told, slept aboard the good ship *Alziera Lima*—they considered anybody who slept in the jungle crazy—and there was no room aboard for us.

By the time the camp was rigged, the sun was high, which meant it wouldn't be worth fishing until the last couple of hours of light. It was a good time to check the hammocks. Even in the jungle, siesta time comes along. Only one thing seemed to have been missing. "How about lunch?" Brennan asked plaintively. "We eat just once a day," Pete told him kindly. "When we get back in from fishing."

Pete is a tall man, a gemmologist, as well as a passionate fly-fisher. He had first met Brodney on the Rupununi River in Guyana in 1972. They both wanted to catch an *arapaima*—reputed to be the world's largest freshwater fish—on fly. It reaches six hundred pounds, but a hundred and fifty-pounder would be a more likely catch. Pete, though, not Brodney, had finally caught one—a mere sixty- or seventy-pounder, but an *arapaima* nonetheless. And on a fly.

He told us this as we swung in our broad and comfortable Brazilian hammocks that afternoon. "Stop mentioning the goddam *arapaima*," snapped Brodney from her corner.

"I don't know what an *arapaima* looks like," I said, pressing the subject.

"Like an *arawana*, only bigger and with a flatter head . . . and I never heard of it," Brodney said bitterly.

"Let's talk about *arawana*. This is an *arawana* trip."

"Now," said Pete, "*there's* a fish, one you have to stalk. Beautiful, greyhounding fish, hits a fly hard. We'll get *lukunanni*, too. . . ."

I told Pete that the nomenclature was becoming confusing. "*Tucunaré*," he said, ignoring my confusion. "*Pavón*, peacock bass. We have two kinds. One with broad black stripes we call *wacu*. Another one with dapplings on its side, like a fawn. We call 'em deer lukes."

That first night, our first fishing night, we took the big dugout a few miles up the Itapera Grande. The signs were bad. No moving fish along the margins. Random casts stirred nothing. Though we'd given the Itapera Grande little enough time, it seemed that the plan was that we should head up the smaller Tapera Pequeno the next day.

In the jungle the first rule is to preserve the civilized amenities. One bathes in the river by flashlight, because only at night do the flies cease their patrols. In daylight it was disastrous not to wear long-sleeved shirts with slacks tucked into socks. "What about the stingrays?" Brennan asked.

"Which of the three venomous kinds do you mean?" Pete asked politely. "Don't worry. They'll not be in the running water where we'll swim."

Later, cleansed and unstung, we gathered on board the *Alziera Lima*. Glenn Bamberg had a great cooking pot full of a brown, meaty stew waiting for us. "Turtle," Brodney said, looking at Brennan and me expectantly. She was disappointed if she expected us to shudder and turn away. Starved since morning, we fell on it like jungle veterans.

When supper was over, we cringed a little at the hideous anthology of river dangers in which we were instructed. The snakes: fer-de-lance, bushmasters, coral. All venomous. Then the crushing snakes: anacondas, water boas. Next the crocodiles, more properly caimans.

"Thought they'd all been converted into handbags," Brennan said. By way of removing that thought from Brennan's brain, Pete swung his flashlight along the bank. Two, three, four pairs of eyes gleamed red in the beam. "Always remember," said Pete, "alligators reflect red, snakes white."

"Except the females," Nelly said.

"Don't fall in the water," Brodney said. "We also have electric eels, all sorts of fangy fish."

"And we have *vampire* fish," said Pete, gleaming wickedly at Brennan.

"You're putting us on," I told him.

"No," he said. "I've seen big peacock bass and catfish come floating dead down the river. Perfect, except that they have no blood. The *biara* have been at them. The vampire fish. Oh, yes, and watch the porpoises. They don't kill you, they just bump you about. Then the piranhas get you." All that day we'd watched the porpoises rolling, huge ones, more than a thousand miles from the sea. I'd always regarded them as friendly creatures.

"But they can't get you in *camp*," Brennan said.

"No," Pete said. "All you have to worry about in camp are the wild pigs, the snakes, the bad spiders, the ticks, the vampire bats. The jaguars won't hurt you. Probably."

"I may sit up a little tonight," Brennan said. "Where did we put the duty-free Scotch?"

"No, seriously," Pete said. "You just have to be watchful. You'll have a net. You'll be high off the ground. You'll have a flashlight in your hammock and a machete within reach. We aren't putting you on. Not that much. Amazonia defends itself fiercely."

Indeed, that night in what inevitably came to be called Fort Brennan, we slept soundly enough, and at first light we were piling tackle into the canoes and pushing up into the Tapera Pequeno.

Within half an hour we could see ahead of us something that fishermen pray for, clouds of screaming, wheeling terns plunging into shoals of baitfish. And as we got closer, we spotted the swirls of feeding predatory fish, great slashings of the water, and all of us were trembling with anticipation that the dreams which had brought us thousands of miles into Amazonia would be fulfilled.

We slid the canoes ashore. Fish were feeding everywhere. As soon as a fly or a lure hit the water, it was taken. "*Tucunaré!*" Pete was shouting. "Peacock bass everywhere!"

The frenzy lasted an hour. At the end of it, one or two of the biggest bass might have gone fifteen pounds. There were other fish, too. *Houris*, silver pikelike fish with heavy scales and Halloween pumpkin fangs. Fish that some of the crewmen had never seen before.

Then, consistent with its infinite variety, Amazonia gave us another kind of fishing. As we paddled upstream on the Branco, gray shadows passed under our boat. More big bass. But this time there was no frenzy. The fish had to be stalked. We beached our boat and waded in with caution, fearing the stingrays. When the peacocks hit they bolted across the shallows. "Like bonefish!" I yelled at Brodney. "And they jump as well!" she yelled back.

And then, before noon, the action was over; the sun was beating down. In attempting to reduce the heat, you dip your hat in the river, fill it and then pour the water over your head. When that proves insufficient you get out of the canoe, kick the rays away and lie down in the shallows, with just your nose out of water. In the canoe again, your clothes take five minutes to dry.

We spent three days at Fort Brennan, in a self-indulgent orgy of catching the Tapera Pequeno's fish, of experiencing the splendors and miseries of the jungle. Among the splendors were the birds: hyacinth macaws, toucans, great tiger herons, bitterns painted like totem poles. And there was the wildness of the peacock bass.

The chief misery: the cabouri flies endlessly attacking. The sub-chief-misery: the cuisine. The second night, the cauldron came up from below with the glassy and reproachful eyes of the bass we'd caught staring out from the oily broth. Amerindians, Brodney said firmly, consider the heads a delicacy. I released all my bass after that.

The nights were time for talk. Once, after we'd eaten what passed for the day's meal, I asked Brodney whether there weren't well-organized fish camps in Amazonia, with ice, beds, air conditioning, good food to come back to after the day's sport.

She made it very clear how much she despised conventional fishing camps. "All that macho stuff," she said. "All that top rod nonsense. All that fishing for the guides. What a pampered aristocracy they are! I like to poop around in my own time, just trying things. All those guys who have to catch the biggest fish and then try to make the woman in camp! I like peace to *fish*, goddammit. People asking all the time if you're *enjoying* yourself. I just happen to have a sullen, glum expression. Doesn't mean I'm not enjoying myself. What I love down here is the freedom from all that."

We might have stayed even longer on the Tapera Pequeno, but

Brodney's questing spirit wouldn't allow it. She'd had enough peacock bass, she said. She wanted *arawana*.

On the trip downstream Brodney and the Gorinskys had spotted what they thought was surefire *arawana* water, but now it was a long way upriver. The Lago du Amaua it's called, a lake system cut off in the dry season from the Branco, so that we would have to carry the canoes in. The area had a guardian, an old man known only as Tertuliani, who — though by lawyers' reckoning he owned none of Lago du Amaua — protected it fiercely from his house at its mouth, his guardianship being all the more effective for the reputation he had along the river as a *condomblé* priest, *condomblé* being a local variation of voodoo.

But it wasn't voodoo that diverted us from Lago du Amaua. Lauro Bamberg thought we might have trouble getting up there in the low water conditions. Temptingly, the chart showed another big lake system that was much nearer: the Lago du Mechede. After much heart searching, we decided to head there.

It was half a day's trip, and in the hottest part of the day we labored to set up what we called, before we abandoned it, Camp Despair. There was more stingrays in the water there than in any place we'd been, a lot of alligators, plenty of water snakes. But no fish. Or no fish of any consequence.

That night we made a hard decision. We had made a four-hour diversion from the main river to head up to Mechede. We would have to add that to the eight hours needed to reach Amaua from Fort Brennan and the time it would take to set up camp again. But it had to be done if we wanted *arawana*. Pete broke the news to the crew that a 5:30 A.M. start lay ahead.

Traveling upriver on a *barque pescero* in the dry season is no fun. You proceed in long zigzags, made necessary by the sandbars. Every couple of hours you inevitably run up on a bar, whereupon everybody gets out and hauls. Very occasionally there is a diversion. Once we came upon a trading boat that had been stuck fast for a week on its way to Manaus. It had *cold beer* in its refrigerator, and a good supply of bully beef and onions. The lunch that followed was the most luxurious meal we had on the river.

Once the Turtle Patrol, the government boat that protects the giant turtle of the Amazon region, caught up with us. Brennan and I had eaten turtle stew and turtle eggs before we had realized the illegality of doing so. A day or so before, Brodney had threatened, only half jokingly, to make a citizen's arrest if a particularly avid egger among the crew went collecting again. Good that she did: we had a clean boat when the law came alongside.

It was dark when we reached Amaua. By the light of a hurricane lamp we set up camp on a sandbar, rigging stakes to sling our hammocks in a kind of defensive square. Beyond the bar was Tertuliani's house. Pete went off to seek him out, to assure him we would only fish for sport, that his precious lake wouldn't be despoiled. He returned with good news. Tertuliani approved of our project. What's more, he would come with us next day and show us the best *arawana* spots. Better still, Tertuliani revealed that in the upper lake there were giant *arapaima*. They were a long way, maybe a day's travel away, though.

That night was the loudest and wildest we had tried to sleep through. The parrots and the monkeys were manic. At two o'clock the first rain of the trip hit us, mercifully lasting only a few minutes but enough to have everyone out of the hammocks. "Did you hear a coughing roar out there?" Brennan said to me nervously at one point. I told him to go to sleep.

But in the morning, leading across the sand to the water's edge were the freshly made pug marks of a jaguar. "All right," I said to Brennan, "you heard a coughing roar."

Tertuliani turned out to be a sun-dried, quizzical old gentleman who sat in his boat with his shotgun across his knee, should he be lucky enough to encounter peccary. He and Glenn Bamberg set off with us, in Tertuliani's boat, towing a small dugout behind the big one. We were running slow enough for trolling, and Nelly let out a plug. Big peacock bass started to hit right away, the striped kind, not the dappled. Eventually the channel had widened to a lagoon and close to the many fallen trees that were in the water we could see fish arrowing. "*Arawanas!*" Tertuliani announced with proprietary pride.

Sometimes other species would beat the *arawanas* to our flies. Tertuliani's lake was full of many kinds of fish. But enough *arawanas* hit to justify all the praise that Brodney had given them. Pale gold ribbons of fish, five- or six-pounders that leapt high. It was all too soon before the sport, as it had done on the Tapera Pequeno, died with the climbing sun.

For Brennan and me, it was the last day. The reverend would be coming in for us next morning. The others, more than likely, would head for the upper lake Tertuliani had revealed on the chance, just the small chance, of finding a *arapaima*. The pair of us were bitten head to foot by carbouri flies, but at least we hadn't been eaten by anything else. Head upstream on the main river until you find us, we had told the reverend. That night, before we turned in, we laid out a bright red tarp on the sand. The boat, pulled into the bushes, wouldn't be all that conspicuous from the air. "I wonder if he'll come," said Brennan.

I asked, "If you couldn't trust a missionary, whom could you trust?" And indeed, in the morning, de Merchant was only a little late. He'd had to land, he said, alongside four boats before he found ours. Soon we were waggling our wings in salutation to Brodney and the others and heading back along the Branco. An hour later, the reverend said he was low on gas but that he could get some on the next river. He brought the Cessna down close to a single, big, new-looking house. "Stay in the plane and don't take any pictures," he said. "The Brazilians get a little sensitive about this area."

From the house, as soon as we were tied up, poured maybe fifty Indians—of the Western Hemisphere sort—all men, most in brilliantly colored, clearly new bathing trunks. They crowded onto the floats of the plane, and one of them, a smiling, handsome young man, began shoving bunches of green bananas through the open cabin window. We grimaced, gestured, smiled back. This type of dialogue went on for some minutes until the reverend returned with his fuel cans. "You'd better give them something in return," he said, "only remember, each one has to have exactly the same. Not money, though. It's useless to them. Do you have a spool of monofilament?"

We did, and that was fine. They could divide it up. We took off pretty fast after that, and Brennan said, "Handsome people. Some of your flock?"

"You've just met the Waimiri," de Merchant said. "The ones who cut up the soldiers and the missionaries. I didn't know they'd be there. They come into that Indian station maybe once or twice a year to trade skins. That's where they got the pants. They were in a pretty good mood today."

The reverend's news about the Waimiri kept Brennan quiet until dinnertime back at the Tropical Hotel. He had been talking for most of a week about the steak he was going to devour when he got back into town. Now we were showered, shaved and ready for it.

In the restaurant, Brennan waved the menu away. "I know what I want," he said. "The biggest steak in the house."

The waiter gave him one of those pitying looks. "I am sorry, sir," he said. "Tonight is Thursday night. The cold buffet only."

"Hell," said Brennan.

"Civilization," I said.

RIVER CAUVERY, KARNATAKA, INDIA

CHAPTER EIGHTEEN

The Maharaja Fish

There are few indeed of the great mahseer, the
quarry of viceroys and princes, left in the rivers of India now, and
the odds are that the species may not survive the century, certainly
not the mightiest strain, the black mahseer of the Cauvery River
in Karnataka province.

INDIA

S UNDAR Raj saw the gang of poachers first,
flashes of white garments among the trees upstream on the far side
of the river. He had the glasses on them before the first dynamite
explosion rocked the valley, and his shirt and sandals were off before
the second dull "crump!" came echoing back. "I must be after them,
sah!" he said. I tried to hold him back. There were at least six of
them over there, and they would have cudgels and knives.

But Sundar was wild with rage. The previous night he had spoken
with sweet reason of how the local poachers should be handled.
"These people are purely uneducated, sah," he had said. "We must
talk to them politely. We must say, 'This is government river, so
please don't poach.' If we say, 'Get out from here!' they will say,
'This is our country. Why now come people using bad words to us?'
So politeness most important!"

Now he was furious. He broke free of me, jumped into the bottlegreen water of the Cauvery River and struck out for the far bank.
There was no way that he could call for assistance. The Indian government allowed him no radio equipment even though he was the
river's chief warden.

And that was a shame, for the fish he was trying to protect from
poachers' dynamite was *Tor mussullah*. It is the biggest of the six
mahseer species found in India and it reaches more than one-hundred-

fifty pounds—a fish "beside whom," Rudyard Kipling wrote, "the tarpon is as a herring."

I had no means of telling if Kipling was right or wrong. For a week in India's deep south, in Sundar's company, I had been after a big one without success. This is not unusual in mahseer fishing, and the experience had not eroded my obsession with the fish. It is, as you shall see, a creature that has obsessed fishermen in India for a long time. In the century before this one, in the upper echelons of the Raj, catching one's mahseer was a rite of passage like killing one's tiger. Hardy Brothers, the prestigious British tacklemakers, advertised uncrushable hooks for the great beasts, and shipped out steel-cored, split-cane rods by the dozen to maharajas who might need them should a viceroy come calling. The social apogee of the mahseer was reached in January 1922, when the Prince of Wales, later the Duke of Windsor, fished as the guest of the Maharaja of Mysore, now the state of Karnataka, on the Kabini, a large tributary of the Cauvery. Unfortunately, HRH had to be content with an eighteen-pounder while, somewhat undiplomatically, his companion, Admiral Sir Lionel Halsey, landed one of sixty-eight pounds.

A fine fish, but not exceptional. As early as 1906, Mr. C.E. Murray-Aynsley had taken the first mahseer weighing more than one hundred pounds, and in 1919 came a 119-pounder, which would stand as an all-India record until 1946. This fish was taken by Lieut.-Col. J.S. Rivett-Carnac, who wrote in a contemporary magazine of a difficult fight which ended when his host, a Mr. P.F. Bowring "gaffed him beautifully in the throat." The colonel, as an accompanying illustration reveals, wore a Custer-style mustache, while Mr. Bowring was rather plump.

That is the kind of story on which obsessions feed. I had come across it in a dusty file I was examining early in 1984, when, through the network of contacts one builds in a lifetime of fishing, I had begun to hear whispers of a river in India where this great crimson-finned, golden-scaled maharaja of a fish still thrived in numbers. My chief contact at that time was an Englishman named Bob Howitt, who, until he was hit by mahseer fever, had been a diamond buyer for De Beers. He had first picked up the bug in 1972 in an antique bookshop in Salisbury, England, where, browsing, he had come upon Henry Sullivan Thomas's 1877 classic, *The Rod in India*. He promptly fell under the spell of this long-ago-and-far-away fishing. He headed to India and there found a most depressing state of affairs.

"Rightly or wrongly, the rivers had been looked after as preserves for sport fishing by the British and the maharajas," he told me. "Nobody ever used dynamite then. It would have been worse than jail if the Maharaja's men caught you. But, unhappily, after Indian independence nobody had a plan for fisheries conservation or development in the rivers. You can't explain to a villager about conservation. Hunger is hunger." The Indians routinely bombed or netted the fish they needed, greatly depleting the population. Then, in 1957, the Indian government began a much-needed damming program, but again there was no thought of fish conservation or protection.

Despite such negative prospects, Howitt persisted in his quest, and everything began to come together at last when he met a young angler in Sivasamudram, a town near the Cauvery's prime fishing stretch. This fellow was the hero of the local fishermen, a native superman who habitually fished with three hundred yards of sixty-pound-test line wound around a cotton bobbin, who clambered down sheer rock faces into the most difficult gorges, and who, more than once, had been pulled into the river by a great mahseer and had swum with it until it was exhausted. This paragon was, of course, my own courageous companion and guide, Sundar Raj. From him Howitt learned of a barely accessible stretch of the Cauvery River where there were still giant fish. "What made it special was that, at the top of the stretch, the Cauvery runs right off the Deccan Plateau, at the Gaganchucki and Barachucki Falls, a straight drop of four hundred feet," Howitt told me later. "Then, twenty-five miles downstream at Meke-datu, there's another set of falls, so that between the two is a perfect fish trap. And, until very recently, the jungle was close to impenetrable here, and a lot of the bank is still tough to reach, with high cliffs and huge, tumbled boulders."

Howitt spent six months learning all that Sundar Raj could teach him, and in that time caught fish of ninety-two and eighty-eight pounds and fifteen more of at least fifty pounds. Then, in 1981, the diamond market crashed, and Howitt soon decided to go back to India. This time he was on a much grander mission than mere personal fishing. "I had decided," he said, "to make the mahseer famous again."

He began by appealing to the Indian government. "I told the officials, 'This river is still rife with big fish. It can be protected. Don't knock your national treasure, the tiger of the fishes, on the head. Protect it as you did the tiger!' " This was the thrust of a campaign which ended triumphantly in 1982 when the state of Karnataka granted the travel company Howitt represents a ten-year lease on sixteen magical mystery miles along the Cauvery and let Howitt cut in jeep trails and construct two fishing camps.

Early this year I headed there myself. The journey started in earnest at Bangalore when I climbed into an old made-in-India British Morris Oxford, a classic family car of the 1950s, called an Ambassador on the subcontinent. Progress was ambassadorial, slow and stately for one hundred twenty miles until we hit the exuberant explosion of temples and palaces in pink, blue and gold that is Mysore City, the ancient capital. It is now one long jam of motorized rickshaws and carts drawn by the *amrat mahal*, cattle with sweeping, lovingly gilded horns. The Ambassador bulled through, horn blaring. The landscape changed, becoming hillier with fewer villages. The road became a red dirt track and narrowed, climbing for ten miles and then diving into a series of corniche bends until the Cauvery gleamed silver below us. On its banks were the tents of Bimishvirri, one of two fishing camps. Sundar Raj himself was waiting to welcome me with his crew of river guards-guides, immaculately khaki clad, standing at attention alongside the camp jeep.

Believe it or not, the Cauvery is a river to make a Scottish salmon fisherman homesick. You would imagine that a river in the south of India would be like Kipling's African "great gray-green, greasy Limpopo River, all set about with fever-trees." But the Cauvery was a wild, clear torrent, now crashing through the jungle, now crammed into gorges, now opening into broad pools. It looked fine for the gear I unpacked, big bait-casting reels loaded with twenty-pound monofilament, heavy metal spoons and saltwater plugs. And I'd also brought, a touch hopefully, a No. 11 fly outfit, bought originally for tarpon in the Florida Keys.

Sundar looked over my plugs and lures skeptically. He said, "Sah, no sah. Here we are using only ragi. Come, sah, and I will show you." He vanished into the dark recesses of the cooking tent and emerged with what looked like two large, rusty cannonballs left over from the Indian mutiny. "Ragi paste, sah," Sundar said cajolingly. "Very good. Made with millet flour, aniseed, cardamom and rice powder." I was aghast. Had I come all this way to dunk *doughballs*? In all the eulogies to the fish I had read, nobody had ever mentioned doughballs. I said as much to Sundar.

"Oh, sah, up in north, in Nepal, plug and spoon very good killers," he replied. "But small fish there. Here big fish want the natural bait. Best is ragi." He went on anxiously, "Don't worry, sah. This way I get you one fish, at least twenty-five- to thirty-pounder. Then after, we try plugs and spoons."

It was the only game in town. In this river, whose rapids looked perfect for plug or spoon, it was ragi or nothing. Sundar's watchful corps of guides wanted it that way and were reluctant to let me stray too far from the deep pools. And not entirely without reason. The very first evening, we set out to fish a pool called *Hati Mudu*, or Elephant Pool. There was a beach of white sand which looked to be a comfortable place to sit and dunk ragi. I said so to Sundar. "Oh, no, sah, this is home of marsh mugger," he said. A marsh mugger, it turned out, was a fourteen-foot, flesh-eating crocodile. I got Sundar's point.

We would fish from the "island" instead, he said, pointing out to a big flat rock in the middle of the river. I looked around for a boat but saw none until Sundar turned over what I had taken to be a smooth brown rock.

I saw that it was—of all things—a coracle. There are only two places in the entire world where you find coracles, and the other is close to my birthplace in Wales, where they have been used for netting Atlantic salmon since the time of the pre-Roman Britons. Riding one is like sitting in a giant sugar bowl. But it's the perfect craft in a fast, turbulent river; you float on the water, not in it, and you bounce off or slide over rocks with ease.

But the old Welsh salmon fishers I knew, whose coracles are constructed of tarred canvas over wood frames, would have tut-tutted over Sundar's craft. Made of bamboo and buffalo hide, the crude needlework left gaping holes. Sundar was surprised at my concern. "We will get across *easy*, sah," he said. "The water comes in not very fast." He was close to being right. We crouched in the bottom of the coracle while the Cauvery flowed into it. Maniacally Sundar paddled, maniacally I bailed with a pink plastic bowl. As we reached the rock, the water was only up to our knees.

All this took a long time, and it was five o'clock before our balls of ragi, the size of kiwi fruit, hit the water. The time didn't matter, Sundar said. "These fish have migrating habits, sah. They go up and down the river, and here they start feeding at five-thirty. You having nibblings yet, sah?"

Yes, I told him, I was having nibblings, but I didn't think they came from a fifty-pound mahseer. Sundar told me that first, small fish made nibblings, then nibblings stopped, then along came monster fish and your rod went *chock chock bang!*

An hour went by. At intervals the bait was changed. Once, after a stronger-than-usual nibbling, I hauled in an X-rated creature a foot and a half long, with enormous, gristly lips and bright red eyes. "A pink carp, sah! Very, very big one, sah!" said Sundar dutifully, but he had the grace to grin. In the Cauvery, I would soon learn, there were all manner of carp, red, black and gray carp as well as pink, all of them with a distressing appetite for ragi. But as dusk fell, all small-fish activity ceased for a minute. Then came *chock chock bang!* I hauled back the rod. For a moment there was the feeling of having hooked a brick wall that pulsated. Then, nothing.

"Oh, sah," Sundar said reproachfully, "you are too soon." I reeled up. There on one barb of the big treble hook hung a giant, translucent scale, a good two inches across. "Forty-pound, fifty-pound fish, sah," said Sundar. "But now we must go home before dark." He looked over his shoulder with some care for a moment; then we were in the coracle again, taking a wet ride home.

In camp it was time for warm Indian vodka and an inspirational tale from Sundar: "You know, actually, sah, my age is seven when I start fishing, and in my short life, for I am twenty-nine years old, I hate to catch any other fish but mahseer, the big monster fish. In my hometown, Sivasamudram, people will fish for anything, carp, eels, anything. But I hate that. I like *crash!* So one day, I am trying from morning until night with no bite. At a quarter to five, *ker-lang ker-lang!*, the thunder starts, then big rain. I find a beautiful cave and I sit in it until the rain stops in half an hour. Now there is mud smell and sticks floating and suddenly I see a huge fish rolling in the rapids. Very small head but a huge monster body, a female. I change my hook to a very big one and I put on some bait. It goes to the bottom and sticks, as if a huge snag had it. But it is the monster! My line goes *jag,* slack, *jag,* slack, then *zee-zee-zee.* Then *chirk chirk!* The line is burning in my fingers, thick line, and the fish is a hundred yards up the river. *Chirk chirk!* I am not worried. I have three hundred yards of thick line. The fish changes her mood, comes downstream into a full deep channel. I am standing on a rock, but now, *chah, chah, chah!* the line is going one-hundred-fifty yards, one-hundred-seventy yards, two-hundred yards. I am jumping from rock to rock, but soon my three-hundred yards is finished. Now I have covered more than half a mile. I cannot control! I am losing skin! One mile more, I am chasing the fish and jumping rocks. Suddenly there comes a big pool! I try to cross by the rocks, but I am dragged into the water. Now I am 97.5 percent tired, and I am worried I will lose my life. I decide to stop chasing fish. My line goes stretch, stretch, *stretch*. Then, *pa chuff!* It is broken.

"I sit for a long time, just thinking. I think she is easy a 170-pound, 180-pound fish, because I could feel. Some people come to pull me out of the river. They had watched. 'Excuse me, please sah!' one says. He is much my elder. 'I am fishing for thirty years, I am experienced person. I tell you that this is not a fish. This is a ghost.' I tell him it is a monster mahseer. 'No, a ghost,' he say. 'It try to pull you under a rock.'

"Then my mother comes. She tells me I must not go more than two miles from home in future. She tells me I must be home by 5:30 P.M. I tell her, 'I am a big fisherman. And this is my first big fish.' But I am at that time only eleven years old so I obey what she says to do." Every evening thereafter, to accompany Indian vodka at tent temperature, Sundar told stories of great fish hooked on ragi.

My own first mahseer was considerably more modest, a fourteen-pounder that still made me work for ten minutes on an outfit that would be adjudged heavy for big Atlantic salmon. But it *was* a first. I looked at it for a long time as it hung in the water at my feet before I released it. Its sides were a magnificent brassy gold, crosshatched with proportionately enormous scales, and the fins were a vivid scarlet. The lips, though, were extraordinary, protrusible like a sturgeon's, and leather-hard, but toothless. Instead, like some fish of the drum family, the mahseer is equipped with formidable pharyngeal (throat) teeth, grinders that could crush an incautious hand. The power of that smallish fish made me more eager than ever to go after them in a more sporting, less static way. I wanted to range about on the river, to begin casting flies or spoons instead of merely dunking doughballs. Why not?

It was siesta time, the afternoon of my second day, when I learned why that sort of thing was discouraged. It had been a less than peaceful siesta anyway. First there had sounded the jackhammer persistence of the song of what early representatives of the Raj called the brain-fever bird. "You're *ill*, you're *ill*, you're *ill*," it whistled. Then troops of langurs arrived to raid the tamarind trees and had become engaged in a noisy running battle with the camp dogs. Then a new note—human voices raised in grievance—had been added. A half-dozen khaki-clad guides whom I hadn't seen before had arrived in camp. I asked Sundar what the trouble was.

"These people, sah, are worried about elephants," he said. They were an anti-poaching squad encamped ten miles upriver. With little rain in three months, the elephants migrate to Cauvery River. "Sah, the elephant is a danger creature. Sometimes he use front leg to stomp you, sometimes kick. These guards have big tusker problem, sah. One big male up there gone musth crazy [a rutting-season frenzy]. Last night, when they sleeping, tusker came right behind their tents, trumpeting. They throw three, four thunder flashes [firecrackers] at them. Elephants ran into the valley, but one hour later they are back among the tents. So these people, sah, they have run here to ask for protection."

By coincidence or not, that evening, as we walked up the jungle path to fish, Sundar grabbed at my shirt, pulled me down and pointed. "Little bit dangerous, sah, they have babies," he hissed. Ahead of us, maybe fifty yards away, twelve wild elephants, very dark, were moving down to the river. There were two calves and at least two big tuskers. Sundar did the time-honored wind check with a pinch of dust. "O.K. for the moment," he said, "but if they come, what you must do is throw your hat away, run zig-zag, then jump in the water." On that cue, the lead male turned and looked straight at us. His trunk went up. "Little bit dangerous," Sundar repeated unnecessarily. The tusker shook his head, then moved ponderously into the water. The rest followed. There would be no fishing there that evening, and now I understood the insistence on static fishing with ragi. This was no place to go roving, after all. "In olden days, this was a tiger area," Sundar said one day. "Very thick forest. There were no villages, only forest, and an adult male tiger must have twenty-five square miles. . . ."

In the valley of the Cauvery, it was possible to see, almost before one's eyes, the shrinking of this jungle. Along the banks, bands of itinerant illegal woodcutters were common, sometimes forty or fifty strong. One saw their campfires at night on hillsides that were almost bare. The wild elephant herds were smaller, too. "Local people made too much poaching for ivory, but they only got a little bit of money for a pair of tusks from the city dealer," Sundar said. "But when dealers sold them, it was for much more."

There were still enough spectacular sights in the Cauvery valley, though, to enliven my continuing siege of the mahseer. Once, in a single frame, so to speak, rounding a river bend in the coracle, I came upon a peacock, a sambur stag that must have weighed more than four hundred pounds and the black bulk of a wild boar. Before my time was over, there would also be sloth bears, jackals and three leopard sightings.

None of this was bringing me any closer to my big fish, although Sundar remained unflaggingly optimistic and there were small mahseer aplenty. Every time I suggested that it might be a good idea if I walked up the river a way and tossed a plug into the white water, I had the same response: "Too many elephants, sah! Too many very bad, wicked cobras!"

I came close to mutiny when, out of sheer honesty, Sundar revealed one possible reason for our non-success. Six miles upriver, a Swiss TV crew had been fishing earlier in the month. "Swiss people catch two ninety-pounders, two seventy-pounders, two sixty-fours, a sixty-two, a fifty-six, a fifty-one," Sundar said. "Also lose seven or eight monsters. These fish will not hit again till next season. We handle them tying ropes around them, tagging them. They are really disturbed. And we have been fishing these same pools for two or three weeks now."

Disgusted, I decided to give the fish a break. There was a small pilgrimage I wanted to make anyway. "Tell me," I asked Sundar, "where would I find Mr. J. de Wet Van Ingen?"

"Oh, sah," said Sundar, "anybody in Mysore will tell you."

Yes, indeed. Once, in the heyday of the Raj and big-game hunting, the Van Ingens' Mysore taxidermy business was one of the largest and most famous on earth: 130 men were employed there in 1922 when Eugene Van Ingen, the firm's founder, was deputed to accompany the Prince of Wales when he fished the Kabini River. Eugene was then the acknowledged mahseer king of all India.

Two years before HRH's visit, Eugene's elder son, J. de Wet, who was then eighteen, had already served notice that he would be following the family tradition. He took a fish from the Cauvery that weighed 107 pounds. In 1946, that same "young" Van Ingen, by then middle-aged and elegant, black-mustached in the military "toothbrush" style, caught a 120-pounder, an all-India rod-and-line record that still stands.

The elegance was still there when I visited J. de Wet in Mysore this spring. It was accented by a perfectly knotted yellow silk ascot, and a notable and humorous spryness, although he is now eighty-three years old. "Dear me. Not much to show you, I'm afraid," he said as I looked about his great taxidermy emporium. He looked me straight in the eye. "There's no hunting now, but there seem to be a hell of a lot of bears and panthers knocked down by buses or found drowned *after*, seemingly, taking a bullet in the head. . . ." We walked through long rooms filled with reconstructed skeletons of beasts. Finally, in the last room, was what I had come to see. High on a wall, flanked by the heads of tigers and tuskers, the sun flashing on its great golden scales, was that 120-pound mahseer.

Even now, almost forty years on, there was the modest reluctance of his generation to talk about an achievement. He had already printed an account of the fight, in the *Bombay Natural History Journal*. It told how he had driven to the upper Kabini, fearful that it might be in flood, and how that evening there was thunder. To change his luck after a fishless day, he assembled a light rod equipped with a four-inch Silex reel and tied on a spoon. When the big fish hit he had to clamber into a coracle to stay with it. The fight was long and brutal, and in the end, he had to beach the huge fish. "It was an old hen fish," he wrote, "and I had a great feeling of remorse in killing such a fine [one]."

Next morning, Van Ingen and I drove eighty miles up-country to the place where the old angler had taken his record fish. There was nothing to be seen but a gleaming plain of water; the Kabini was dammed in the 1950s. J. de Wet stood beside me, trying to puzzle out where the river had flowed. He found a clue. "You see where the big tree sticks out of the water?" he asked. "I remember a seventy-seven-pounder being taken just there where the tree is. By a Captain Fremlin." The old eyes stared into the distance. "Oh, they don't give a damn about sport in India today, you know," he said.

Later, back at camp, I found that Howitt had arrived from Nepal and was urging Sundar, now that I had but two days left, to pull out every stop.

Ashore, we worked out a plan for my last day that would take us hiking a couple of miles up to Sambur Pool. Next morning came the drama of the dynamiting and Sundar's wild plunge in pursuit of the gang. As he swam away I sat on the rock, reflecting. Many carp, catfish and small mahseer floated belly up past me. The massacre was quite terrible. This, I could see, was a problem that would not be solved easily or soon. "Sah," Sundar had told me earlier, "these people do what work they can, like carrying stones and firewood-selling. They get only seven or eight rupees a day, like sixty of American cents. For fish you can get forty rupees a pound. You can buy some dynamite, very easily, for ten rupees from contractors. We cannot control them."

Sundar was out of sight now across the river. I suddenly realized that I was no longer under guard. I looked down the jungle trail. It seemed elephant- and cobra-free. I took off the ragi doughball and tackle. I clipped on a four-inch Swedish spoon and set off.

A hundred yards down the bank I came upon one of those medium-deep, medium-fast runs that would hold salmon if this were a salmon river. I started to fish it down methodically. About twenty paces on, my lure jammed hard in a rock. Then the rock started to move into midstream, *chirk chirk!*, slowly at first, then gathering momentum. I was calm. This, I knew, was monster fish. "Sundar! Sundar!" I yelled shrilly. There was no response, of course, and now the big fish was more than seventy yards away from me, on the far side of the river, trying to crash the rocks. I crammed down the drag, the line hummed in the light breeze and the rod doubled over.

I managed to stop him short of the rocks. He surged downstream, keeping up a steady pressure. Then, suddenly, there was no weight. I reeled in. The spoon was still there. The hook had never set prop-erly. I worked my way up the river back to camp. I kept casting. I didn't have another hit.

That evening, my last at camp, I heard Sundar's saga about the poachers. The gang had sat on the hillside laughing at him as he toiled up to them. They had rolled rocks down at him when he drew too close. He retreated, swam the river again and headed back to camp to call up reinforcements from the visiting guards who had fled from the elephants. Together, they had brought some of the poachers into custody. Sundar shouted, and from temporary im-prisonment in the cookhouse, under escort, came three of them. They did not look especially villainous. In spite of the hot night, their thin bodies shivered. "There is no excuse!" Sundar shouted at them severely. "You should be in jail, three, four years!" He gazed at them fiercely, but his anger had already ebbed, and realism had replaced it. "Next time, six years of jail!" he yelled, but he was already gesturing to the guards to release them. They slipped off into the night.

I told him about my fish, how it had gone *chirk chirk!* against a heavy drag.

"Oh, sah!" he said. "A monster fish! Only monster go *chirk chirk.*"

"Well, there you are," I said. At least, I consoled myself, I'd felt the *power* of a big mahseer. Maybe I could try again, lest the best river in India be wrecked, like the others. It didn't seem likely, but if I did, I thought I would travel viceroy class. It seemed to me that the sprightly J. de Wet could still guide the way to a big one.

And I'll bet he wouldn't use ragi dough.

CHAPTER NINETEEN

Greetings from Christmas

A magical mystery tour . . .

CHRISTMAS ISLAND

O N T H E 24th, after passing the line, land was discovered. Upon a nearer approach it was found to be one of those low islands so common in this ocean, that is, a narrow bank of land enclosing the sea within." So runs the journal of Captain James Cook. On his third Pacific voyage, commanding the ships *Discovery* and *Resolution*, he had sailed north on December 9, 1777, from Bora Bora to seek a landfall on the West coast of North America, but had begun to see "boobies, tropic and men-of-war birds, tern and some other sorts" as early as December 16.

Not until Christmas Eve, though, did he observe from the south-west how the ocean "broke in a dreadful surf" on an uncharted atoll some 110 miles in circumference. He waited until Christmas morning before sending in boats, a channel into the atoll's lagoon having been discovered by no other than twenty-two-year-old William Bligh, later captain of His Majesty's Ship *Bounty* but then principal navigation officer aboard *Resolution*. Bligh's men were far from mutinous on this occasion, and they rowed back from the atoll with more than two hundred pounds of fish, to be supplemented later by three hundred green turtles.

Cook, meanwhile, had taken sightings and had placed the atoll at latitude one degree fifty-nine minutes north, longitude 157 degrees fifteen minutes west, just above the equator in mid-Pacific. Eighteen days later he would discover Hawaii and eventually proceed to arctic Siberia and Alaska. He would remain anchored at this isolated landfall long enough only to plant some yams and coconuts, observe an eclipse of the sun and dub the atoll Christmas Island ("We kept our Christmas here"), thus sowing the seed of two centuries of postal

BOOBIES, CHRISTMAS ISLAND, MID-PACIFIC

confusion, because an earlier British sailor, Captain William Mynors of the East India Company, had so named another tropic island, that one in the Indian Ocean, back in 1643.

Nearly 206 Christmases later, though, no more than a quarter of a mile from where Cook's anchor chains had rattled down in twenty fathoms onto clean sand, I was expecting no mail but making further discoveries by the minute, such as the fact that my tackle box full of popping plugs — enough to last through half a dozen seasons of striped-bass fishing on Cape Cod — was emptying faster than Macy's at closing time on Christmas Eve.

Our flat-bottomed boat, which strictly speaking should never have left the lagoon, was riding the swells close to the barrier reef of Christmas Island, and I could look through twenty-five feet of flashing neon-blue-and-green water down to white lanes of sand that cut through the dark coral. I put on my penultimate red-and-white popper, sent it whistling sixty yards toward the breakers and began yanking it back. The surface commotion caused by the plug suddenly broadened into a wild eruption of the sea as a huge brown shadow came up behind it, engulfed it, screeched away with it and buried it in the coral.

I hadn't expected anything else, nor that big Eddy Currie would fail to give a joyous peal of laughter. "What you want with that too-big devil for, anyhow?" he spluttered.

As a matter of fact, I wasn't entirely sure. In his log, Cook had remarked on "an abundance of fish" around the island. Alone, that vague statement wouldn't have brought me to an atoll 3,415 miles from Los Angeles. But recently the first outriders of that special class of sport fishermen to whom abundance isn't an especially important word had been making the long pilgrimage.

What had brought these sun-visored and khaki-clad veterans of the Caribbean and Central American coastal flats to Christmas, in the way the sighting of a distinctly rare bird draws birders to an obscure estuary, was a report that on this distant coral interruption of the ocean, bonefish could be caught on fly.

For decades now, the speedy and subtle bonefish has been the target of the saltwater fly-fisher. Hold on, though. These were *Pacific* bones. So? Aren't there millions of bonefish in the Pacific? Don't the Hawaiians catch them all the time?

Well, yes, certainly, one of those sun-desiccated anglers might reply, but only in deep water, not on the flats, in the skinny ankleto-knee-depth shallows where they can be artistically stalked. Hadn't the archpriest of the art, Lefty Kreh, written in his seminal *Fly Fishing in Salt Water*, ". . . as far as fly-fishermen are concerned, [bonefish] are found only in Central America, the Caribbean and the Florida Keys. In all other areas, bonefish feed in deep water, inaccessible to fly-fishermen." Kreh could hardly be blamed for that statement; no doubt it will be corrected in future editions—but oh, how joyful to be a Christmas pioneer, to catch Pacific bones on the flats and prove Kreh wrong!

And so, sparsely, since the early part of this year, a handful of fly-fishers had done just that. By the time my 727 began its approach to Casady Airfield on Christmas Island last month, a hemisphere had just been added to fly-fishing history, and I was looking forward to being part of its early chapters. I was unaware then that I would be sidetracked by Eddy and his devils.

The first morning I fished, Eddy, a massively broad and tall islander who was new as a guide but old in the ways of fish and outrigger canoes, had, instead of heading for the bonefish flats inside the lagoon, gone straight through the reef gap to the ocean side of tiny Cook Island, where the great navigator had first anchored.

"Try for *te rereba*," said Eddy now. I looked blank. "Hawaiian men call *ulua*," he said impatiently, "you call trevally." I placed it. Trevally was the Aussie name for one of the *Carangidae*, a member of the jack family but one that, like the related Gulf permit, ventured into very shallow water. I'd heard that they, too, could be caught on fly in the Christmas lagoon—gentlemanly sized fish of ten pounds or so.

This didn't seem to be what Eddy had in mind. Already he'd picked out a thirty-pound outfit that I had brought along in case I got a shot at wahoo or yellowfin tuna, and now he rummaged in my tackle box and came up with an immense blue-and-white surface plug that had proved itself on Nantucket stripers. "Throw long way," he said succinctly. "Bring back fast."

And so began four successive mornings of attrition. The typical scenario, in fast sequence, went thusly: The splash of a plug, the appearance of a brown shadow, the explosion in the water, the screaming reel, the thumb foolishly blistered once or twice trying to slow a big devil down, the hang-up in the coral, the break-off. Once in a while the trevally would decide to head for the open sea, and if it were small enough, under thirty-five pounds, say, I'd get it in. Most of the time, though, the life expectancy of my lures was somewhat less than that of a tail gunner over Berlin circa 1943.

There was no point, I thought, that fourth morning, in giving the last of my poppers the chance to live to see Cape Cod again. On it went, and was summarily crashed. "Big Devil," Eddy said, laughing infuriatingly.

"How big?" I asked him.

"Seventy pounds," he gurgled.

"Last plug," I said.

Eddie stopped laughing. "Last plug?" he said. Something had put him on his mettle. "Take up slack," he said. He started the motor and we inched in, following the line, suicidally close to the breakers. "I see him," Eddy said, tossing the anchor over. Then he dived over the side and I, too, could see in the clear water the line running under the coral and the big trevally hanging on the other side of the reef, the plug across his jaws like a bone in the mouth of a bull mastiff, with Eddy's dark shadow approaching him.

There was no chance, of course, even if the weaponless Eddy had been able to grapple him with bare hands. A shake of the great head, and the fish—and my plug—was gone forever.

"Bad devil," said Eddy, back on board again, shaking his own head. It was a losing game, and we both knew it. "We better go 'way now, catch some bonefish. Moon is right, big bonefish on this moon. They get a hex in the belly, come in from the deep ocean. We should go to Paris."

I knew where Paris was—right across the channel from London, naturally, and ten miles north of Poland. Nobody lived in Paris these days, but London had 740 people, Poland 175, and down the road from London there were 350 more in the settlement of Banana.

When Captain Cook arrived, he had noted that "should anyone be so unfortunate as to be accidentally driven upon the island . . . it is hard to say that he could be able to prolong existence." Since then, the island has received occasional, thin emigrations from the Gilberts to the south when workers have been needed for copra production, but much more ominous temporary visitations have occurred.

And they have left their mark. The village of Banana, for example, is served by an airport with a runway of 6,900 feet, capable of handling big jets; there is an even bigger, and quite deserted, airfield at the uninhabited southeast end of the island. If you drive from Banana to London, moreover, suddenly, among the coconut palms, you will come upon a complex of deep-dish antennas and mysterious white constructions agleam with stainless steel that look as though they came off the cover of *Analog*, the science-fiction magazine.

All of which is somewhat extraordinary for a coral atoll, which, if you discount its tiny sister atolls of Fanning and Washington, must be the most isolated on earth. Honolulu, on the nearest landmass of consequence, is 1,335 miles away. Christmas Island is also part of the world's newest nation. Until July 1979 it was attached to the British crown colony of the Gilbert and Ellice islands. Now a new flag of blue waves, golden sun and soaring white seabird flies over it, symbol of the nation of Kiribati — pronounced kiri-bass — which comprises thirty-three ocean specks straddling the International Date Line, 264 square miles of land scattered over two million square miles of Pacific.

And for the moment, in spite of that airfield and the sci-fi buildings, it is still one of the world's remote places, with only a ham-radio link with Tarawa, Kiribati's capital, 2,015 miles away. Since 1981, though, it has had an air link with the outside world; Air Tungaru, Kiribati's national carrier, flies there once a week from Honolulu.

And, of course, it is possible to have lunch, or at least a picnic, in Paris, so named by a nineteenth-century Catholic missionary, something of a freebooter, who quit the Church to raise copra on the island. Now in Paris there are only a few scattered stones left of Father Rougier's settlement and, as we found after lunch, many acres of bonefish flats and bonefish by the thousand. As it turned out, these fish were as particular as any much-cast-for sophisticate that swims around the Florida Keys, but because they are in army-corps strength they offered many more opportunities. They also hit Florida fly patterns and made the line scream out in the same way. Inevitably, there were many small ones, but there were also plenty of five- and six-pound fish and, once, an eight-pounder. For the record, Lefty, there *are* Pacific bonefish for the fly rod.

After Paris, London turned out to be bustling. Under a drying copra stack a few locals sat around drinking beer beneath a sign that read: E TABU TE MOOI BEER IKAI AO TE TAKAKARO, which forbade loitering and the drinking of beer, the legitimate place for which turned out to be Ambo's Bar on the wharf. At Ambo's a blue-water sailor from Tarawa with flowers in his hair told us his name was Rudolph and apologized because, he said, "I am not very much pretty, I am ugly brute," but nevertheless invited us to join him inside the wire-mesh fence that surrounds the bar so that the local cops can seal it off should trouble come. Gilbertese sailors you can find in all the merchant fleets of the world, and Rudolph was a cosmopolitan. "You like Christmas?" he asked. "It is like Florida. It is flat and it snows not too much." We couldn't linger, though: Eddy's father, Eberi, was waiting for us downtown.

Outside Eberi's house, kids played a kind of blackjack, called kemboro, for Australian pennies—for some strange bankers' reason, Aussie dollars are the currency on Christmas—and in the backyard lay all manner of detritus—old truck motors, two propellers, recognizably from a DC-4. Eberi is an upstanding man in his fifties, father of ten, who had come to the island in '58 from the Gilberts to oversee the London copra plantation and, almost immediately, had found himself in the most hideous period in the history of Christmas.

In a while he was to say of those days, "The military officer told us all to stand in the tennis court the soldiers built and bring a cloth. Then he said, 'Three minutes, one minute,' and we put our cloths over our heads, shut our eyes and faced north as we had been told. We were all frightened. Even the name 'bomb' frightened us. We had heard of this bomb."

World War II, which had ravaged the Gilberts, passed by Christmas Island, but in June 1956 a small party of British troops came ashore at London. In a month there were two thousand of them; a year later, three H-bombs were exploded at eighteen-thousand feet about thirty miles south of the island. Between then and mid-1962 there were at least twenty-six more shots. Each time the Christmas Islanders were gathered together and told to protect their eyes against the flash. Toward the end of the span the British were joined by U.S. forces, who also tested bombs, and it was 1969 before they all went home, though some Americans returned briefly in April 1970 for Apollo 13's splashdown.

Huge quantities of matériel—trucks, mighty generators, a complete communications system—and a couple of intercontinental-sized airfields were left on the coral, explaining why Eberi now hefted a prop blade onto his mighty shoulder and following Christmas Island etiquette said to his visitor gravely, "Please take this home with you. I have many."

In 1975, a U.S. team established that by then there was no measurable radioactivity on Christmas Island, but there was cause for a slight fission when Eddy said, "I show you the graveyard on the way back."

The graveyard turned out to be nothing but a vast monument to military profligacy. Lined up in hundreds among the fleshy-leaved saltbushes, hub-deep in the tangled vines of pink-flowered Sesuvium, lay the rusting carcasses of American Dodge trucks, British Bedfords, cranes, bulldozers still painted with regimental insignia and the ironic graffiti of hot and homesick soldiers. IVOR THIRST, one of them had scrawled on the cab of his truck, but his seat was now occupied by aggressive red and blue land crabs, and overhead, like great marine vultures, a dozen man-o'-war birds sailed.

"My father tall as me, hey?" Eddy said as we drove on. I'd noticed both men were taller than other islanders, but it was still a surprise when he said, "My great-grandfather Scotland man. In 1868 he comes, with cons."

For a moment I wondered wildly, was there a penal settlement on the island? "Cons?"

"Sure," said Eddy. "He sell cons. Single-bullet kind. Where my family come from, down in Gilberts on Maiana Island. He come for trading, he sell cons to people on my side of the island. They have very easy war because people on other side only got spears. My people make him like a chief or a king, they give him a quarter of the island, he marry my great-grandmother, stay there till he die. He was big, smart fellow."

Indeed, as I looked at him now, I could see in Eddy the genes of that rascally old Scot, as I could in Eberi's pale blue eyes. I told Eddy that back in Scotland there was a popular folk-song group with his name — the Corries. "You send me?" Eddy asked. "I got some Scotland blah-whee music already. I like this. Can you sing Scotland music?"

Not the pipes, I told him, but we headed down the road from the graveyard to my uncertain rendering of *Annie Laurie* until we were in sight of the island's only hotel, called, naturally, the Captain Cook — twenty-four rooms, twelve with air conditioning, $8 extra, and one bungalow, proprietor Mr. Boitabu Smith.

Built, like the houses in London and Banana, of old barracks material, the Captain Cook should really have been called the Somerset Maugham; over the bar a massive fan moved lazily above a heterogeneous collection of expatriates. There were ex-colonial British unlikely to go home again — like Peregrine Langston, now a fishing guide, a cloth badge pinned to his shirt proclaiming him the local International Game Fish Association representative — and there was the polyglot crew of the five-thousand-ton container ship *Fentress*, out of Ponape in the Marshalls, which, in a memorable moment of inattention the previous week, had run ashore on the reef close to London. There were sun-hardened American fly-fishers, like Doug Merrick from San Francisco and Kathryn and Clive Rayne from Carmel, California. There were four other Americans, an esoteric collection of radio hams who had spent weeks on an uninhabited atoll to the southwest called Jervis, earning the envy of all other hams worldwide because they were the first to receive and transmit from there. And, explaining the space-age construction up the road, a tableful of technicians from the Japanese equivalent of NASA sat planning how they would track a satellite to be launched from their homeland in January, since for them Christmas Island was Tracking Station No. 3. Assisting them were three disconsolate electronic geniuses from Santa Barbara who were hoping to be off Christmas by Christmas.

Not that happy, either, was a solitary New Zealander whose baggage had been left behind on one of the six island stopovers he had made on the way from Auckland. He greeted us with an N.Z.-style "Gid-day" and proved to be Richard Anderson, a senior field officer of the New Zealand Wildlife Service, on loan from his government to help newborn Kiribati with its conservation problems.

And after a beer or two he confided that he reckoned he would soon be the most unpopular man on the island. "You love cats, right?" he said. "Nearly everybody loves cats. And it's worse here because cats are pretty special animals in some Polynesian cultures. But I'm the feller that's been sent to get rid of them, right down to the last bedraggled moggie. That's if these people want Christmas to go on being the most special bird island in the Pacific. And, God knows, it's been knocked about enough *without* the cats."

There were, he explained, more than two thousand sneaky, lanky, hungry, feral cats on Christmas, an island where Tom has all the advantages and Jerry is, well, a sitting booby. One reason Anderson had been drafted was on account of the experience he'd had in his own island country of planning an anti-feral-cat campaign to rescue the last thirty kakapos in the world, flightless parrots that the cats would tackle even though they weighed ten pounds and more.

"Here, though," he said, "they mostly hit the shearwaters and terns that nest on the ground. And, man, this little speck in the ocean has a huge importance. Seventeen million seabirds nest here, frigate birds — man-o'-wars — boobies and shearwaters that range for hundreds of miles out to sea to feed but can't land on the water. They have to have a home to go to — this little island.

"They took a terrible battering in the H-bomb tests, millions of them blinded by the flash and millions more young starved to death when the tests coincided with the breeding season.

"Now cats are the deadly factor. With time — and when the airline shows up with the traps I brought — I can probably handle the cats. But nobody is going to love me because the pet cats are going to have to go as well — the Kiribati Government's passed an ordinance to that effect — but how do you tell people their pets are doomed? One other problem I have is that the government can't even spare me a vehicle."

He made me feel guilty. I had a pickup and Eddy, just to go fishing. "Want to head out to one of the bird islands tomorrow and maybe try some fishing on Saturday?" I said.

"Blerry airline got my blerry fishing tackle as well," said Anderson. I told him there was tackle aplenty, waited a moment for him to square his conscience — but how could he work, anyway? — and we were set.

Next morning on a trip to Motu Tabu, one of the bird islands, Eddy was plainly uncomfortable about the expedition. "Don't mess with any bird," he told me. "Don't kill any. Don't eat 'em." It would be much later before I realized he wasn't making a case for conservation but was taking the Gilbertese name for the island — the Forbidden Isle — seriously.

Once we were on the white sand beach of Motu Tabu, it was plain that nothing would be easier than to harm the entirely fearless creatures. "Tameness is hazardous to their health," Anderson said laconically, something the first European sailors discovered when they found big, gannetlike birds sitting in the heliotrope trees waiting patiently for their necks to be wrung and so named them "boobies." Now, as we picked our way through the ground vines among the nesting terns and noddies, they showed no inclination to fly off, nor did the extravagantly handsome red-tailed tropic birds feeding young as big as themselves, nor did the broiler-size booby chicks, fluffy and wacky enough to star in *Sesame Street*. Translucently white fairy terns whirled overhead, then fluttered close to examine us. Out on the bonefish flats, now stripped by the tide, a golden plover from arctic Alaska was overwintering like a fly-fisher from the U.S.

We'd met Katino Tebaki, the local conservation officer, when we landed on Motu Tabu. Anderson said, "He and two assistants have to look after all of Kiribati, not just Christmas, and they don't even have a Jeep. All over the world conservation is tough, but on this poor and isolated island it's murder."

Katino, of a new generation of Gilbertese, had trained in England with the Nature Conservancy and in Hawaii with the Fish and Wildlife Service. As he cradled a tropic-bird chick on Motu Tabu he said, "Richard's told you about the cats, but the islanders eat birds, too, and it is hard to blame them because their fish and coconut diet is so monotonous. But at least there's no market now for the tropic-bird tails they used for ladies' hats, because they've gone out of fashion." I caught a sharp look of anguish on Eddy's face that I would understand later, but now Katino was bending to release a blue-gray noddy from entangling vines. "A lot of them die this way," he said, "but more by the cats."

When we returned to the boat there were bonefish in the shallows like idlers on a street corner, and blue, flashing trevally came raiding the tiny snappers that fed under coral ledges. "Fish tomorrow," Eddy said, "but I'll see you at the dancing tonight."

At ordinary tourist hotels, the local *folklorique* show tends to be tired and commercial. At the Captain Cook, though, the dancing was frenetic, savage, the Micronesian choruses overlaid by a shouting soloist giving the theme, as a shantyman did on the old sailing ships. Meantime, I thought I recognized the face of the girl who was wildly stamping and gyrating out front. "You met her at the farm," Eddy said.

On Christmas, where there is no soil to speak of, I'd been to see a tiny establishment where cabbages and tomato plants were grown semi-hydroponically, in moldering coconut husks carefully contained in rusting file cabinets left by the military. "That's Mekara," Eddy reminded me. "Best dancer on the island" — and now I recalled the shy girl who had appeared with a wheelbarrowful of what, at 50¢ a pound, was probably the dearest cabbage on earth. I also recalled Mekara's sad story: When the Christmas Island dancers were scheduled to perform in Honolulu, each had to fill out a visa application for the U.S. consul in Fiji. Mekara had been too honest on a previous application. Under "purpose of visit" she'd written, bluntly, "Marriage." She didn't make it to Honolulu.

Eddy disappeared, returning with cups of toddy, a slightly sparkling drink made of three-day-old sap from palm trees. It was as strong as Burgundy. "Tomorrow," he said, "we'll go for a big trevally, my way. You can get bonefish as well, in the lagoon, back at Y-site."

Y-site—the stark name was yet another military inheritance—was deep in the inner lagoon. "Not too many peoples know about this way to fish, but some peoples know." He chuckled mysteriously and took a little more toddy. "Tonight I'll make special oil," he said. "For magic."

"Magic?" I asked.

Eddy began to explain, entirely seriously. "These trevally," he said, "I can catch, kill, eat. They not my devils. My devils you see yesterday. Tropic bird, man-o'-war bird. Also sailfish, manta ray, porpoise. I must not hurt my devils. If I eat them I die, very quick, two or three days."

Now I remembered Eddy's concern over the tropic birds on Motu Tabu; remembered, too, that barely a generation separated him from tribal life on the Gilberts. I remembered a little anthropology also, about the extended family system of Micronesians and their old animist religion, with its tabu creatures—different ones for each family.

The toddy was low again. I fetched more. "You want to talk to my big ghost-devil?" Eddy asked confidentially. "She is Neikana. She comes like a very old woman. I can hear her in the night sometimes, messing with the dishes in the kitchen. We go."

We left the party, heading through the star-bright dark toward London, and came to a rusting group of oil storage tanks, left, of course, by the military. "We bring her a smoke," he said as we parked the pickup, and I followed him to a recess between two tanks. He struck a match that showed a neat circle of coral, inside it three stones that made an arch. "Light a cigarette now," he said. "Take three puffs, lay it down. You can leave the whole pack. And some matches. This devil likes to smoke. Now you tell her what you like to have. Tell her you want big trevally." It was dark, warm and mysterious. I wished.

"Good for get womans, too, if you want to make more wish," he said.

"I thought you told me you went to church," I said evasively.

"I stop when I'm fifteen; one day I will go again," said Eddy. "My father go back to church when he is fifty, when he is old and don't like womans. Also because my mother burn up his magic book and don't make cookings for him. My devil woman is better than church because she say, have a good time, make a big party. She gives you what you want right away without waiting."

In the morning, what had passed at the storage tanks seemed a little remote. With Richard Anderson we headed to Y-site, and it was a pleasure to see him hook his first bonefish. "Nearly as good as our *kawahai* at home," he said, which was wild praise from a Kiwi. We both immersed ourselves in the limitless world of the bonefish flats, drifting away from where Eddy had run the boat ashore, drifting back when the equatorial sun demanded we drink some cold water.

By then Eddy was busy. He had brought his own trevally outfit, a mighty surf rod left behind by a previous client. Now he was wrapping his leader in an oily palm frond, threading it into a baitfish and leaving the hook clear. "Devil in this oil," he said matter-of-factly, tied the rig to his line and plopped it out into the deep lagoon channel.

It was time to wade the flats again, picking up bones, small trevally, too, on the fly rods. You lose your sense of distance very quickly on the flats, and when I first looked back the boat seemed tiny. Nonetheless, I could see Eddy's big rod, which he had set in a holder, bouncing wildly. I shouted, and the three of us started to run through the shallows to the boat. By the time we got there, little line remained on Eddy's spool, but his mighty muscles had the boat off in seconds and the pursuit was on.

This time the big devil had no coral to plunge into, but there was heavy work before he was shimmering like a great moon at the side of the boat. "Not too big devil," Eddy said, " 'bout fifty pounds. We get them eighty pounds sometimes. Maybe Neikana don't like your cigarettes much." He went off into gales of laughter.

"What's he talking about?" Anderson said. "What cigarettes?"

"Just his old woman," I said.

Back at the Captain Cook, at forty-eight pounds the trevally drew admiring attention at the scales, whatever Eddy might have thought, and clearly merited a picture. Hovering nearby was Tekira Mwem-wenikeaki, who worked for the government, and I asked him to steady the fish while I took a shot.

He did not demur but seemed a little tentative about holding it. When we were through, I urged him to take the fish.

Tekira was clearly torn. Trevallies, even big ones, are delicious.

In the end, though, he explained haltingly that no one in his family cared for *te rereba*. He slipped away, and other, eager hands stretched forward for the fish. Eddy, meantime, was having trouble stifling laughter. "Tekira," he spluttered, "can't eat trevally. This is devil for his family."

"But he went to the University of the South Pacific," I said.

"He still don't want to die in two, three days, though," said Eddy.

"I'll tell your wife about these tricks," I said. "She'll stop cooking for you."

"Sometimes she go away now," Eddy said seriously, "but then I put special oil on my hand, and she back in two days."

It wasn't surprising, therefore, that Eddy wasn't at church in Banana next morning to hear the Rev. Been Timon, in formal Gilbertese wear of white shirt, tie and black wraparound skirt, admonish his congregation to worship God, not Mammon. The call to service had been made by the striking of an iron bar against an old nitrous oxide cylinder left by, of course, the military.

Neither, naturally, was Eddy one of the white-robed choir that after service sang in sweet harmonic Gilbertese first *Hark the Herald Angels Sing* then *Joy to the World*, practicing for one of the special events that in little more than a month would mark Christmas on Christmas Island — a grand competition among the choirs of London, Poland and Banana that would follow the morning service and the midday Christmas feast of pig roasted in an earth pit. A basket of food would be the prize, said the Rev. Timon, and all three villages would assemble for the occasion at the *maneaba* (the open-air meeting place) in London.

They can expect Eddy, presumably, in about a quarter of a century, around Christmas 2008 A.D. Maybe not even then.

CHAPTER TWENTY

Last Cast

A WHILE back, I was surf-fishing near Cabo
San Lucas at the southern tip of Baha California in Mexico and I'd
been doing very well. Red snapper, yellow snapper, various grou-
pers, jack crevalle, even a miniature hammerhead shark I'd beached.
The action was non-stop, even a little wearying after a few hours.
"Last cast," I said, and heaved. Bang! A meaty striped pargo, pre-
mium eating and all of eight pounds, hit the bait. "This one we'll
keep," I said, and waded out to cast again.

"Stop!" cried the voice of a young man from Abilene, Texas,
named Brad Harelson. He was a recent graduate of Texas Lutheran
on a vacation trip and he was also fishing the beach. Now he repeated
his plea. "Hold it," he yelled over the roar of the surf. "The Goddess
of the Last Cast may be listening!"

Sunfried brains, I decided, and I threw out again. But the fish had
stopped biting as if a switch had been thrown.

Later, Brad elaborated. "Okay," he said, "you're out fishing and
it's about time to go. It's so dark that you wonder if the fish can see
your lure. You say, 'This is the last cast,' you chuck it out and a
nice sierra mackerel or something hits it. You get it in and, damn,
you see there's more of them out there.

"But you quit. You do *not* throw out your lure again. You declared
a last cast and if you cast again, boy, you may have messed yourself
up. Because if the Goddess of the Last Cast was watching, she is
really going to frown on you. So what you say is, 'The Goddess
came through for me! I'm not casting anymore! I'm in touch with
the universe and everything is shining on me!' "

Yes, well, I told myself, it's getting late and there's a full moon.
After Brad had left I started to fish again. I caught nothing. I caught
nothing for the next several days, at the end of which I had completely accepted what Brad had said.

And last July I bore his words in mind when I went back, briefly,
to Wales and to *Ystrad Twyi*, the green Vale of Towy, where this

book started. A gap had opened in the journalistic schedule that had brought me to London and I knew that my old friend Peter Williams, now retired, had taken a summer place close by the Llanwrda fishing we'd shared before I'd left to live in the U.S.

So I called him. There'd been a summer flood ten days earlier, he said, a lot of water and a big run of the sea-going brown trout we called sewin. In sewin fishing, though, ten days is a long time. There'd been some prodigious catches when the fish first hit the river. Now, though, Peter said, the sewin had turned shy. Every one you caught had to be earned the hard way, flyfishing after dark, which would mean a 10:00 P.M. start this time of year. The good news was that the fish had not yet moved on upstream, and that there were big ones around. The night before, a twelve-pounder had hit a Black Spider, so he'd heard, down Manordeilo way. In the meantime my room awaited me.

It had been more than twelve years since I'd fished the Towy, heading out through the Swansea suburbs of a summer evening, cursing the traffic for all of the thirty-five tortuous miles between me and the river. This time, though, once I'd sliced down the freeway from London I found that Swansea had become an irrelevance: a six-lane highway bypassed both the city and every bumbling tractor and farm truck until I was deep into the green shire of Carmarthen. That was the first change, though to begin with it seemed the only one. I stopped, by tradition, at the bridge spanning the Towy in little gray Llandeilo, and the river was summer level, low and clear. Swallows were skimming the roof of the white farmhouse in the field below the bridge at which once, long ago, Billy Nathan and I had received a specious "permission to fish." Later I would be alarmed to learn that three wine bars serving quiche lunches had sprung up in town and that, a quarter century late, Llandeilo had caught up with Haight-Ashbury: a small group of elderly flower children, almost certainly the last colony surviving in the United Kingdom, could be seen on its streets now and then.

That was no concern of mine. More fundamental by far were the tidings I had from Peter when we met. The Towy had always been a vagrant of a river, prone to change its course when the big winter floods cut into its soft banks and changed the lie of its gravel bars. In the old days this had affected me only in yearly increments, but now I had to accept better than a decade of dereliction in one news bulletin. "The Island Cottage pool has gone completely," Peter said, "and you wouldn't know Glantowy."

"Come on," I said. On the Towy, although you lost a few, you won as well: the years would have created new runs, new pools. And a career as one of Her Majesty's judges had put Peter in the habit of casting a cold eye on most things. "How about the Top Pool?" I asked him.

This time he conceded a slow smile. "Ah," he said with relish. "The Killing Ground."

And so it was on the Top Pool that I spent my fishing time on the Towy that summer, a very short time, a couple of hours on each of two warm, velvet-black Welsh nights, starting each one by wading into the top of the run at twilight as the bats fluttered across the shadow of the hill to the north, in a cave in which the wizard Myrddhin, born in these parts and known to Anglos as Merlin, lies imprisoned by the treachery of his mistress Vivien until Arthur shall come again.

As the darkness settled, I'd work down the pool, casting, until I was waist deep. The first night was a strange one. I took a sewin early on the obligatory No. 6 Black Spider, a fish of a couple of pounds maybe, and for the next twenty minutes I hooked fish after fish, one a very big fish. I lost them all. Not once was I broken. Each time the fish seemed well-hooked, jumping repeatedly. But each time it got off. I checked the fly frequently — sometimes in the blackness your backcast can drop low enough to nick the barb from the hook. But, no. Each time the hook was perfect.

And so to my last night. This time I fished so long without a pull at the fly that I believed I was doomed to a blank. But then, it must have been close on midnight and just after I'd told myself that this was my last cast, the Black Spider was taken with such savagery that it jolted my right wrist, and under the trees on the far side came a wild threshing of the water. Not overly wild, though. This was a manageable three-pounder. I worked him onto the shingle, unhooked him, despatched him and moved to go into the water again. Maybe the fish were just starting to come on. I thought of that twelve-pounder from Manordeilo . . .

And then I thought of a beach in Mexico and the Goddess of the Last Cast — and it had been a last cast I'd declared just now, even though it was a silent declaration. I wanted to come back to the Towy again. The twelve-pounder could wait. I reeled up.

I KNOW A GOOD PLACE

《　》

was set on the Linotron 202 in Bembo, a design based
on the types used by Venetian scholar-publisher Aldus
Manutius in the printing of *De Aetna*, written by Pietro
Bembo and published in 1495. The original characters
were cut in 1490 by Francesco Griffo who, at Aldus's
request, later cut the first italic types. Originally adapted
by the English Monotype Company, Bembo is now
widely available and highly regarded. It remains one
of the most elegant, readable, and widely used
of all book faces.

Composed by Crane Typesetting, West Barnstable,
Massachusetts. Printed and bound by Maple-Vail Book
Manufacturing Group, Binghamton, New York.
Designed by Richard C. Bartlett.